LIZZY'S WALK OF
Faith

LIZZY'S WALK
of
Faith

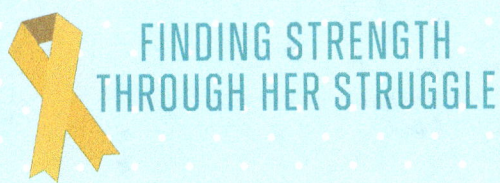

FINDING STRENGTH
THROUGH HER STRUGGLE

By John and Jennifer Wampler

With Hannah and Daniel Wampler

LIZZY'S WALK OF FAITH
Finding strength through her struggle

All Scripture quotations, unless otherwise indicated, are taken from the Holy Bible, New International Version®, NIV®. Copyright ©1973, 1978, 1984, 2011 by Biblica, Inc.™ Used by permission of Zondervan. All rights reserved worldwide. www.zondervan.com. The "NIV" and "New International Version" are trademarks registered in the United States Patent and Trademark Office by Biblica, Inc.™

Scripture quotations marked (GNT) are from the Good News Translation in Today's English Version-Second Edition Copyright © 1992 by American Bible Society. Used by permission.

Interior Layout and Design by Stephanie Anderson
Book Cover Design by Abigael Elliott
Editorial Team: Cindy McCachen and Traci Matt

ISBN:
979-8-89165-167-8 *Paperback*
979-8-89165-168-5 *Hardback*
979-8-89165-169-2 *E-book*

Published by:
Streamline Books
Kansas City, MO
streamlinebookspublishing.com

LIZZYSWALKOFFAITH.ORG

Family is forever. 💗 Here's a glimpse of us, John, Jennifer, Hannah, and Daniel, joined by our faithful companion, Memphis, in 2024. As we embrace the present moment, John holds a cherished photo of our beloved Lizzy, whose spirit continues to inspire us every day. #FamilyLove #ForeverInOurHearts 📷

ABOUT THE *Authors*

JOHN AND JENNIFER Wampler are the heart and soul behind Lizzy's Walk of Faith Foundation, based in Columbia, Missouri. Alongside their cherished pets—their Anatolian Shepherd dog Memphis, and cats Oreo and Peaches—they reside in a home filled with love and memories of their beloved daughter, Lizzy.

Their journey is marked by resilience and purpose, driven by their unwavering commitment to honoring Lizzy's legacy. Hannah and Daniel Wampler, Lizzy's siblings, are now navigating their own paths as college students, each carrying forward Lizzy's spirit of kindness and perseverance.

Every September, during Childhood Cancer Awareness Month, the Wamplers host Lizzy's Walk of Faith 5K Walk/Run—a heartfelt tribute that raises funds for cancer research and supports families battling pediatric cancer. To date, their foundation has contributed over $200,000 to cancer research and more than $100,000 to families in need.

Join the Wamplers and their dedicated supporters, in person or through the virtual event option, this September for a day of hope, remembrance, and solidarity. For more information about their inspiring journey and ongoing efforts, connect with them on

Facebook at 'Lizzy's Walk Of Faith Foundation,' on Instagram at 'lizzyswalkoffaithfoundation,' or visit their website:

LIZZYSWALKOFFAITH.ORG.

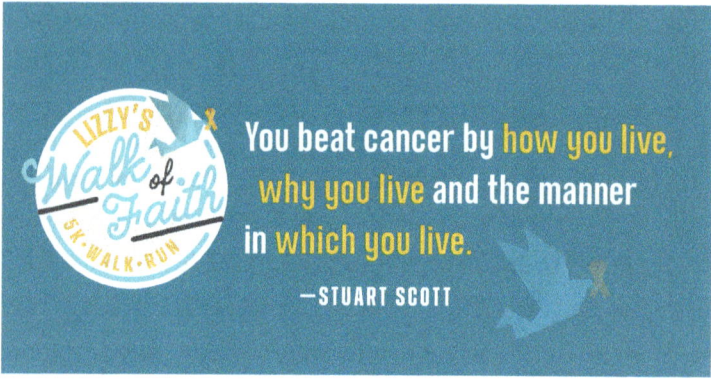

You beat cancer by how you live, why you live and the manner in which you live.

—STUART SCOTT

#stronglikelizzy

When something's wrong

Always look on the BRIGHT side.
July 1st

On July 1, 2017, in the craft room at St. Jude Children's Research Hospital, Lizzy Wampler created this painting. The profound sentiment written on the canvas, which she later expressed during her interview with *The Today Show,* was one of her life mottos: "When something's wrong, always look on the bright side."

WE DEDICATE THIS BOOK to the brave children battling pediatric cancer, to the resilient survivors, and to those desperately awaiting a cure. You are not forgotten. Our heartfelt gratitude extends to all the oncology doctors, nurses, and staff who tirelessly serve these precious children.

We also acknowledge the unwavering support from businesses, family, and friends throughout our journey, and their ongoing dedication to Lizzy's foundation. To our devoted Lizzy's Walk of Faith Board, your commitment helps us heal and realize all that Lizzy inspired us to achieve.

Thank you to the community and all of the people who have participated in our Lizzy's Walk of Faith 5Ks, and to the Mizzou students who helped add life and joy to these events.

Finally, we dedicate this book to our daughter Hannah and our son Daniel. Your unwavering love and support for Lizzy, and your invaluable contributions to this book, mean the world to us. We love you and thank you for being our guiding lights on this journey. We wish you nothing but the very best.

CONTENTS

Psalm 91

1 Whoever dwells in the shelter of the Most High will rest in the shadow of the Almighty.

2 I will say of the LORD, "He is my refuge and my fortress, my God, in whom I trust."

3 Surely he will save you from the fowler's snare and from the deadly pestilence.

4 He will cover you with his feathers, and under his wings you will find refuge; his faithfulness will be your shield and rampart.

5 You will not fear the terror of night, nor the arrow that flies by day,

6 nor the pestilence that stalks in the darkness, nor the plague that destroys at midday.

7 A thousand may fall at your side, ten thousand at your right hand, but it will not come near you.

8 You will only observe with your eyes and see the punishment of the wicked.

9 If you say, "The LORD is my refuge," and you make the Most High your dwelling,

10 no harm will overtake you, no disaster will come near your tent.

11 For he will command his angels concerning you to guard you in all your ways;

12 they will lift you up in their hands, so that you will not strike your foot against a stone.

13 You will tread on the lion and the cobra; you will trample the great lion and the serpent.

14 "Because he loves me," says the LORD, "I will rescue him; I will protect him, for he acknowledges my name.

15 He will call on me, and I will answer him; I will be with him in trouble, I will deliver him and honor him.

16 With long life I will satisfy him and show him my salvation."

Lizzy just kind of dove right into memorizing Psalm 91, and it offered her peace during her time at St. Jude.

PREFACE

ULTIMATELY, we'll all leave this world someday. But our actions *do* matter and will leave lasting impressions. We hope Lizzy's story inspires you to live your life in a way that is filled with joy, wonder, and indescribable courage.

Click on the QR codes found throughout the book to see additional photos and videos of Lizzy.

Lizzy and Jennifer met Chip and Joanna Gaines at the St. Jude Target House, where their mutual admiration was immediate. Lizzy was so overwhelmed with the moment that we thought she might faint. It was unusual for a ten-year-old girl to idolize celebrities from a home improvement show, but if Lizzy could have chosen anyone in the world to meet, it would likely have been them. #ChildhoodDreams #ChipandJoanna #Idols 😆😆😆

FOREWORD

I N NOVEMBER 2017, Chip and I had the honor of visiting St. Jude in Memphis, Tennessee, for the first time. The week before our trip, Chip had a spur-of-the-moment idea to launch a fundraiser called "Operation Haircut." The concept was simple: the more money we raised beforehand, the shorter Chip would let the kids at St. Jude cut his hair during our visit. What began as a last-minute initiative to raise funds unexpectedly led to a profound connection with a beautiful and remarkable young girl named Lizzy.

Do you know the feeling you get when you meet someone you instantly feel connected to? The feeling as if you have known them forever? That's exactly how we felt when we first met Lizzy. Her smile lit up the room, and her laughter was infectious. Lizzy possessed a magnetic personality which captivated everyone with her curiosity, conversations, and stories.

Despite battling bone cancer, Lizzy, a radiant ten-year-old who adored singing and playing the ukulele, exemplified extraordinary resilience. She taught us that light can shine through even in the darkest moments and that hope always finds its place. Our time with Lizzy served as a gentle reminder to cherish each day as a precious gift, recognizing that every minute is too valuable to waste.

Leaving St. Jude that day, Chip and I were profoundly changed. Lizzy's optimism, joy, and hope left an indelible mark on our hearts. She inspired us to seize every moment, especially those unexpected encounters that cross our path. Lizzy ignited a passion within us, urging us forward with gratitude, reminding us to use our time on this earth wisely and to face adversity with hope and love.

Spending time with Lizzy was an incredible gift that enriched our lives and reshaped our perspective. Her story changed us; we believe it will do the same for you.

Joanna Gaines

CHAPTER 1

Lizzy's Arrival

OUR PRECIOUS LITTLE GIRL

Jennifer

A S THE CRISP FALL DAYS of 2006 settled in, a whisper of anticipation swept through our home. It was during this season
that the joyous news unfolded: I was expecting our third
child, a precious little girl. John and I, filled with boundless excitement, eagerly awaited the arrival of our newest family member.
With our cherished daughter, Hannah, now five, and our spirited
son, Daniel, at three, our hearts overflowed with happiness at the
thought of expanding our family. This long-awaited addition felt
like the fulfillment of a cherished dream, marking the beginning
of a beautiful new chapter in our lives.

The years leading up to this moment were marked by transi-
tions and challenges. We had recently made the difficult decision
to uproot our family from Fort Worth, Texas, bidding farewell to

dear friends and a cherished church community. The circumstances surrounding our departure were distressing, leaving a lingering ache in our hearts. Anyone who has experienced leaving behind a community they poured their heart into understands the depth of that hollow feeling.

Our destination was Missouri, a place that felt unfamiliar and foreign to me. While others marveled at the vibrant fall foliage and serene landscapes, I found myself yearning for the vast blue skies and warm Texas sunshine. Surrounded by dense trees that seemed to enclose me like a suffocating embrace, I struggled to find my footing in this new environment. Though my perspective would eventually shift, in those early days, I couldn't shake the sense of loss for the life we had left behind.

A dear friend once likened this tumultuous period to a wave crashing upon the shore—leaving us feeling empty and adrift, yet gradually drawing us back until we found ourselves whole again. But in that moment, John and I felt as though we were navigating uncharted waters, unsure of what lay ahead in this new chapter of our lives.

Then, amid the waves of upheaval, came the unexpected news: I was pregnant with our third child—a precious little girl. John and I were elated at the prospect of expanding our family. It felt like the fulfillment of a cherished dream we had held onto for so long. With Hannah and Daniel already filling our home with boundless love and laughter, we eagerly awaited the arrival of this newest addition. Anticipation crackled in the air, and our hearts overflowed with joy as we stood on the brink of a beautiful new chapter in our lives.

With this newfound hope, the days seemed to fly by with barely a moment to spare. Yet, amid the busyness, we couldn't shake the anticipation of baby number three's arrival. The impending birth felt like an eternity away, with time dragging on as we eagerly waited for the newest addition to our family.

One particularly amusing memory that perfectly captured that era of my life was when I ventured into small stores with Hannah and Daniel in the stroller while heavily pregnant. Each time, I couldn't escape the amused glances and comments from strangers, with remarks like "Boy, you will have your hands full" or "Boy, you will be busy" echoing in my ears. It was as if everyone was predicting a chaotic future of relentless chasing after not just one or two, but three little ones.

The moment that truly stands out is when, during one of our shopping escapades, Hannah gazed up at me with curious eyes and innocently asked, "What do they mean you will be busy, Mommy?" It was a moment of innocence mixed with impending chaos. Despite feeling a surge of emotions, I couldn't help but chuckle at the adorable confusion in her eyes. It was a bittersweet reminder of the beautiful messiness that awaited us.

Finally, on May 8, 2007, at Cox South Hospital in Springfield, Missouri, our patience was rewarded. In the quiet halls of the hospital, our precious Elizabeth (Lizzy) Joy Wampler made her grand entrance, turning our hopes and dreams into a beautiful, breathtaking reality.

Cradling Elizabeth Joy in my arms, surrounded by John, Hannah, and Daniel, a profound sense of wholeness washed over me. At that moment, it became unmistakably clear that our family had reached its perfect, complete form. No more additions—just us, a cozy family of five. With some dark times behind us, we knew the most joyful and light-filled days of our adventure together were ahead.

Capturing pure bliss with my little Lizzy. Her infectious smile and that adorable bow on her tiny bald head always melted my heart. Dressing her up was like playing with a living doll. 💝 #MotherDaughterMoments #BundleOfJoy #LittleDoll

From the moment we met Lizzy, it was clear that like her middle name, she possessed an inherent joyfulness that endeared her to everyone she encountered. I remember the routine of strapping her into her car seat, her big blue eyes meeting mine with that sweet baby smile of hers. In those moments, amid the chaos of the day, I always felt an overwhelming sense of love and joy wash over me, as if everything else just faded away. Her disposition, even as a baby, was consistently sunny, and her magnetic personality had an uncanny ability to attract people. I vividly recall navigating the aisles of the grocery store with her in tow. Every so often, I'd steal a quick glance over my shoulder, only to find a total stranger beaming at Lizzy and waving enthusiastically. Lizzy's face would light up with an infectious smile as she eagerly waved back, effortlessly charming even those she had just met.

Lizzy embodied the spirit of a true risk-taker. Her natural ability to throw herself into the fray was evident. Confidence and boldness seemed woven into her very being; an unwavering resolve to never be left behind. As a three-year-old, she taught herself to swim, an endeavor prompted by her desire to keep pace with her older siblings. I vividly recall telling her to wait by the pool's stairs while I tended to the other children. The next thing I knew, she propelled herself into the water, swimming towards us with an unspoken determination that seemed to declare, "I refuse to miss out on the fun they're having."

Another image stands out like a cherished snapshot frozen in time. As a toddler, dressed in a vibrant pink snowsuit, she was a pint-sized warrior. I can still almost see her, perched atop her saucer sled, eyes gleaming with a mixture of adventure and excitement. The hill before her was nothing short of colossal, yet she was fearless. All I remember was a rosy blur against a pristine white background as she propelled herself down the icy hill. What struck me most though was not the fearless descent but the uphill journey that followed. Most of the other children were complaining about the arduous task of dragging their sleds up the steep hill. But not Lizzy. She simply seized her saucer and ascended without a word of complaint or a plea for assistance.

Little did I know, as I watched her conquer that snowy slope, that this very strength and inherent toughness would be the bedrock of her journey. Looking back, it seems like this very ordinary winter day was a glimpse of Lizzy's resilience and extraordinary spirit—a spirit that lingered long after the snow had melted. Those images of Lizzy's strength are forever engraved in my heart.

As a teacher's aide in her preschool class, I had the privilege of observing Lizzy's interactions with her peers and witnessing the development of her infectious personality—an experience not all parents have the opportunity to enjoy. Working at the school not only gave me an opportunity to soak up her childhood and stay close, but it also provided the practical benefit of easing the financial burden of sending three children to a private school.

Lizzy was spunky, her mischievousness stemming from an exuberant sense of fun rather than causing trouble. One particular memory stands out: I vividly recall a day when I was in charge of lining up the children as they returned from recess. To my surprise, I watched Lizzy playfully tap the shoulder of the little boy in front of her, and when he turned around, she planted a sweet kiss on his cheek. I couldn't help but exclaim, "Lizzy!" Her response was a gleeful giggle, leaving no doubt that her actions were undeniably cute.

While Lizzy cherished her friendships, the adoration she held for her brother and sister was unparalleled. Her bond with Daniel was a special one; she would gleefully immerse herself in hours of playing with toy cars at his side. However, a tender revelation one day unveiled a deeper truth—her fondness for cars was eclipsed by her love for Daniel. In a shy, whispered confession, she disclosed that her enthusiasm for the toy cars stemmed not from a genuine interest but from an earnest desire to spend time with her beloved brother. Her commitment to their shared play was so convincing that had she not disclosed her secret, I would have remained none the wiser.

There was a five-year gap between Lizzy and her older sister, Hannah. While their ages often set the stage for sibling clashes, Lizzy's love for Hannah remained unwavering. As a middle schooler, Hannah was navigating the tumultuous waters of self-discovery,

Throwback to elementary school days. Daniel loved karate and rocked a new mohawk. Hannah was busy with piano lessons while Lizzy enjoyed twirling around the dance floor. Such a fun age for all three! Photo by Jess White @jjwhiteartist. #Siblings #Memories #ElementaryDays 🥋 🎹 👚

striving to carve out her unique identity. In this quest, she sometimes felt as if Lizzy was shadowing her every step, inadvertently amplifying the natural desire for separation that comes with adolescence.

I distinctly recall a particular instance when Hannah hosted a sleepover and, amid the giggles and secrets shared in hushed tones, she extended the rare invitation for Lizzy to join the gathering in her room. For Lizzy, this was a slice of paradise, a ticket to the world of big girls, as she reveled in every moment spent in Hannah's company.

Lizzy was no different from countless other young girls who harbored a deep-seated passion for singing and dancing. She possessed a vivid imagination and a fervor for performance that was truly infectious. Whenever she heard the enchanting notes of "Let it Go" from the beloved movie, *Frozen*, it was as though she transformed into a radiant princess, twirling gracefully around the room, her voice echoing the lyrics with an unmatched enthusiasm. She was definitely a ballerina at heart.

Recognizing Lizzy's innate talent and unbridled enthusiasm, we made sure to nurture her artistic abilities. It was evident she had a natural love of movement and expression, so we enrolled her in gymnastics, ballet, and hip-hop dance classes. Her grace and flair were undeniable, and she effortlessly became the star of the dance floor. She wasn't shy about her dreams and aspirations, proudly sharing with everyone that she wanted to become a professional ballerina on ice when she grew up, a dream she carried with her like a precious secret, waiting to be unveiled to the world.

Lizzy adored school and seemed to have a natural zeal for learning. The mere mention of homework was enough to set her into action; she thrived on the challenge, driven by an internal motivation that needed no outside nudging. Her love for organization was remarkable, reflected in her impeccable penmanship—a testament to her meticulous nature. She loved to read, eagerly consuming each installment of *The Great Mouse Detective* series, losing herself within its mysterious world of mousedom. When Lizzy made a new friend, she would admire their intelligence and academic skills, traits she highly valued. She also loved it when her friends embraced healthy eating habits. Unlike my other two children, Lizzy told everybody that she loved science. We wondered where that passion might take her in the future. I

Cherished moments at the Aviary Cafe in Springfield, Missouri, with my little Lizzy in 2015. Standing tall on a chair to match Dad's height, her smile lights up our favorite spot. 🧡 #FatherDaughterTime #AviaryCafe #PreciousMemories

remember finding her science experiments, water bottles mixed with all sorts of concoctions, all over the house. Her heart danced with the rhythms of nature, finding joy in the company of animals and the playful textures of slime.

Much like her dad, Lizzy exuded an infectious spirit that was akin to a party waiting to happen. It was as if she had a magical touch, capable of infusing merriment into even the most mundane moments. Lizzy possessed an extraordinary ability to perceive the silver lining in virtually any circumstance, making her the quintessential embodiment of a glass-half-full perspective. She definitely knew how to look on the bright side of life.

Her vibrant personality was akin to a sparkling firecracker, igniting joy and excitement wherever she went, without the need

Lizzy, the youngest of all the grandkids, held a special place in our family. Every summer, the cousins would gather at Grammy and Pop Pop's, filling their home with laughter and joy. The days were spent running back and forth between the house and the Highland Springs Country Club swimming pool, creating cherished memories that would last a lifetime. ☀️ #July4th #FamilyFun #Memories of loud or obnoxious displays. Instead, her presence radiated an inherent sense of fun and courage that drew people towards her. Lizzy approached life with an adventurous spirit, seemingly intent on wringing every drop of experience and delight from each moment. She lived her life to the fullest, embracing every opportunity that came her way, leaving no stone unturned in her quest to savor the richness of existence.

From an early age, Lizzy displayed a profound love for attending church and seeking knowledge about God. Her heart was drawn to prayer, and she approached matters of faith with remarkable openness and acceptance. She delighted in the summer weeks our family spent attending Kanakuk Camp in Branson, Missouri, where she won the "Sweet and Caring Spirit" award. Her early years were spent in a private Christian school, where her spiritual foundation was carefully laid.

When it was time for Lizzy to switch from a Christian school to a public school, I couldn't help but feel a bit nervous. I wondered if we had done enough to nurture her faith during the time at the Christian school, especially since she was starting in second grade. But to my relief, it quickly became clear that her faith was still strong in the new environment.

Lizzy's teachers in the public school consistently provided feedback that highlighted the unwavering outward expression of her faith. An anecdote that stands out is when students were asked to bring three items from home representing themselves. In her selection, Lizzy included her beloved Barbie doll, reflecting her passion for imaginative play. Her headphones made the cut, signifying her love of music and dancing. But it was her decision to include her Bible, a personal symbol of her faith, that truly encapsulated her character.

Cherished memories at Kanakuk Camp in Branson, Missouri, courtesy of Pop Pop Wampler's thoughtful gift. Lizzy's dream came true after eagerly watching her siblings enjoy the camp for years. 🏔️ 🎒 #KanakukCamp #DreamsComeTrue #Grateful

Though the public school setting was diverse in belief, Lizzy approached it with an admirable blend of acceptance and unwavering conviction. She had an innate ability to seize opportunities to share her faith without making others feel awkward, a quality that seemed to define her character. Lizzy's teacher, who shared her beliefs, was impressed by Lizzy's willingness to openly share her faith. The teacher remembered a time when Lizzy filled out a "student of the week" questionnaire and stated that the most important thing about her was that she was a Christian. It was impressive to see a second-grader confidently sharing her faith without feeling pressured, even in situations that could have been challenging. As a mother, I couldn't help but feel a swell of pride witnessing Lizzy's unwavering commitment to her beliefs, tucking these moments into my heart and cherishing them as precious reminders of her character.

John and I found ourselves constantly amazed by the depth of Lizzy's empathy, a remarkable trait that truly distinguished her. She possessed an unwavering focus on others, perpetually attuned to their needs and emotions. Even at her young age, Lizzy had this uncanny knack for discerning when someone was feeling sick or needed a dose of encouragement. This was vividly evident during a challenging period in second grade when John fell severely ill and had to be hospitalized, his diagnosis revealing Type I diabetes.

John's illness took its toll on all three of our children, including Lizzy, who was especially close to her dad. As a devoted daddy's girl, Lizzy felt the impact deeply. She loved to go on daddy-daughter dates and spend time together being silly. Witnessing her care for him amid his health struggles was profoundly moving. Her sensitivity to both his emotional and physical state was remarkable. She would always ask, "Dad, are you okay?" Then she would offer soothing foot massages to help alleviate his discomfort, her actions a testament to her attentive nature and genuine concern. She turned to prayer as a source of solace and hope.

Specifically, I remember hearing about one instance where Lizzy, in her classroom, earnestly asked the children to pray for her father. Her teacher later conveyed this touching gesture to me, underscoring the impact of Lizzy's heartfelt plea for her dad's well being. The way she rallied support through prayer, enlisting others to join in, left a profound impression on everyone. Her actions spoke volumes about the unwavering faith and compassion of a child.

I recall another touching moment when Lizzy, a preschooler, stirred me from sleep in the dead of night, seeking assistance after a bed-wetting incident. As a seasoned parent on my third child, I thought I knew the ropes of handling such occurrences. However, Lizzy had an unexpected response. In the midst of the clean-up, she tenderly placed her small hand on my cheek and uttered, "I'm so sorry, Mommy. I know you could be sleeping right now."

The sincerity and empathy in her voice caught me off guard. I had a profound realization that, even at such a tender age, Lizzy

John and all the kids soaking up summer fun in Wisconsin! Great memories made with Jen's family. #FamilyTime #Fatherhood 🧡

possessed a remarkable sensitivity to the feelings and needs of others. Her innate understanding and consideration for my well-being left an indelible mark, a touching display of the compassion that transcended her years.

Lizzy's caring nature extended to almost everyone in her life. Whether accompanying me on shopping trips or spending countless hours with her brother and sister building intricate LEGO creations, Lizzy seemed to thrive on heart-to-heart discussions about the simple joys of life as seen through the eyes of a child. Lizzy's love knew no bounds; she had a way of making every person she was with feel like the most important person in the world at that very moment. She didn't hold back; she spoke the truth. Lizzy was fearless and rose to almost any occasion, yet her personality was soft, not abrasive. She could be timid, yet brave, showing remarkable strength in vulnerable moments. She was the girl with whom everyone wanted to be friends, and Lizzy befriended them all. It didn't matter the gender, age, or race, as long as they had a good heart, Lizzy was their friend.

Playfully nicknamed "Wizzy," a fusion of her first and last name, Lizzy was a beacon of infectious humor. Her comedic timing was a constant source of joy to those around her. You never knew what was going to come out of her mouth. I remember one incident John recounted when they entered a crowded elevator. Lizzy, with her usual uninhibited charm, piped up, "Dad, remember the rules—no farting on the elevator!" Her spontaneous wit brought laughter to the enclosed space, leaving strangers bemused and amused in equal measure.

Another notable moment unfolded during a driveway basketball game on Halloween. Initially, Lizzy wasn't enthused about her clown costume, complete with oversized fuzzy hair and exaggerated face paint. Yet given our budget constraints and my hectic schedule as a mom, I hadn't the time to search for an alternative. Despite her initial disappointment, Lizzy embraced the situation with a positive outlook, allowing her natural humor to shine through. As she darted toward the basket, she unleashed her playful side, breaking into the "Running Man Dance" with infectious energy. Watching her utter goofiness and spontaneous antics, infused with grace and humor, never failed to impress me.

Another particularly memorable instance occurred during Thanksgiving of 2015 when she observed me delicately removing the turkey's giblets and other internal parts before cooking. At that moment, Lizzy declared with conviction that she would never make turkey for her family when she grew up. It was too gross! Her candid and humorous perspective on such everyday experiences always added a touch of levity to our lives.

Perhaps every parent believes their children are extraordinary, and in that sense, I am no exception. In the tapestry of our lives, John and I were fortunate to be blessed with three remarkable children. Many families share in the joy of having wonderful children, but it's often only in the face of change that the true depth of that blessing becomes apparent. Through the routine days of shuttling kids to various activities, hastily preparing supper before the next event, and tackling homework, I made a conscious effort to soak in every moment with my kids. Now, more than ever, I am grateful that I did.

Lizzy, our precious baby, was a radiant and beautiful soul, and the privilege of being her mother is an honor I hold dear. Expressing the magnitude of what she meant to me proves challenging, for words often fall short in capturing the essence of such profound emotions. She was simply a normal child who possessed some truly exceptional traits of empathy and perceptiveness. But, we always had a sense that she was an "old soul" in a little girl's body. We didn't understand it at the time, but looking back, it seems as though God, in His wisdom, endowed her with extraordinary qualities, perhaps as a subtle preparation for the unforeseen trials that awaited us in the future. Lizzy's presence in our lives was a gift beyond measure and the echoes of her impact continue to resonate, leaving an indelible mark on our hearts.

CHAPTER 2

In the Blink of an Eye
OUR WORLD CHANGED FOREVER

John

I N THE FALL OF 2016, we were busy with the relentless demands of parenthood as we raised our three children. At the time, Hannah was navigating the challenges of homework and her first year in high school while Daniel, a bundle of uncontainable energy, charged through the inevitable awkwardness of middle school. And then there was Lizzy, our fun-loving nine-year-old, who attended fourth grade near our home in Columbia. Aware that the fleeting days of elementary school were drawing to a close, Jen eagerly participated in every party and field trip, not wanting to miss a single moment.

It was in the middle of these seemingly routine days that the ordinary facade shattered, revealing an unexpected journey we never imagined. Jen, attuned to the subtle differences of motherhood, noticed an extra layer of clinginess in Lizzy, a tendency that unfolded more noticeably during their evening snuggles. Simultaneously, both of us caught glimpses of a limp, favoring her left leg. Initially brushing it off to mere "growing pains" given her age, we continued on our course, blissfully unaware of the storm brewing on the horizon. Little did we know that these shifts were a prelude to the next chapter of our lives.

In God's perfect timing, looking back, we see the divine orchestration of our paths aligning with the right people at the right time. Many times our eyes look so far down the road that we miss divine appointments, connections, and opportunities right in front of us. We want to get to this place or that. When things happen differently than we expect, we get frustrated, discontented, anxious, and unsettled. We have to learn how to stay fully present and content wherever God places us. Believe me, I know—it's not easy to trust that God has us in the right place at the right time.

One of the paths I firmly believe God orchestrated in my life was working for Tiger Pediatrics. They were one of the largest pediatrician offices in the area, and I found myself in hog heaven for several reasons. First, I've always had a passion for servant leadership and helping people, so being at the front desk allowed me to indulge in this love every day. Secondly, I've always considered myself a kid at heart, and nothing brings me more joy than connecting with children, making them laugh, and ensuring they feel at ease in a doctor's office. Moreover, my role at the front desk was a perfect fit as I was recovering from a previous foot injury and needed a desk job until I was fully healed up. So not only was I able to indulge in my passion for servant leadership and helping others, but I also had the opportunity to spread laughter and joy to children before they went in to see the doctor. It truly felt like the right place for me to be at that moment in my life.

The staff welcomed me with open arms and reminded me what a real team looked like. Greeting children and parents as they walked through the doors, bantering with coworkers, and fostering a light-hearted atmosphere became not just a job but a rewarding and satisfying part of my daily life. We discovered a sense of companionship in the simplest and everyday moments, be it sharing jokes, indulging in playful pranks, or even crafting amusing videos together. "Wamp It Up," a playful spin on my last name, became our office's signature phrase, embodying my passion for amplifying humor and inspiration in any situation.

I remember, like it was yesterday, when Lizzy and Daniel were laughing, having fun and wrestling in his room. I was preoccupied with something else down the hall when I heard her bloodcurdling scream. This wasn't just a whimper or small cry that most parents normally ignore. As a father, I knew this was serious and, along with Jen, rushed to Daniel's room to investigate.

The next day, we scheduled an appointment with Lizzy's primary care doctor, Dr. Adam Wheeler, at my place of employment, Tiger Pediatrics. I distinctly recall Lizzy's painful walk and limp as she made her way to the examination room to see Dr. Wheeler. Her facial expressions showed grimacing, evident strain, and a visible struggle walking. Initially I assumed it was just a strain or bruising that would soon go away. Cancer didn't cross my mind at that point; it wasn't even on my radar.

Dr. Wheeler had a sense of urgency when he examined her knee. Although the swelling wasn't immediately visible to us, his seasoned eyes noticed something living below the several layers of the skin (subcutaneous) and effusion. He ordered an X-ray later that day and worked quickly to get her into an orthopedic doctor the next day.

Jennifer

THE NEXT DAY I took Lizzy to see our local orthopedic specialist, Dr. Vikesh Gupta. John didn't take off work to go along because neither one of us thought the problem was anything serious. We reasoned that it was probably a hairline fracture or swelling that would result in a few weeks on crutches and a return to normal life.

However, Dr. Gupta escalated the seriousness of the issue. In the dimly-lit room, examining the X-ray, he stated, "This could be one of two things. It could either be cancer, or it might be a bone infection." I struggled to fully grasp his words. Wasn't it simply a hairline fracture? The doctor immediately sent us to get an MRI for further clarity.

Lizzy was in the room with me when Dr. Gupta shared this devastating news, but in her young mind, she didn't pick up on the word "cancer." She had no clue as to the severity of either of those diagnoses. She was just a typical fourth grader out of school and getting special attention with her mommy in the doctor's office. Also, when the doctor ordered crutches and a little brace for her leg, she was almost excited. She couldn't wait to go back to school and show her friends. So at that point she was shielded from the pain and worry of the situation.

However, John and I weren't so fortunate. We didn't know the results of the MRI until the next day. We were both in denial and immediately got online and googled "bone infection." At that point, we couldn't process the word "cancer." Of course it couldn't be that! We found that bone infections were serious but treatable. I remember calling my mom and telling her, "Here's what the doctor just said to me." She was like, "No, no, no. It's not cancer. It can't be." So the next day I took Lizzy to Dr. Gupta's office in the orthopedic clinic to get the MRI results.

John

WHILE JEN AND LIZZY went to Dr. Gupta's office, I went ahead and worked at my regular job (across the street) at Tiger Pediatrics. I was sitting at the front desk checking people in for their appointments when Dr. Wheeler walked by. He stopped and said, "What are you doing here?" He obviously knew the severity of the situation, but I did not. I was thinking that Jen would call me as soon as they heard the results.

Dr. Wheeler looked at me and said, "You need to be there now. You need to be at the appointment with your wife!"

I was like, "Oh crap. This must be more serious than we thought." So, I scrambled to get my stuff and find someone to cover my position. Quickly I texted Jen that I would be right there and made my way across the street.

Jennifer

WHEN I RECEIVED JOHN'S TEXT, I had a sinking feeling. Why would Dr. Wheeler tell him to come? Upon checking in for the appointment, another unusual occurrence unfolded. Kelly Scott, a nurse practitioner and close friend, came into the waiting room to meet us. Although we knew she worked in the office, she didn't normally come to visit us in the waiting area. But that day, she offered hugs, words of encouragement, and even asked if she could pray with us. Although we agreed, lingering questions persisted in my mind: Why is she here? Why did we need to pray? Deep down, I think I knew. This was serious. It was a sinking feeling as if a rug had just been pulled out from under me.

John

HURRIED TO THE PEDIATRIC orthopedic clinic as quickly as possible, finding Jen and Lizzy waiting to be called into a patient room. While I tried to maintain a facade of strength for my family, inside I was a nervous wreck, uncertain what the future would hold. We entered the doctor's office where Lizzy sat on my lap, with Jen right beside us. Dr. Gupta, accompanied by his assistant, delivered the news—words that hit like a sudden storm. His pace was swift, and he used terms unfamiliar to me, each carrying life-altering weight. These were the words we weren't prepared to hear: "We believe your daughter has cancer."

In total shock and disbelief, I asked how to spell what he saw on the X-ray since I had never heard of it before:

O-S-T-E-O-S-A-R-C-O-M-A.

Using my pen and yellow notepad, I frantically tried to transfer the doctor's words to paper. In the following moments, I got a crash course in bone cancer, discovering that approximately one thousand new cases of osteosarcoma are diagnosed each year, with roughly half of them affecting children and teenagers. I quickly learned that osteosarcomas are bone cancers that come in different types, or grades, and based on the rapid progression of Lizzy's cancer, she probably had a high-grade, fast-growing variety.

I tried to hold it together and ask questions. What is our next step? Where do we go now? What does this look like? The onslaught of uncertainties swirled, each one a heavy stone added to an already burdened heart. Dr. Gupta continued by outlining the subsequent course of action, which involved scheduling a meeting with a pediatric oncologist, Dr. Andrea Evenski. She would conduct a surgical biopsy to provide detailed insights into the specifics of Lizzy's cancer.

By this point, Lizzy was in tears, and Jen soon followed suit. I remained seated, thinking, "I have to be strong for my family." The room was engulfed in an atmosphere of disbelief, shock, and indescribable pain. It marked one of the most devastating moments of our lives. Our grief journey had just begun.

Jennifer

AS JOHN ACCOMPANIED LIZZY for her biopsy, I found myself behind the wheel, driving the other kids to school. The decision to let Lizzy undergo surgery without me was a heavy burden, torn between being there for Hannah and Daniel as well. It marked the beginning of a delicate balancing act of emotions—caring for Lizzy while trying to maintain normalcy for the other two. As Hannah and Daniel began to grasp the seriousness of the situation, I had to navigate their fragile emotions while coming to terms with the sudden urgency of Lizzy's surgery. Despite my efforts to shield them from the harsh reality, I couldn't escape the painful truth that some things were simply beyond my control.

I hurried back to the hospital to be there when Lizzy awoke. Climbing into bed beside my daughter, I held her close as she stirred, clinging to her favorite teddy bear, "Buttercup." It was surreal to see my innocent girl coming out of her first surgery. Even though the procedure was minor, every moment involving my child felt monumental.

The biopsy, a significant surgical procedure involving anesthesia, entailed the extraction of a portion of her bone and the tumor from her femur using a long needle. Unfortunately, osteosarcoma, known as the dandelion cancer, has a propensity to spread easily. Initially encapsulated within the tumor, any disruption can cause it to rapidly disseminate, resembling the dispersal of dandelion seeds. Although Lizzy's cancer hadn't spread initially, it began doing so shortly afterward. The uncertainty lingers: Did the biopsy trigger the spread, or was it an inevitable progression? I often contemplate if alternative measures could have been taken.

The biopsy results took a couple of days to arrive. Seeking a second opinion, we requested that the biopsy samples be sent to two distinct individuals in different locations—one in Columbia and the other in Florida. Regrettably, both opinions were the same: Lizzy was diagnosed with osteosarcoma.

The next few days were a roller coaster of emotions as we navigated the depths of our despair and tried to be a pillar of support for Lizzy in the unimaginable battle she was about to face. We simply couldn't believe it. In just a matter of days, Lizzy found herself relying on crutches, an unexpected addition to her nine-year-old world. Surprisingly, she approached this new accessory with a sense of fun, blissfully unaware of the gravity that loomed within her diagnosis. As questions from curious onlookers started to trickle in, Jen and I found ourselves caught in a web of uncertainty, hesitating to disclose the looming truth. We didn't yet know what to say. It was as if, in the simplicity of those crutches, we clung to the last vestiges of normalcy, reluctant to utter the word that would shatter the illusion—cancer.

Lizzy struggled to maintain a sense of normalcy. After the surgery, she wanted to go back to school, trying to maintain her regular routine. I informed her teachers that she had cancer, and the news left them heartbroken. Yet, despite it all, Lizzy struggled to grasp the gravity of the situation. In her mind, the upcoming surgery was a mere event with a straightforward resolution—surgery, a Band-Aid, and then back to normal. Looking back, those fleeting days of normalcy were slipping away rapidly; after the diagnosis, nothing remained ordinary.

One instance vividly illustrates Lizzy's lack of comprehension. A few weeks later, her beloved older cousin, Olivia, visited her in the hospital. Innocently, Lizzy asked Olivia if she ever had cancer as a child. Olivia, moved by the question, couldn't hold back tears as she clarified that she hadn't experienced cancer. Lizzy's inquiry seemed to stem from a childlike innocence, as if cancer were something kids aspire to have, and it's simply a part of growing up. It revealed her genuine lack of understanding that cancer is not a common occurrence, and when it does happen, unfortunately, children don't always get the chance to grow up.

John

DURING THE NEXT few days, nothing seemed to matter. This was Thanksgiving week. Life around us continued as people shopped at the mall, prepared Thanksgiving dinner, and enjoyed a break from school. These were the furthest things from our minds. We found ourselves merely going through the motions, sensing we were standing on the brink of something significant, yet unable to grasp the enormity of what lay ahead.

It was also a grieving time for all of us. Jen had eagerly volunteered for every school party—Christmas, Valentines, Easter—immersing herself in the joyous celebrations that now felt bittersweet. As a father, I was overwhelmed with a myriad of emotions, unsure of how to navigate the situation. Lizzy, once caught in a whirlwind of activity with dance lessons, gymnastics, and church events, found her vibrant schedule abruptly interrupted by the weight of a diagnosis. The realization echoed in the silence, emphasizing the void left by the absence of those once-beloved activities. It wasn't just a diagnosis; it symbolized the countless moments slipping through her fingers, an unwelcome pause button pressed on the rhythm of her vibrant life.

When Dr. Evenski returned with the results of the biopsy the day before Thanksgiving, she tried to prepare us for the challenging path ahead. She conveyed the urgency of initiating chemotherapy immediately to gauge its impact on the tumor and ascertain the potential for recovery. The plan included subsequent rounds of chemotherapy, tumor removal, and amputating Lizzy's leg to prevent the cancer from spreading.

Hearing these words immediately plunged us into a realm of significant decisions. Where would she be treated? What do you mean "amputate her leg?" Would that really be necessary? Surely there would be some other option besides amputation! Seeking guidance, we asked the doctor what she would do in our situation. She mentioned several hospitals nationwide which are known for providing effective treatment for pediatric cancer patients.

Uncertain, I started gathering information and asking questions. I toured our local children's hospital, but it didn't seem like the right fit for us. Despite its closeness to our house, we didn't feel at peace with the idea of choosing it.

So I widened my search to find the best place for Lizzy's treatment. My parents, Dee and Anne Wampler, encouraged us to explore treatment options at St. Jude Children's Research Hospital in Memphis, Tennessee. St. Jude is known worldwide for their expertise in treating osteosarcoma in children. Sam Hamra, a close family friend who I had grown up playing tennis with, offered to make a call to St. Jude to see if he could get us in. So we decided to explore this option and include it on our list of potential treatment choices. (Little did we know then that Sam was on the board of St. Jude and was even distantly related to its founder, Danny Thomas.)

I began calling hospitals around the country seeking answers to the swirling questions in my head. No answer. Heck, it was Thanksgiving. Of course there wouldn't be anyone there to answer the phone. However, when I contacted St. Jude, someone answered promptly, leaving me in a state of surprise. "Oh my gosh," I said. "I can't believe you guys answered the phone. It's Thanksgiving." The response was warm, welcoming and full of empathy and understanding. "Well sir, cancer doesn't know any holidays. We're always open."

Subsequently, they began answering my questions and almost immediately put me at ease. They exclusively focus on childhood cancers, and osteosarcoma is their specialization. Additionally, St. Jude offered a limb-sparing surgery, a procedure our local hospital couldn't provide. If Lizzy qualified, they could remove her femur with the tumor and then put a titanium rod in place of the bone, preserving her leg and averting the need for amputation. Despite the merits of our local hospital, all signs were pointing toward St. Jude.

Initially, we didn't comprehend that choosing St. Jude meant Lizzy would reside there for eight months—rarely returning home. We initially assumed we could commute for treatments. However, numerous aspects of this journey became clear only as we navigated through it.

Qualifying for treatment at St. Jude involved adhering to specific criteria, and it was explicitly stated that no treatment could start before arriving at the hospital. Although the local doctors were eager to start Lizzy's treatment immediately, they waited until after the Thanksgiving holiday. Thankfully, this meant Lizzy met the necessary criteria. St. Jude maintains a policy of never denying families based on financial situations or insurance, but due to being a research hospital with limited capacity, they sometimes deny children who have started treatment elsewhere. Additionally, a referral from a doctor was essential. So Dr. Wheeler diligently processed and submitted the paperwork while friends and relatives fervently prayed for the referral. During this waiting period, we were acutely aware that the earlier Lizzy could embark on this journey, the sooner her path to healing would begin. Jennifer reached out to friends and relatives through Facebook to let them know what was happening.

NOVEMBER 24, 2016

Here's an update on our current situation. Over the weekend, we've dedicated much time to prayer, sought counsel from parents of other children battling this type of cancer, consulted with family members, and conferred with doctors. Following these deliberations, we've decided to pursue treatment for Elizabeth at St. Jude Hospital in Tennessee. We've already submitted a referral and are now awaiting a response.

We appreciate your prayers for continued healing and guidance. Pray for a quick response so she can begin her healing cycle as quickly as possible. It is a tremendous amount of responsibility to make such important decisions for your child in such a short amount of time. Right now, I am loading Elizabeth up with healthy vegetable juices and other cancer fighting remedies. We have cut down tremendously on all sugars.

Thank you for all the love you have all sent our way. We will let you know if we get her into St. Jude and what the next phase of our journey looks like. Blessings to each one of you.

Over the weekend, we received a call from St. Jude, instructing us to pack our bags for a two- or three-week stay and bring Lizzy to the hospital on Monday morning. Grateful for their guidance, we immediately began preparing for the journey ahead. Right away, a whirlwind of tasks demanded our immediate attention. Questions swirled in our minds, and with a sense of urgency, we gathered the essentials—clothing, birth certificates, insurance cards, social security numbers, and emergency contacts. Our family's intricate web of life needed to be temporarily disentangled for Lizzy's treatment journey to begin. During the first phase of treatment, we would stay on campus at the St. Jude Tri-Delta House, sponsored by the sorority my sister and cousin had been part of at Southern Methodist University in Dallas, Texas. We embarked on this journey, unsure of what the future would hold.

NOVEMBER 28, 2016

Wonderful news!! Elizabeth is Tennessee bound!! She will be headed there with John tomorrow to St. Jude. I will switch places with him on Saturday. We are so grateful!! Osteosarcoma is the number one cancer they treat there!! I am thankful for every prayer, the help of family as they advocated for Elizabeth to their friends on the St. Jude board, and Elizabeth's pediatrician here in Columbia, Adam Wheeler. Adam helped put in her referral and helped speed up the process tremendously. He is a wonderful doctor and has made himself available to us through this process. Thank you everyone for your faith!!

Although we primarily relied on driving during the subsequent months, the urgency to initiate treatment immediately led us to opt for a plane for this initial journey. Our community swiftly rallied around us, and my dad, along with his law partner Joe

Passanise, arranged for a private plane piloted by our good friend, Terry Marshall, to transport Lizzy and me to Memphis. With my arms filled with a coloring book, journal, and a variety of toys to keep Lizzy entertained, we boarded the plane on November 28, just four days after Thanksgiving. This emotional journey from Columbia, Missouri, to Memphis, Tennessee, will always stay with me, marking the initial chapter in Lizzy's long and challenging treatment journey.

NOVEMBER 29, 2016

I'm learning this journey is a series of highs and lows. We were celebrating the fact that sweet Elizabeth will be receiving some of the best medical care we can give her. Then came the realization of what this will mean for our family. We aren't wallowing in it, just reflecting. Daniel and Hannah, in particular, are unsure when they will see Elizabeth again. They're understandably saddened by the prospect of me missing their Christmas band concerts. Their minds are consumed with questions like, "Will Elizabeth be home for Christmas?" We're certain that everything will come together step-by-step. Praying God's grace.

Lizzy is pictured here on the Monday following Thanksgiving 2016. She is on her way to St. Jude Children's Research Hospital to be admitted as a patient. Our daughter, admitted to a cancer hospital? It can't be possible. We just couldn't believe it.

Lizzy standing tall, full of hope and innocence, outside St. Jude Children's Research Hospital in Memphis. Little did she know the courage she would show within those walls. 💛 #HopefulBeginnings #StJudeStrong

CHAPTER 3

The Wrecking Ball

A WORLD WE NEVER KNEW EXISTED

John

THE NEXT MONTH seemed like a blur with all semblance of our normal life thrown out the window. Cancer took over our life. We were in survival mode. Osteosarcoma became public enemy number one. Boy, did we fight it with everything we had—Lizzy bravely leading the charge each day. Jen and I, in our attempts to navigate this challenging journey, became like ships passing in the night. We established a routine where each of us took a two-week shift being with Lizzy, followed by two weeks back in Missouri. Throughout this tumultuous period, we strived to maintain as much normalcy as possible for our other two children, all while caring for Lizzy.

I took the first shift. I will never forget the moment we arrived at the front door of St. Jude Children's Research Hospital. Lizzy, with her blonde hair, crutches, and brace, exuded both beauty and bravery. Before entering, we paused at the statue of Danny Thomas, the founder of St. Jude. This sight instilled a glimmer of hope inside of us. Learning how Danny Thomas, a prominent figure in television, film, and radio, had pledged to build a shrine to St. Jude Thaddeus in gratitude for his success, provided us with inspiration. As he gained more notoriety, he fulfilled his promise by establishing a research hospital dedicated to eradicating childhood cancer. Fueled by private donations, St. Jude champions the noble cause of providing treatment to children regardless of race, creed, or economic status. Today, Danny's daughter, Marlo Thomas, carries forward the torch, ensuring that the legacy endures.

Standing before that statue, I was gripped by a mixture of fear and hope. I felt a deep sense of apprehension about the uncertain future ahead. Despite the anxiety, I took a picture of Lizzy beside that statue, clinging to the hope that she too would find a miracle like Danny Thomas did.

Globally, the American Childhood Cancer Institute estimates that 300,000 children are diagnosed with cancer each year, a staggering number that underscores the urgency of the cause. Sadly, Lizzy is not alone in her diagnosis. Around the world, approximately eight to nine hundred new cases of osteosarcoma are diagnosed annually, about 65 percent of which affect children and teenagers. St. Jude has been a beacon of hope, contributing to the remarkable transformation of childhood cancer survival rates. Since its inception in 1962, the hospital has played a pivotal role in elevating the survival rate for childhood cancer from a mere 20 percent to an inspiring 80 percent. We were praying, and had good reason to hope, that Lizzy would be included in those triumphant survivors ("US Childhood Cancer Statistics," acco.org).

Walking through the front door of the hospital, I was overwhelmed with emotion. The scene unfolded like a war zone—children in wheelchairs, some with no limbs, others with eye patches, no hair, and crutches. It was a diverse array of challenges and conditions, a deep reminder of the breadth of struggles these kids were facing.

We completed the admitting process, and Lizzy was given a bracelet with her identification number. Armed with our insurance card, I headed to the finance department, unsure how we would manage the costs of Lizzy's care. It was then I learned that her treatment would be entirely covered. They assured me, "We are going to pay for everything. You're not going to have to pay for anything. If you get a bill in the mail, please disregard it." The realization of the extent of St. Jude's generosity and awesomeness overwhelmed me. I hadn't previously grasped that the patients and their families wouldn't have to pay a dime. It was a profound moment and blessing for our family, like the greatest gift and stress reliever I could have received.

Throughout our stay at St. Jude, we consistently found ourselves amazed by the exceptional generosity extended to us. A notable example was our interactions with the valet attendants, who quickly became familiar faces as they parked our car daily. Given the time-consuming process of getting Lizzy and her necessary equipment in and out of the car, these attendants were unfailingly friendly. It was heartening to experience their helpfulness, but we were surprised to learn that tipping them was not allowed. For those without a car, a free shuttle was available to navigate the campus. St. Jude ensured that every conceivable need was provided for, adding to our sense of gratitude.

Initially, I had concerns about the additional costs of being away from home, particularly for food. However, St. Jude had that covered as well. They provided a meal card for the cafeteria, essentially making all our meals free. Additionally, we received a $200 debit card each week to help pay for additional food and grocery expenses. Remarkably, throughout our time in Memphis with Lizzy, whenever we took her to a restaurant, we seldom paid. I would estimate that 80 percent of the time, someone in the restaurant would quietly cover the cost of her dinner. Memphis proved to be an incredibly supportive and welcoming city, especially for pediatric patients.

St. Jude's patients are also provided with housing, and it's all offered free of charge through partnerships with major corporations. During our time there, we had essentially three options: Tri Delta Place and the Ronald McDonald House for short-term stays, and the Target House for longer-term accommodations. We utilized all three during our time at St. Jude. As these housing options are spread out—such as the Target House being three miles from campus—transportation is provided each day for patients and their belongings. Since our time at St. Jude, an additional housing option called the Domino's Village, catering to both long and short-term stays, has been introduced. All these options were bright and cheerful, providing the appropriate level of housing for our needs at the time—whether it was a hotel room or suite for a shorter stay or a fully-furnished two-bedroom apartment at the Target House.

We made one of the two bedrooms in our Target House accommodations Lizzy's craft and play room. We hung up twinkling lights, filled it with stuffed animals and had a desk there for her to work on special crafts. We even covered the twin beds with matching yellow comforters and pillow shams—anything we could do to make it feel like home. She loved having her own space. It helped to have time to do normal kid things. Since so many of her days

Caught in a moment of childhood innocence amid the challenges of treatment. Lizzy's room at the Target House was her sanctuary, where she found solace in conversations with her dolls. 🧡 #ChildhoodMemories #Sanctuary

were spent in the hospital, in pain and in a wheelchair, it was so nice to have a place to get away fromit all.

Moreover, whenever Lizzy required overnight treatment, she was admitted to the Chili's Care Center. This arrangement allowed us to pack up everything and stay with her there for three or four days during her treatment. Packing was no small task, given the multitude of items needed for her care—medicine, large and heavy equipment, and more. Additionally, Lizzy always insisted on having her toys and stuffed animals. Parents were required to bring their suitcase along with their own pillow, and we even brought a mattress topper to enhance the comfort of the provided bed.

Ironically, even in a hospital primarily dedicated to children with terminal diseases, there is such a spirit and atmosphere of joy and hope at St. Jude. Everyone from top to bottom, including the staff, doctors, nurses, and even security guards, just seem to exude this joy and positivity. They all seemed to have such a servant mindset. I will always be grateful for them. At that time, our life was such a whirlwind of emotions—almost like a roller coaster. There were moments filled with hope and excitement, knowing everything would work out with the help of the doctors. Then there were instances of great anxiety and deep despair, where life appeared utterly hopeless. Jen, in her quest for information on the Internet (a place she wasn't supposed to be), would unearth both positive and mostly distressing news. It was during those challenging times that I confronted dark thoughts, realizing I could potentially lose my nine-year-old, blonde-haired, blue-eyed little girl. Throughout these tumultuous times, having the St. Jude staff by our side made such a difference.

During Lizzy's time away from her usual schooling, she worked with teachers and tutors at St. Jude to keep up with her classmates in Columbia. The St. Jude Imagine Academy, led by a team of thirteen dedicated teachers, is recognized as a special purpose school by the Cognia accrediting agency. Despite our hope for Lizzy's swift return to school once her treatment was complete, the cognitive effects of chemotherapy made it clear that reintegration wouldn't be easy, despite the intensive tutoring efforts. Grateful for the school's attempts to maintain a sense of normalcy for Lizzy, we found brief moments of relief knowing she was well supported. The unwavering kindness and patience of the teachers provided Lizzy with a much-needed distraction, offering her some routine during her scheduled eight-month hospital stay.

Embarking on adventures with Lizzy was always the highlight of my days in Memphis. Whenever I arrived, I couldn't wait to whisk her away from her normal routine of hospital appointments and treatments on whirlwind escapades filled with excitement and joy. "C'mon Wizzy, let's go have fun and fly a kite," I'd suggest eagerly, and in no time, we'd be laughing as Lizzy, with her bald head shining under the sun, expertly maneuvered the kite while I snapped pictures of her radiant smile. But our adventures didn't stop there; we'd indulge in gastronomic delights at our beloved restaurant or candy haven, reveling in the sheer delight of every bite.

Some days, we'd unleash our inner explorers, venturing into the wilds of the zoo or delving into the mystique of Graceland, immersing ourselves in the legendary realm of Elvis. The thrill of attending Memphis Redbirds baseball games would have us cheering at the top of our lungs, and the spectacle of the ducks parading through the opulent lobby of the Peabody Hotel would never fail to dazzle us.

Yet, in the whirlwind of excitement, there were moments when Lizzy wasn't feeling her best. But even then, our adventures didn't halt; instead, we'd cozy up indoors, watching movies or diving into captivating books, cherishing each moment spent together, regardless of the circumstances. With Lizzy, every moment was an adventure waiting to unfold, brimming with laughter, love, and unforgettable memories.

One of my favorite memories was our trip to Shelby Farms Park. Lizzy and I jumped in a paddle boat and had the time of our lives! I can fondly remember laughing, joking and cutting up as we paddled and explored the lake around us. Full disclaimer—this

John's spirit of adventure lifted Lizzy high above the clouds as they soared along with the kite.
#FatherDaughterBond #AdventureTime

was highly against the doctor's orders due to the port in her chest. Of course, we made several funny and silly videos that I'll cherish forever. We captured Lizzy's video message that regardless of what battle you are facing, to take the time to laugh, live life, and make the best of your time together as a family. Additionally, life doesn't stop and isn't over if you have a setback.

John and Lizzy paddleboating at Shelby Farms Park.

Another day, Lizzy rode a horse for the first time. I was a nervous wreck because her body was so frail and fragile. Yet here was my little daughter, not only courageous but living her best adventurous life doing something for the very first time. Her bravery inspired me to be open to trying even more new things.

Jennifer

INITIALLY, WE WERE uncertain about the duration of Lizzy's treatment. In those first appointments, I would be on the speakerphone with the doctor, discussing the protocol and understanding what her treatment plan would entail. Although Lizzy had a sizable care team, Dr. Michael Bishop emerged as Lizzy's main oncologist, overseeing the majority of her care. Dr. Bishop was upfront with us, conveying that we needed to brace ourselves for a long and tough journey. He likened the chemotherapy to a wrecking ball, aiming to eradicate the cancerous cells. But he also acknowledged that it would impact some healthy cells along the way. Lizzy's chemotherapy was expected to take about nine months, using a cocktail of three chemo drugs. In tandem with the medication, she would undergo the limb-sparing surgery to remove the tumor. If everything unfolded according to plan, Lizzy might be declared cancer-free by August of the following year.

While there were instances when both John and I were with Lizzy, the majority of the time, we were separated—one of us in Missouri and the other in Tennessee. Throughout our journey, despite the physical distance, we stayed connected through texting and FaceTime. Whenever we traded places, embarking on the six-hour drive (393 miles) one way down Interstate 55, we usually brought the other two kids with us. This allowed our family to be together, even if just for a few precious hours. Occasionally, commitments like ball games or school events kept the other two kids from joining. There were times when one of them had a cold or fever and couldn't be around Lizzy. But mostly, Hannah and Daniel came with us because they wanted to be with their sister. Lizzy did get to come home for a few days at Christmas and a weekend here and there, but otherwise, she didn't return home during her treatment. Lizzy's absence was greatly felt in our home. We all missed her so much!

Due to the intensive care required for Lizzy and the necessity of being present at all her appointments, it eventually became difficult for me to continue my job. I held the position of general manager at a cleaning company that supported City of Refuge, a non-profit founded by Dr. Wheeler's wife, Jen Wheeler, to help refugees. Despite attempting to work remotely from St. Jude, I often struggled to hear clients on the phone due to poor reception in the hospital. I reached a point where I had to tell Jen that I could no longer manage both responsibilities. Although she didn't want me to leave because she knew we needed the income, it was just too much.

Under ordinary circumstances, leaving my job wouldn't have even been a consideration for me, as I've always been acutely aware of our financial situation. However, when you find yourself backed into a corner, faced with the choice between staying to care for your sick child or going out to earn money, one instinctively prioritizes the child's needs above all else, hoping that everything will somehow fall into place. Likewise, John also had to transition from full-time to part-time employment, resulting in a loss of benefits. Lizzy became our top priority, and we entered into a mode of survival.

The first time I drove down to relieve John and take over caring for Lizzy remains seared in my memory. As I drove into Memphis and caught sight of the skyline, crossing the bridge, I saw the illuminated St. Jude hospital sign looming before me as both a beacon of hope and despair. Overwhelmed, it was hard to fathom that my daughter was there as a cancer patient.

When I finally got inside, the gravity of the situation hit me like a tidal wave. There was Lizzy in a wheelchair with John and her nurse, the IV already attached to her line—a stark reminder of the double Hickman surgery she had already undergone without me. I couldn't bear to look at the lines protruding from her once flawless skin and tiny body, directly connected to her heart. Seeing her in such a vulnerable state tore at my heartstrings, sending waves of anguish through me. Yet in that moment, I knew I had to summon every ounce of strength within me to be there for Lizzy. Being separated from her and enduring this agonizing time in the hospital was a new and excruciating trial for us both.

When John left me in Memphis to drive back to be with Hannah and Daniel in Missouri, fear gripped me tightly. I was alone, carrying the weight of the instructions for Lizzy's chemotherapy regimen. With each passing moment, the directives seemed to grow. The nurse meticulously detailed how I was to care for her, stressing the importance of avoiding contact with her bodily fluids during the four to five days of her chemotherapy infusions. I was tasked with the delicate responsibility of bathing her while she was attached to the double Hickman line, which must never get wet. How could I manage all of this by myself? With no medical experience and almost fainting at the sight of a needle, the thought was overwhelming. It felt like too much to handle.

It was also incredibly challenging to witness the nurses entering her room, fully gowned and masked, preparing to hook Lizzy's IV up to the chemotherapy drugs. The awareness of the potential dangers that even a single drop of the fluid could pose and then realizing that such potent substances were being given to my daughter was overwhelming. As someone deeply conscious of health, strictly adhering to organic products and avoiding chemicals in shampoos and lotions, this new reality was profoundly difficult for me as a mother. I felt utterly helpless in the face of it all.

As we talked about the potential side effects of the treatment, the experienced nurse delicately brought up the subject of Lizzy losing her hair, advising me to prepare for it. Even though I was hesitant to acknowledge this possibility, I tentatively voiced my hope that Lizzy might not lose her hair. With compassion, the nurse assured me, acknowledging the inevitability while providing comfort.

That moment, when I realized that Lizzy would eventually lose her long, beautiful blonde hair, marked the onset of my profound grief and deep sorrow. Her hair had always been her defining feature, and realizing it would soon be gone made the harsh reality of our situation sink in. I wasn't just a nightmare; it was real. I vividly recall a few weeks later, when I returned to Missouri and found myself sitting on the kitchen floor, overcome with emotion. Clutching Lizzy's pink princess robe, I desperately searched for even just one strand of her hair, a poignant reminder of the loss that lay ahead.

The days at St. Jude stretched on endlessly. Every day, despite Lizzy already being a registered patient at St. Jude, she would be checked in, provided with a new wrist bracelet with her medical record, and then given a printed schedule of her appointments for the day. The appointments ranged from physical and music therapy to psychiatry sessions, DNA testing, or consultations with the oncologist. Each was prearranged, sparing us the task of scheduling. Some days might include five appointments, creating a mammoth juggling act.

In the midst of this routine, if Lizzy ever developed a fever or faced complications, everything would be put on hold so we could rush her to the emergency room for immediate attention. Yet this was the rhythm of our daily life—every single day. Occasionally, we might get a weekend off, and Lizzy cherished those times when there were either no appointments or just one, making it an easy day. However, even on these "off" days, there lingered the possibility of returning to the hospital. She might need platelets or fluids due to a recent procedure or chemotherapy. Consequently, St. Jude essentially became our home. Despite the hardships of sickness, there was a strange sense of joy associated with it. Being there with Lizzy became our world, and it became her world as well.

The staff at St. Jude quickly became cherished additions to our family. From the dedicated doctors and nurses to the friendly faces at Starbucks greeting us with a smile, to the volunteers outside the cafeteria who eagerly offered to hold my tray so I could push Lizzy's wheelchair and help her choose her food—there were countless individuals whose kindness shone brightly during our darkest days. Their warm smiles and helpful gestures served as a source of daily encouragement for us, like medicine for Lizzy's spirit.

As parents, we were constantly on standby—ready to jump into action when needed. Even though there were always nurses and staff nearby to care for Lizzy, whenever one of us took a break to take a shower or retrieve something needed for her care, she would text the parent in Missouri to inform us that the other parent had temporarily left the hospital. It was a manifestation of her anxiety that reared its head throughout her illness. Being alone, far away from the only home and friends she had ever known, presented a challenging situation for her. While we constantly reassured her, she simply needed the comfort of knowing that one of us was always nearby—either by phone or in person.

As the night wrapped around us, our anxiety and stress did not lessen, for Lizzy's struggle with cancer persisted into the darkness. Our nightly routine was filled with tender embraces, heartfelt prayers, and Lizzy's soft whispers before drifting into restless sleep, knowing another early morning awaited us at St. Jude. She found comfort sharing the full-size bed with me but returned to the twin bedroom when John took over to escape his snoring. Throughout the night, Lizzy's discomfort was palpable, her body wracked with twitches and groans from the nerve pain following her surgeries.

As a light sleeper, I grappled with each disturbance, a painful reminder of her ongoing struggle. Her frequent trips to the restroom, exacerbated by chemotherapy-induced fluid intake, further disrupted our sleep, adding to the relentless cycle of exhaustion. These nighttime trials compounded a new form of anxiety, one I had never known before. In the quiet darkness, my mind raced with thoughts of Lizzy's healing, the uncertainty of her future, and the unbearable weight of the possibility of her not being cured.

After enduring those nights filled with darkness, I often woke up early, allowing Lizzy a few more minutes of sleep, and quietly brewed my first cup of coffee. It was in these moments that a profound sense of loneliness would wash over me. I couldn't help but imagine the hustle and bustle back home—wondering how my other children were doing, picturing them getting ready for the day, contemplating the events they might have in the evening. The weight of the days, weeks, and months I was missing from their lives bore heavily on my heart.

As I sipped my coffee, I often found support in sending John a text. Our connection during this time was vital. I missed our shared morning coffees dearly, and exchanging loving texts and prayers became our lifeline, a reminder of the bond that held us together despite the miles between us. The strain this ordeal placed on our marriage and family was immense, and almost unbearable at times.

At St. Jude, a profound sense of community naturally blossoms among the families. However, it's not universal; rather, it depends on one's willingness to reach out and connect with others. Often this connection forms around children battling the same type of cancer, as you frequently find yourselves in the same clinics. These families, hailing from all corners of the globe, share in each other's stories. Despite diverse backgrounds, they're united by the gravity of circumstances, forging an unspoken bond that transcends language and culture.

Yet, in the bustling halls of St. Jude, loneliness would occasionally creep in because the constraints of Lizzy's hospital regimen seldom allowed for deeper connections to form. We'd occasionally attempt to arrange "playdates" among the children. But truthfully, it rarely came to fruition. One child might be too ill, undergoing surgery, or grappling with a weakened immune system or pain, making it nearly impossible to synchronize our schedules. Instead, we'd settle for fleeting glimpses of each other in the corridors of St. Jude, each pushing their child in a wheelchair or watching them walk with leg braces down the corridors.

So in those quiet mornings when I awakened early, I'd send up prayers for all those precious families and their children. Then I'd plead with God, asking Him to carry me through yet another day, to watch over my precious little girl, and to guide our family through this unfathomably difficult and dark season.

A typical morning as Lizzy walks to the car on our way to St. Jude for a day packed with appointments.

CHAPTER 4

Sharing Lizzy's Story

A JOURNEY OF
FAITH, FAMILY, AND COMMUNITY

John

JEN AND I disagreed about creating a Facebook page and sharing Lizzy's story. I was still in private mode and believed that we should keep it within our family. However, when Jen emphasized that people needed to know about Lizzy's journey so they could pray, I realized she was right. While our current residence is in Columbia, Missouri, our network extends across the nation. Jen grew up in Wisconsin and has also called Maui home. Meanwhile, I trace my roots to Springfield, Missouri, and together we spent eleven years in Texas. We had gathered so many friends that were familiar with our children and our family and were eager to offer support through prayers. The main objective of creating the page was to streamline this process and make it easier for everyone involved. Looking back,

I am especially grateful that we documented the journey on the page, as it now serves as a collection of memories for us.

So, even before heading to St. Jude, we started the Facebook page, separate from our personal profiles. Jen, already familiar with creating small business pages, took the lead in setting it up and writing it. Initially, it was Lizzy's idea to name it "Lizzy's Mean Tumor," and we used that name for a while. While it was amusing and endearing, we wanted a name with more depth, allowing people to connect and find inspiration. Early on, we changed it to "Elizabeth Joy's Walk Of Faith" (now "Lizzy's Walk Of Faith Foundation"). We have continued to use this name as we established a foundation and organized walks to build support for children battling cancer.

Initially, the number of followers on Lizzy's page was small, but it rapidly gained momentum as individuals wanted to share her courageous journey with their friends and family. Witnessing Lizzy's resilience and spirit touched the hearts of many, prompting an outpouring of support and interest in her story. By the conclusion of Lizzy's journey, the number of followers exceeded 9,000, a testament to the profound impact she had on countless lives. Her page became a community united in solidarity, compassionately accompanying our family through every triumph and challenge along the way. It was in this way that we shared Lizzy's cancer story with the world, shedding light on the devastating impact of childhood cancer.

When Jen and I look back on many of these posts, we don't remember writing them. We were just in the moment and wrote from the heart. We had to get it out. There would be no way for us to rewrite them again in that same way. (Jen wrote all of them unless specifically indicated.) So in the upcoming chapters we'll unveil snippets from the posts we shared throughout Lizzy's battle with cancer, along with further insights and explanations about our lives during that period. Our fervent hope is that you'll not only catch glimpses of Lizzy's journey, but also immerse yourself in the myriad of thoughts, worries, and emotions that defined our experience during that significant time. By sharing these heartfelt posts, our intention is to provide you with a deeper insight into the challenges encountered by pediatric cancer patients and their families. We hope to inspire action, urging individuals to join us in the pursuit of improved treatments and, ideally, a cure for childhood cancers.

NOVEMBER 30, 2016

One BIG reason to be thankful today: We received a great report from our oncologist that the cancer did not spread into Lizzy's lungs. Celebrating the first downs before the touchdowns!! Thank you all for your prayers and support. Please know that it is making a difference, and we can feel your love. We give thanks that things are as good as they are. I hope you will hug your family a little bit tighter. I know we will!

I was able to FaceTime with John and Elizabeth. Elizabeth was a little sensitive tonight. It was good for her to talk with mommy, Hannah, and Daniel. John showed me the port. It's hard for me to look at that stuff. I'm sure it's not difficult for doctors or nurses, but it's hard for me. I just tell myself that they do this thousands of times a year, and we will get through all of this. The surgery went fine, and the port is in place. John, the doctors, and I will all have a conference call tomorrow to discuss her bone scan and the road map of walking all of this out.

DECEMBER 1, 2016

I am probably overtired but I changed Lizzy's page to her full name, Elizabeth Joy. I think it's a mom thing. I just kept thinking about how I love her name and wanted to see her full name if I was going to be looking at this page for a while. I know we need your faith and love as John and I are happy to give you our faith and love for your battles. We will keep you updated on all important things, and we really want to share all the victories we discover along the way. Celebrating victories together can be so helpful at times.

DECEMBER 1, 2016 *(John)*

Here is a sweet letter that Lizzy wrote to me today.

> *Dear Dad,*
>
> *I can't belive that I'm your daughter!! You are so special and kind. Thank you for a taking care of me. And pushing me in the wheel chair. Sorry if I throw up in front of you. I felt so dizzy and hot I almost lost my balance. I love you soooo much!! You are a very kind gental men and a good sport. Thank you for the pajamas and the coat that you bought me. I will guarantee that the Cowboys will win!!!*
>
> *To: Dad*
> *From: Elizabeth*

John had been keeping a journal for each of our kids since they were little. So, when John was with Lizzy, he would lovingly sit with her and encourage her to write. It was during those times that she composed heartfelt letters. It was one of those tender "daddy things" he did, creating precious memories and keepsakes of their bond.

DECEMBER 3, 2016 *(John)*

Lizzy and I enjoyed our time together at The Pyramid. It was good for her to get away and focus on something else. In the next few days she'll face a battery of tests to prepare her body for the upcoming treatment. Heart, kidney, ears, bones to name a few. Next, she'll meet with the physical therapist to customize a wheelchair and crutches just for her size. She is not allowed to put any weight on her right leg due to her bones being so brittle. The doctors are protecting it from being fractured which would delay upcoming treatment.

I am very impressed with her doctors, nurses, and nurse practitioners. They thoroughly take their time explaining everything in a transparent practical way. Lizzy's pain level is eight out of ten. Doctors have taken her off of ibuprofen and put her on morphine.

DECEMBER 5, 2016 *(John)*

Elizabeth knows you are praying for her! She knows God has His angels around her. We've taught her that we believe in the power of prayer. Thank you so much for standing for victory with us!! I took a picture of Elizabeth saying goodbye to her bedroom that she just decorated this weekend. I remind myself that our goal here is to give her many more Christmases to come. If one Christmas is not as planned, it's OK. Thank you for walking with us. Knowing we aren't alone is truly helping us piece this all together.

Very productive and informative day! Dr. Neal will be Lizzy's orthopedic surgeon. Bright and sharp guy who showed us exactly where the tumor is and his plan to surgically remove it. It will be a six-hour surgery followed by a week in the hospital as an inpatient. Here's the game plan that is subject to change: 1) Ten to twelve weeks of chemo. 2) Surgery. 3) Three to four months of chemo.

Tomorrow, twenty-thousand people will be on campus for the St. Jude Marathon. Looking forward to getting Lizzy outside for some fresh air. Might even visit a popular pizza place and cool toy store for Lizzy! Really appreciate everyone's support through texts, emails, and messages. Have a great weekend!

DECEMBER 5, 2016 *(John)*

Today Lizzy underwent a full body bone scan (PET scan) to see if the tumor spread throughout her body. Hope to hear the results soon. I was proud of her since she did not need to be sedated, and she took it like a champ! The doctor wanted her to lay down and relax, so we both watched a part of *Home Alone*.

Tomorrow, Lizzy will have a double Hickman Lunan Line (central line) surgically placed in her vein just above her heart. This will allow her to receive her chemo treatment for the next eight to nine months. The doctor is allowing me to be in the operating room for a brief time to be with Lizzy until she falls asleep. Daddy needs to be strong!!

Here is a letter Lizzy wrote (complete with her special spelling) to me as she was thinking about tomorrow's surgery:

Dear Dad,

Thank you for ALWAYS being the man of the house. I ALWAYS feel safe around you because I ALWAYS know you are a trustworthy friend and a good, good dad. I love you sooooo much! Thank you for buying me those cool Lego sets! I love them a lot!!!! Right now I have my ivy in and tomorrow I have surgery. 😞 Thankfully I will be asleep. I have a Hickmen line in my chest and it will not be pretty. I feel protected because 100's of pepole are praying for me!! I will always know that angles are protecting me and God is ALWAY by my side. We are going to stay in Tennise for about 8 to 9 months. I will have cemo for awhile. So can't wait for that!!

To: John Christian Wampler
Love: Elizabeth Joy Wampler

DECEMBER 5, 2016

I've often heard people say that when you go through a catastrophic event, life is boiled down to three things: faith, family, and friends. Lizzy was blessed to have visitors from Missouri and Texas the past two days. There is no way we can go through what we're going through without a strong faith in God, supportive family, and amazing friends that have overwhelmingly stood by our side. Here is another letter Lizzy wrote to John in her journal while sitting in one of her favorite coffee shops, Tamp and Tap:

Dear Dad,

I love you soooo much!!! You are the best dad ever!!! Right now we are at Tamp and Tap. I'm sitting in the red chair writing in your journal while you are posting pictures of me on Facebook!!! Thank you for paying the bills, pushing me in the wheelchair, and driving me to cool places like Tamp and Tap, Blue City Cafe, Hueys Central Barbeque, Candy Store, Lost Pizza Co., and other cool places!! I feel bad when you tell pepole about your foot and you say that every step is painful, and it hurts when you walk. I pray that your foot will get healed and

you can run, play tennis, and do other stuff. When mom
is with me, I will miss you like CRAZY!!!!

Love: Elizabeth Wampler
To: John Wampler

DECEMBER 5, 2016 *(John)*

One nurse suggested we go to the Peabody Hotel to watch the march
of the ducks. It was only seven miles from the hospital. It was such a
wonderful break after being in the hospital all week. It made us feel
a part of Christmas, and I enjoyed watching her have fun! We are
praying her lab work stays good so she can come home for Christmas.
That would be so wonderful to have the family together. Thank you
for praying for her and for our whole family. We love you all! Here is
another sweet letter from Lizzy:

Dear Dad,

*Thank you for always being by my side wherever I am.
You are the best dad in the whole wide world!!! I love
you sooooo much!!! When Mom gets here, I'm going to
be sad because you are going home with Hannah and
Daniel, and it would just be mom and I. :(I miss you
already. Every time you close the door, I start crying
cause I miss you soooo much!!*

To: John Wampler
Love: Elizabeth Wampler

P.S. I hope the Dallas Cowboys win!!!

DECEMBER 6, 2016

John and I just finished a conference call with Dr. Bishop, who will be overseeing Elizabeth's chemo treatments. Great news, there are no signs of any other tumors on her bones or in her lungs! It is localized to one bone!

DECEMBER 6, 2016

Elizabeth is all settled into her new room for the next three to four days. This is where she'll receive her treatment. This is the most amazing place! I am in awe with how kid-friendly everything is and how the staff genuinely care for her. Lizzy can set her room to any color she wants. Also, there's a cool Xbox Kinect that she can play. There is an attached parent suite where I can stay with a full-sized bathroom, desk, and is very spacious.

The child life specialist, Megan, is always so friendly and takes special care of Lizzy making sure she is comfortable, at ease, and understands from a kid's point of view the totality of what's happening. In fact, she has made such an impact on Lizzy's life that when doctors and nurses ask Lizzy what she wants to be in life, Lizzy tells them she wants to be a child life specialist. Today, she took the time to make friendship bracelets and talk about her upcoming treatment. Everyone tells us the key to staying sane and having a successful stay is connecting with other families and kids. Lizzy is now about to get her first treatment. Gotta go.

DECEMBER 7, 2016

As the list went on and on of the medicines they were going to be giving her over the next eight months, my heart did not faint. I wrote down the areas we can target our faith to help see Elizabeth onto victory. Elizabeth starts her first round of chemo tonight! Here are the basics of what we are believing when we pray:

1. That the chemo will directly kill all tumor cells in her body.
2. The chemo does not damage her heart, her liver, nor her kidneys.
3. That she would not have fertility problems in the future.
4. That she would not get extremely sick during her chemo sessions.
5. She would not lose the ability to have beautiful hair. If some falls out, let it grow back just as beautifully.
6. That she will be included in the seventy percent who live cancer-free without complications.

Thank you, I believe you all are mighty people of prayer, and we are praying daily for this miracle. To walk away cancer free with no side effects, to me, is a major miracle.

Thank you!!

It was difficult for everyone in the family when Lizzy began losing her hair. The hair that remained became dry and brittle, looking thin and stringy, prompting us to cut it to shoulder length. It seemed so unfair that she had to go through this.

DECEMBER 8, 2016

First, I wanted to say I am so thankful for my son Daniel. I'm humbled by his heart toward God. Here is his card to Elizabeth. Such a great kid!

Dear Lizzy,

I miss you soo much. It's not the same without you at home. I pray you get better and the cancer will leave your body. For now on, every day when you wake up say God is good. You know why? Because GOD IS GOOD!

Also don't think this is your fault because its not and you did nothing wrong!

Love,
Daniel

P.S. Remember God is Good!

Also, I want to shout out to Daniel's basketball team. I heard almost the whole team wore pink socks at tonight's game in honor of Elizabeth. So great!! Then, I want to thank Cedar Ridge Elementary and all the students and teachers who wrote Elizabeth cards. She is enjoying reading each one! Her stomach has been queasy, and she has thrown up several times. The nurses are amazing from what John says. It's my turn tomorrow and I can't wait to see her. I'll be praying my whole way while I drive down to Tennessee.

DECEMBER 10, 2016

It's hard to know what to say. Our day was very slow moving. John showed me the ropes and then headed home. Daniel and Hannah needed Daddy as well. Our day was very simple, and I'm realizing this may be how the next several days, weeks, months may be. Elizabeth needs to go to the bathroom very often as they are making sure her kidneys are being flushed after this first round of chemo. This is not an easy task with a huge brace on her leg.

Elizabeth only threw up once today but has felt queasy pretty much all day long. We went on a short walk. I've gotten good at putting the IV pole in the right spot while pushing her wheelchair. I saw one father chasing his one-year-old around with his IV pole. That did not look easy. These IVs are attached to the central line in their chest.

Elizabeth didn't last long on our walk. Mostly felt like throwing up. Sat for ten minutes on the couch for a nice change. We both took a nap this afternoon. When she is up, she is mostly complaining of her stomach hurting. She finally got some morphine and will be out for a while.

I met a nice lady who has been here since June with her son who has osteosarcoma. His cancer spread to his lungs before they got here and then to his thigh. His leg was amputated, and I saw him walking around with his prosthetic. The cancer is in his other leg as well. His name is Zac, and I believe he is eleven years old. They are a wonderful Christian family from Virginia. This is his second time battling cancer. He had Hodgkins Lymphoma four years ago. Zac's mom told me that her key to getting through all of this is staying thankful for all the good things. Even if they are small—just stay thankful. Otherwise, you will go down a dark hole, and it's not good for anyone.

So I'm going to read and wait for Elizabeth to wake up and help her swish her mouth with some kind of solution that prevents open sores from forming (from the chemo) in her mouth. And that is our day. Through this I know God is with us. He is holding our hands each step of the way. There honestly is a peace that I have; sure, I cry, but I am not without hope! 🧡 🧡 😊

Before meeting Zac, I had never seen a child with an amputation. It was a shock that was further compounded when I realized that he lost his leg because of the same cancer afflicting Lizzy. As I learned about the journeys of other children facing similar challenges, I found myself forming tunnel vision. My focus narrowed to see only my child as a whole. I think it is a coping mechanism necessary to maintain some semblance of sanity in spite of the madness surrounding us.

DECEMBER 12, 2016

Quick update of our lives while at St. Jude. I'm doing this to just help people understand what people go through during their chemo treatments. Just to educate, not to make anyone sad. I'm learning a lot.

I snuck downstairs while Elizabeth was still sleeping (she had already thrown up and gone to the bathroom but went back to sleep) and had a quick breakfast. St. Jude gives each parent an $8 meal card. Such a blessing. I like sitting by the window as it looks like a fun museum and not really a hospital. Then I spent the day getting our stuff ready to move to the next spot they need us. They say patients do a lot better when they are out of the hospital. We will be staying in the family housing in between treatments. We will always return to the hospital for each of her chemo treatments.

What this means, though, is John or I become Elizabeth's nurse. I had several meetings with IV line nurses, a pharmacy nurse, parent counselor, and regular nurses.

Taking care of a chemo patient is a big deal!! Elizabeth has a five-pound backpack filled with her fluids that are attached to her central line in her chest. I've been taught how to take care of that line. Then there is all the medicine she needs. Mostly for nausea.

It's quite the learning experience. Life just kind of pauses when things like this happen. I'm amazed at the people I knew who had cancer. I never before understood how it impacted their life. One of the nurses here was a patient of St. Jude when she was ten years old and had exactly what Elizabeth is fighting!! She had a lot of wisdom to share!! It was encouraging to see a lovely young lady who is married and perfectly healthy after going through osteosarcoma!!

We did have a wonderful FaceTime as a family. John prayed for all of us, and it was sweet watching the kids talk to each other, there were some tears. Anyhow, we are thankful for so much still. This is just a hard season but we will get through it!! Blessing to all of you praying.

DECEMBER 14, 2016

St. Jude provides a shuttle to take patients from their housing to the hospital. Elizabeth cannot walk at all on her leg, so ninety percent of the time she is in a wheelchair. This can make traveling and bathroom breaks more challenging. She has physical therapy a couple of times a week. She has been very nauseous and has been throwing up all her meds. Therefore, we carry a five-to-seven-pound IV bag attached to her chest line everywhere we go. I also give all her meds through her chest line now. Praying for the nausea to subside!

Elizabeth had been wanting to go to the gift shop to buy her friend a teddy bear. We got it and found her friend!! She is from India. I talk with her mom every day. It's nice to have someone who understands to talk with. Elizabeth has a ton of patience. We had to sit in one doctor's office for two hours talking about medicine, upcoming procedures, and giving her IV medicine. She went to sleep around four p.m. today after being at the hospital since eight thirty a.m. today. I'm amazed at how God's grace is constantly equipping me (all our family) to continue on this journey. I won't lie. There are many times my knees want to buckle.

Navigating Lizzy's cumbersome wheelchair in and out of the car posed a new obstacle, complicating our daily activities. Each bathroom break or fluid connection necessitated a laborious transition. Though I tried to shield Lizzy from feeling burdensome, the experience underscored my deep admiration for those who confront similar challenges daily. Whether it was grocery runs or quick errands, the routine of unloading and reloading the wheelchair left an indelible mark on my memory.

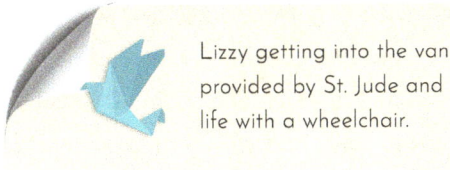

Lizzy getting into the van provided by St. Jude and life with a wheelchair.

DECEMBER 16, 2016

The kids sure miss each other when they are not together. Here is a sweet letter Lizzy sent to her sister, Hannah:

> Dear Hannah,
>
> I miss you so much! You are the best sister I can ever dream of! I miss you and love you. You are the greatest gymnastics player in my opinion. You are a smart and gifted and talented girl!! Every day I cry cause I miss you sooo much! I love you. Thank you for always being thier for me when times are tough.
>
> To: Hannah
> Love: Elizabeth

The city of Memphis was also a big part of our community as we walked through pediatric cancer. Because of the legacy of St. Jude, the people of Memphis are extraordinarily attuned to the challenges of children with cancer. Everywhere we went, we found people willing to open their hearts to our little bald-headed girl in a wheelchair.

One good example of the city's outpouring of love was when we met Santa Claus. During our first Christmas at St. Jude, Santa prayed for Lizzy when we visited the Memphis Pyramid Bass Pro Shops. We were brand new to town and still in a state of shock regarding Lizzy's diagnosis, not knowing how we would manage to stay in Memphis for the next nine months. In the midst of our uncertainty, Santa patiently took his time to ask questions, laugh, and joke before praying with her. It was a tearful moment but one that showed us that we can find community everywhere.

DECEMBER 17, 2016 *(John)*

I wanted to get a picture of what Elizabeth and Jen look like walking around the hospital. This is how most parents, if they are the only caregiver with their child, have to make it around the hospital. As you can see, getting anywhere can be a challenge. Bathrooms, getting on and off shuttles, etc. It's an all-day event sometimes at the hospital! I've noticed the volunteers seem to have such joy helping families. Let me tell you, it's a true ministry!!!

We wanted to take the time to thank each of you that have donated through the GoFundMe page that our friend set up. We've never been in this position or season before and know this is quite humbling. We are so grateful and thankful. We literally feel your prayers and support!

The great basketball coach John Wooden said, "You cannot live a perfect day without doing something for someone who will never be able to repay you." Joy shared is joy doubled! Wherever you are in life, get in the way if someone you know is on the way down. Walk in on someone you can help when others are walking out. Jen and I firmly believe there are no unimportant jobs, no unimportant people, and no unimportant acts of kindness.

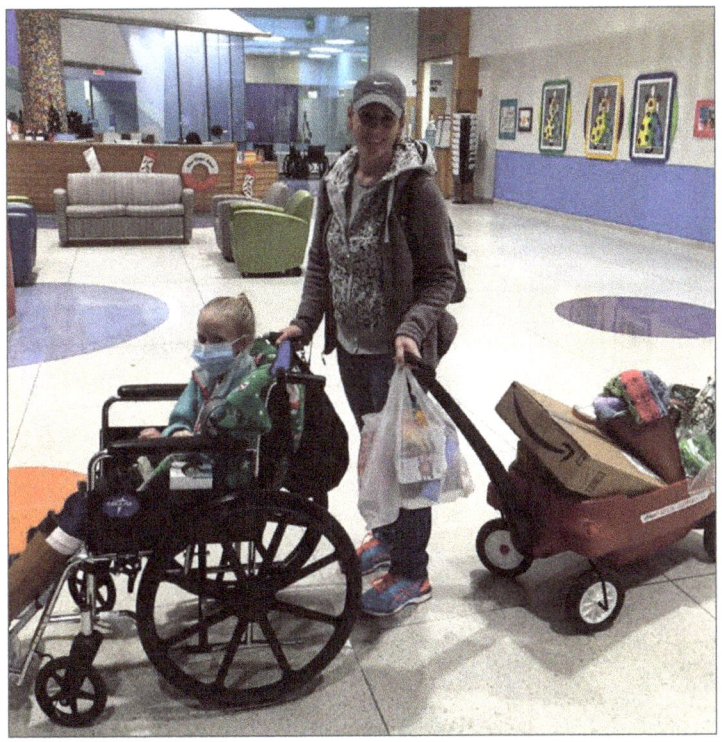

Elizabeth and Jen, navigating through St. Jude with love and strength, accompanied by essential equipment for Lizzy's journey. 📱 ❤️ #StJudeStrong #LoveAndStrength

One of the reasons I married my wife is because she lives to give. We both have discovered that people are far happier giving than receiving. This is our greatest passion and joy! You and I were created to be an answer to someone in need.

Wishing all of you a very merry Christmas and happy New Year! Love John and Jennifer

DECEMBER 17, 2016

We are so happy They have released Lizzy to go home for Christmas. 🌲 🌲 🌲 🌲 This will be so good for her! John will bring her back to start her second round of chemo on the 28th. This will be such a wonderful break!

DECEMBER 23, 2016

We are home! 🧡 John and I were exhausted yesterday. We literally fell into each other's arms! We both are carrying so much for the family helping them make it through this season. I don't think we realized how tired we were until we saw each other!

The kids just adored seeing each other. I know it's an adjustment for Hannah and Daniel to see Elizabeth so weak, especially considering her usual strong self. Hannah has been great following her sister up and down the stairs making sure she doesn't fall on her leg or down the stairs.

We've all had to watch as Elizabeth's hair is starting to fall out. It is not fun as a parent to watch her hair come out in chunks as I brush it. We've always admired her beautiful golden hair. Elizabeth handles it beautifully. She just looks in amazement and just moves on. I'm so grateful she is the way she is.

Elizabeth's eyes are bothering her a bit. She keeps squinting, and they seem irritated. She says everything looks blurry. I'm keeping an eye on that.

Our Christmas tree has more presents under it than we have ever had! As usual, John and I give three gifts to each child for Christmas—one big, one medium and one little. So for our kids to have all these gifts through the generosity of others is so exciting for them!!

I'm going to take the kids to the mall today. Hannah desperately wants to push Elizabeth around in her wheelchair. Daniel is concerned because he has no spending money of his own to buy presents for the rest of the family. ❤️ I told him I'd help him. 😊

I'm thankful to be home, yet we guard our hearts from sadness when it comes. I want to soak in each day. Love to you all this Christmas season!

DECEMBER 25, 2016

Elizabeth has had a wonderful Christmas at home in Columbia. We were blessed to have Pop Pop and Grammy with us for Christmas brunch. Pop Pop was explaining eight-digit multiplication to Elizabeth. Daniel was a gentleman and helped Elizabeth get her food. There were many presents to be opened and desserts to be eaten. Enjoying the meaning of Christmas together as a family has been priceless.

We hope you are all having a peaceful Christmas and are with the ones you love. I want to say a special Merry Christmas to some of the wonderful friends I have made at St. Jude—the ones who were not able to go home over the holidays. I pray that peace and healing will be with you on this Christmas Day.

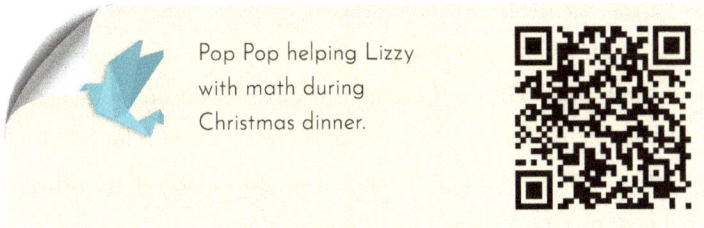

Pop Pop helping Lizzy with math during Christmas dinner.

DECEMBER 26, 2016 (John)

Elizabeth received a wonderful surprise yesterday from one of her best friends, Jacie. Jacie's mom works in the Columbia Police Department Administration Bureau, and Jacie told them about Elizabeth. The CPD

Administration Bureau came together and raised enough money for Jacie's family to get an American Girl doll and wheelchair for Elizabeth! We are so grateful for their generosity and really don't have the words to express how much this means to us and Elizabeth.

DECEMBER 27, 2016

My heart was heavy as I watched John load up the car to take Elizabeth back to Memphis. It's his turn to be her caregiver for the next couple of weeks. I love being able to be here for Daniel and Hannah, yet knowing my other child is going through such a difficult time without me is challenging. When you take care of someone you love during their time of need, there is such a special bond. It is often overwhelming—constantly getting up in the middle of the night, helping her throw up, and getting her dressed. But I wouldn't trade being there for anything in the world.

I know I'm blessed to take a break from hospital life, and I'm certain she will be in wonderful care without me. I often think of the moms who don't have that option and have already been at St. Jude for six months or longer.

I enjoyed watching Elizabeth choose what special items she wanted to take back with her this time. She brought along a medal from her friend Frank. His mom brought him over yesterday so he could give it to her. It's his wrestling medal. He said he won it for her. That meant so much to Elizabeth! I told her she could look at each chemo treatment as a match and aim to win each one!

She also brought along the new Supergirl Build-A-Bear given to her by her friends at Christian Fellowship School. They even added her name to its paw. 🧡 In addition, she included one of her American Girl dolls with its own wheelchair and a ton of new books.

She starts her next round of chemo tomorrow. We're hopeful that it will not do damage to her heart. I am thankful for each prayer you lift up on her behalf. God is truly faithful, and I'm amazed at all of the goodness He has shown to our family during this season. ❤️ Thank you for allowing me to continually update you. Merry Christmas and New Year! 🎄

DECEMBER 31, 2016

John has had his hands full today. He gave Elizabeth a bath and had to wash what's left of her hair. He had to watch her get her flu shots. He moved all of their stuff back to Ronald McDonald House. And while we were FaceTiming, Elizabeth threw up. Elizabeth is in good spirits though. John keeps things exciting and keeps a happy atmosphere for her. She truly is blessed to have him as a father. I'm hoping they can have a nice New Years Eve dinner somewhere tonight. Thank you John for all that you do!! Happy New Year everyone!! Believing for a year of healing and restoration in 2017!

DECEMBER 31, 2016 — *A Letter from Lizzy*

Dear Dr. Wheeler,

Thank you for saving my life!!! You are a heck of a good doctor!! You are very talented and smart. If I didn't have you as a doctor, I wouldn't be here at St. Judes. Always remember that you are an awesome doctor and an awesome person!! I hope you have a happy New Year!!!

-Elizabeth Wampler

CHAPTER 5

Finding Light in the Darkness

LIZZY'S FIGHT FOR HEALING

THE YEAR 2017 was undoubtedly one of the most difficult and trying times we have experienced. It was during this time that Lizzy continued to face the relentless challenges of cancer treatments at St. Jude. At this pivotal moment, cancer treatments, a formidable ordeal that surpasses the bounds of what anyone should endure, became our path. Our fervent hope is that by sharing these moments, you'll gain a deeper understanding of the strength and courage exhibited by children with cancer and their families in the face of adversity.

JANUARY 2, 2017

Look who looks beautiful even without hair! I asked Elizabeth's permission to post these pictures, and she agreed. We encourage her to read these posts. Apparently the lady cutting her hair was very kind

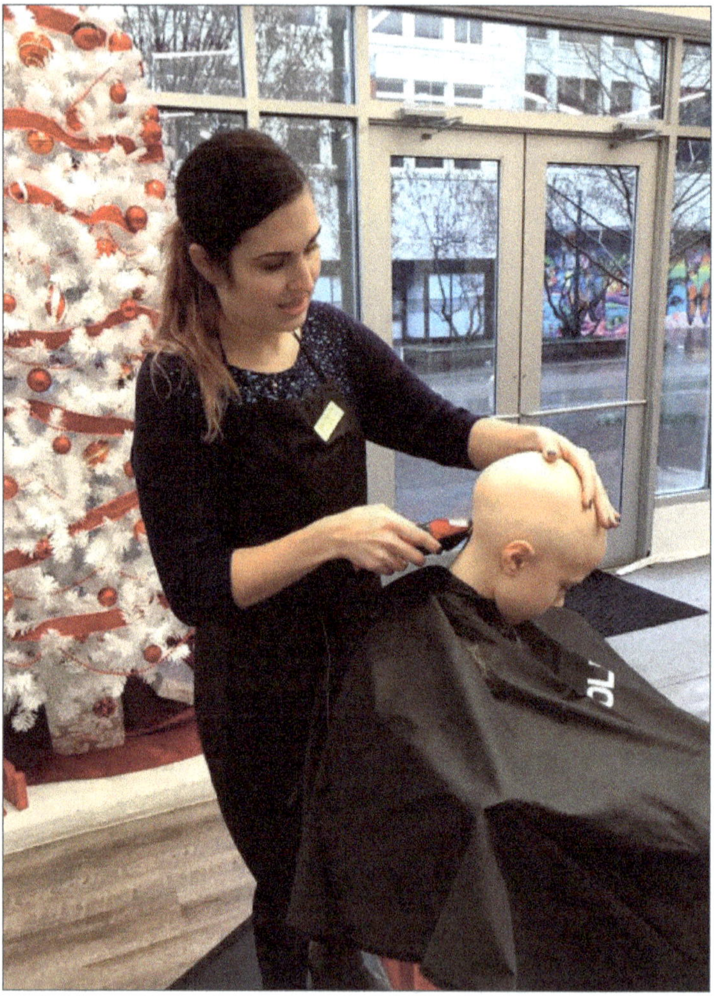

Lizzy bravely shaving her beautiful blonde hair was one of the more emotional moments of our cancer journey. Seeing her bald head made the reality of cancer hit home like never before. 😢#EmotionalMoments

and didn't even charge John for the haircut. So sweet! I know John loves his daughter so much. Seeing her get her head shaved was so hard, yet he felt such amazing love for her. We know she will make it to the other side! Please pray for the following:

1. Elizabeth goes downhill quite quickly. She could be eating one second and then almost fall totally asleep.
2. John was taking her to the bathroom today and she felt light-headed and almost fainted. John had to carry her (and her backpack full of fluids) to the restroom.
3. She told me today that her throat was hurting.

JANUARY 3, 2017

Please pray the doctors find what kind of rash is on Elizabeth's stomach and close to her port. It's important to avoid any infections. It's been going on for over a week now. I'm concerned.

JANUARY 9, 2017

Today is a busy day for Elizabeth. They will be examining her heart to make sure the chemo is not damaging it as well as checking her hearing. They will also be looking at the tumor to see how it's responding to the chemo. Then she will be admitted as an inpatient for her next round of chemo. They waited until this week, when her liver enzymes were a little lower, to start.

This medication, dexrazoxane, was something St. Jude administered before giving doxorubicin. Before taking Lizzy to St. Jude, I met another mom who had a child with osteosarcoma. My friend introduced us, thinking it would be helpful for me to connect with someone who had been through a similar experience. However, when

I asked her how her daughter was doing, she shared that although her daughter had become cancer-free, she tragically passed away from heart failure caused by the chemotherapy. I was shaken to my core and felt utterly speechless.

I vividly recall the moment I learned that St. Jude was providing Lizzy with medication to protect her heart from the specific type of chemotherapy she was receiving. It brought me an immense sense of relief during the constant turmoil of battling cancer. Yet, this journey with cancer is relentless. Just when you start to feel a glimmer of hope, another threat looms around the corner, ready to knock you down once again. It's an unyielding cycle that never ceases to challenge the resilience of hope, always lurking with the potential to shatter it.

JANUARY 10, 2017 *(John)*

Lizzy's third round of chemo is done. For the next 48 hours she'll be in the post-hydration phase. During this time, they will be checking her methotrexate blood levels. She's been asleep all day. Trying to get her up to get rocking on the day! 😝 😝 😝 I want to put her in a wheelchair and roam the hallway. C'mon Wizzy, let's go!

JANUARY 12, 2017

Some of Elizabeth's friends from Christian Fellowship School wanted to host a "Hair-A-Thon" for Elizabeth on January 23. We are so grateful 🧡 Their goal is one hundred people to donate their hair. Thank you 😊 😊

Even though Lizzy was only in the fourth grade, she had attended two schools—Christian Fellowship School for kindergarten and first grade and Cedar Ridge Elementary School for the remaining years. Teachers and families from both schools were so supportive.

As Lizzy was losing her beautiful blonde hair and finally had to have it cut off, one of her friends, Emma, and other students at Christian Fellowship School hosted a "Hair-A-Thon" to raise awareness for children with medical hair loss and to raise funds to help with our expenses. During the event, numerous people cut more than eight inches of their hair to support pediatric cancer. To think that people would sacrifice their hair for Lizzy fills us with so much emotion—even now. Another time, the children did a bake sale during their Christmas program to support us. The bake sale alone raised $3,600 which was then matched by a local company to help with our medical and travel expenses. Jen remembers speaking at the fourth and fifth grade chapel about how "All things work together for good—even in the darkest seasons" to thank them for sharing. Each and every one of those students meant so much to Lizzy and our family.

JANUARY 13, 2017 *(John)*

Today, we did not get a good report. After three cycles of chemo, Lizzy's tumor did not respond the way the doctors had hoped. The tumor appears to be growing and progressing, despite the fact that her pain has decreased significantly. Additionally, after an MRI, PET scan, CAT scan, and multiple battery of tests and X-rays, our doctor is concerned about several spots in Lizzy's lungs and on her other knee. He is not 100 percent sure what the spots are since they are so small. For now, the doctors will treat these concerns as an infection and check the results in three weeks. At that time, if they don't like what they see, they will immediately perform surgery and change her chemo plan.

Jen and I felt we got the wind knocked out of us. The doctor left the room and allowed us to get ourselves together before we faced the kids.

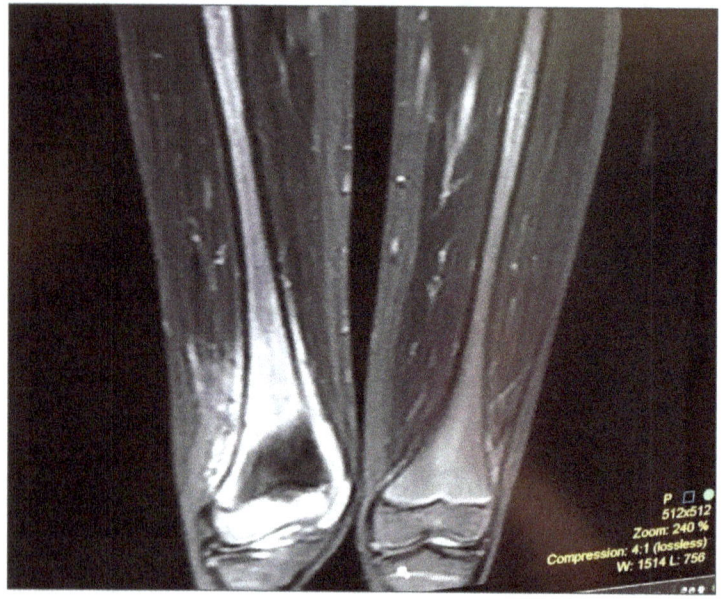

A revealing X-ray capturing the presence of the osteosarcoma tumor that reshaped our lives and ignited our fight against cancer. 💔 #CancerReality

We will pick ourselves up and continue to move forward as we fight this battle together for Lizzy. We will continue to pray, believe, and seek the face of God. Thank you for your continued prayers and support!

JANUARY 18, 2017

The doctors met today to discuss the exact timing of the removal of the tumor. There is a window, not too soon, not too late they are following through their studies and protocol. I told them we were praying for them to have exact wisdom. Praying this cancer continues to shrink, shrivel up, and die.

JANUARY 21, 2017

She finished this round of chemo and then she had a special visitor! Her Uncle Mark drove in just to see her! She was so surprised, and it really meant a lot to her. She is doing well, just very weak and battling nausea. They have given her meds to counter that, so I'm just trying to stay on top of it the best I can.

JANUARY 23, 2017

It has been a rough couple of days for Elizabeth. This last round of chemo has been really hard. She gets extremely nauseous and incredibly weak. This makes it difficult for her to eat or drink. She was in extreme pain last night due to a shot they gave her to help her bones produce white blood cells. At one point she crawled out of the bathroom—unable to stand up even with my help. At times she is overcome by waves of nausea. Yesterday, she started breathing heavily, her eyes rolled back in her head, and she collapsed with exhaustion. After a time, it passed. I have to help her do everything.

We spent the entire day at the hospital today. They are giving her fluids with supplements to help. This too shall pass, I know it will. It just takes a lot of patience to see her go through this. I asked her what cancer treatment is like. At a time when her pain level was high, she said, "It's like being tortured in prison." Despite everything, she remains hopeful and still smiles the moment she has a wave of peacefulness come her way. She is always thanking me for everything I do for her. She is still considerate and kind even as she suffers. At times she kisses my hand as I have to give her medicine through her line. Although she feels sad she is going through this, she is never rude to anyone and just endures with grace. Better days to come!

JANUARY 25, 2017

The doctors are going to move up Elizabeth's surgery to February 13th. I am so happy about that!! No more chemo until after the surgery!

JANUARY 30, 2017

Her absolute neutrophil count (ANC) is back to normal, and she doesn't need a blood transfusion. They haven't had to give her any nausea medicine today other than her Benadryl patch. I've had to give her numerous doses of intense medicines during the past nine days. For now, I'm just enjoying each peaceful day and continuing to hope there is no cancer in her other leg or in her lungs. Scans will probably be next week.

FEBRUARY 3, 2017

Elizabeth is at home for a few days. Today Cedar Ridge Elementary really showered her with love and joy, thanks to their amazing staff and students. Teachers and staff members stopped by to say hello to her. It was heartwarming to see so many people praying for her. The school really wrapped their arms around Elizabeth, giving her gifts, making a donation, and, most importantly, showing her love. 🧡🧡 The kids asked such wonderful questions, and there were a few tears shed during our visit. Elizabeth felt incredibly welcomed, and she cherished seeing each of her special friends. As a mom, I'm just overflowing with gratitude to see my child surrounded by so much love! A big thanks to Cedar Ridge for everything.

As she continued through her treatment, the staff and students at Cedar Ridge kept reaching out. Lizzy was on the student council at her school. She received a certificate for "outstanding leadership" from the student council with all of the members writing encouraging notes and signing the back. It was these little things that meant so much! They even let her come back to school whenever she felt up to it.

We returned home one weekend to find that the children in our neighborhood had secretly held a "Kids for Liz" bake sale selling cupcakes, coffee, and lemonade to support us. Just these kids and some lovely parents raised over $400! Friends gave us tickets to the Mizzou men's basketball game when we needed some excitement. Another time friends held a fundraiser—selling $10 cups of coffee and donuts—to help meet our needs. There was so much kindness poured out.

Friends rallied behind Lizzy by purchasing "Lizzy's Shirts" to show their support. Lizzy even had a hand in choosing the design and colors. Tiger Pediatrics, where John worked, bought shirts for the entire staff and even hosted a "Lizzy Wampler Day." Another time, an amazing teen and his friends did a "Caroling Against Cancer" event in Columbia on Lizzy's behalf. Sullivan Frazee, a nine-year-old, red-headed boy from Rock Bridge Elementary, single handedly raised $400 to help. Our niece, Olivia, helped spearhead a student fundraiser at Belmont University in Nashville for St. Jude. Olivia and her sorority, Kappa Alpha Theta, raised $146,180.78! Countless individuals and groups sent letters, cards, and gift boxes with items to keep Lizzy occupied during the long days of her treatment. We could go on and on about all of the amazing people who stood behind us and allowed God to work through them.

Lots of friends visited us during the many months we were in Memphis. They came from Columbia, Springfield, Fort Worth, and many other places in between to bring love and laughter to our aching hearts. A friend took Lizzy to a Christmas movie. A church brought dinner to the Ronald McDonald House. While there, they felt led to give Lizzy an offering from their congregation. Lizzy had been feeling low and was so surprised she said, "It seems like God knows when I'm down and wants to cheer me up!"

FEBRUARY 6, 2017 *(John)*

MRI, PET body scan, and CT chest scan today and tomorrow. Needless to say, Jen and I are looking forward to a good report. Lizzy's still smiling!! 👍🌕🌕🌕

FEBRUARY 6, 2017

Yesterday while driving back to Memphis, Elizabeth doubled over in pain in the backseat and threw up everywhere in the car. John never complained and immediately took care of her. Of course Elizabeth apologized profusely because she couldn't find her barf bag in time. She's always very considerate. She is in excellent hands when John is with her. It helps my mommy heart not be so sad when I can't be there as well. ❤️

FEBRUARY 8, 2017 *(John)*

Rushed to X-ray to determine why her knee is so swollen and causing so much pain. We will keep you posted. Thank you for praying. I am believing the report of the Lord that she is healed and will be restored.

FEBRUARY 8, 2017

What a hard morning! Elizabeth was in excruciating pain and her knee was really swollen. The doctors were concerned there was a fracture. That is something you do not want with a cancerous tumor. But, after a recent X-ray, there is no fracture. Praise God!

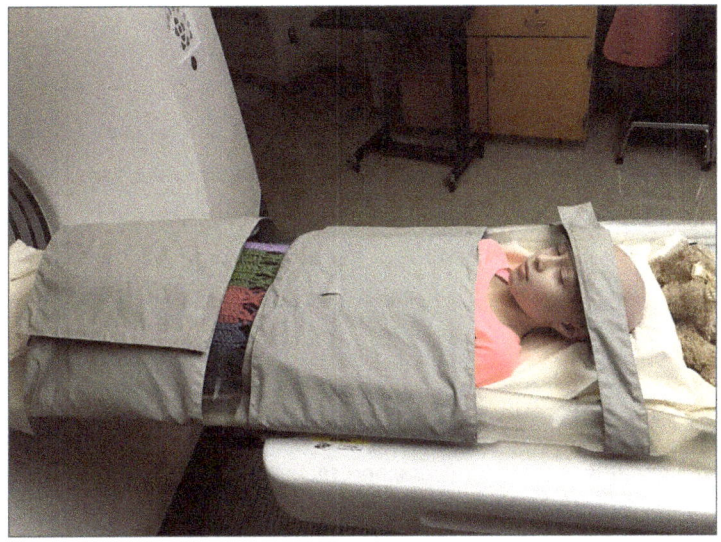

Lizzy, resilient as ever, braves another scan, her strength unwavering despite the discomfort. 💪✨ #BraveLizzy #Resilience

They have given Elizabeth a morphine drip (that she can control) attached to her port. She is very happy about that because of her intense pain this week. The surgery Monday will be such a relief!

Update on all other scans: A few weeks ago the doctors found very small spots in her lungs. We were devastated to learn these might be cancerous. Today's scans showed all but two spots are gone! The last two spots are small and not cancer shaped, so they are not concerned for now. The other spots on her other leg are too small to tell anything. Yay! The tumor has not shrunk but it has not grown either. So I'm not sure if they will change the chemo treatment Elizabeth is on after her surgery. Praying for the right chemo!

FEBRUARY 10, 2017 *(John)*

Today we had our pre-op surgery visit with Dr. Neal. Lizzy's surgery is set for Monday. She will undergo a distal femur resection (limb-sparing surgery) from 8:30 a.m. to 1:30 p.m. Recently the pain from her tumor has been very intense. Monday cannot come soon enough!

Patients with osteosarcoma of the distal femur have traditionally been treated with high above-knee amputation. Today, with earlier diagnosis, approximately 95 percent of osteosarcomas can be resected with tumor-free margins. The functional results are excellent and patient satisfaction is high. They say most patients enjoy a normal lifestyle, with limitations only on running and some contact sports. Thankfully, Jen will be here to support Lizzy during the surgery. Can't wait to see my wife!! ❤️🧡👍🤞🤞🤞

FEBRUARY 11, 2017

I keep telling Elizabeth, this is just a season. She says, "Well Mom, it's really like three or four seasons!" I guess time wise, it is. But I'm just wanting her to know that this isn't where we are staying. She isn't always going to be a kid fighting cancer. Our family isn't always going to be in this place of needing a miracle along with lots of help and support from others. Thank you again for everything, every card, every message, every donation, every meal and act of kindness. We embrace each gift and treasure the love behind it.

We will get to the other side of this season and be able to do all that's in our hearts as a family to do. We all have so much to give back. I look forward to those days ahead. Until then, I do see God at work in this season and am learning and embracing what I can from all of this.

FEBRUARY 13, 2017 *(John)*

So thankful Jen was able to go back with Lizzy to the operating room. We both spoke words of comfort to Lizzy as she was wheeled out. This will be a six-hour surgery, so we'll keep you posted!

FEBRUARY 13, 2017

The first set of doctors just came in and told us they have just finished the first part of her surgery. They removed six inches off her femur and everything went according to plan. The pathologist will examine the tumor in a couple of days so we will know how the chemo has been affecting it. We hope most of the tumor will already be dead. Now Dr. Neal is putting her prosthetic in and all will be done. Celebrating one victory at a time.

FEBRUARY 13, 2017 *(John)*

Surgery is finished and Lizzy is peacefully resting in PACU! The doctors were very happy with the surgery, and there were no complications. Such a joy to hear!

FEBRUARY 14, 2017

Since it's Valentine's Day which is dedicated to love, I think this is appropriate. To love means to sometimes experience pain. The pain of seeing someone you love in so much pain and unable to help. The pain of saying goodbye, if even for a few days knowing it breaks their heart (knowing as a mother I need to take care of my other two children). This pain is so hard, and yet I know I am blessed beyond measure to have:

1. A husband who loves me and whom I love dearly. ❤️❤️
2. Three beautiful children who I've had the privilege of loving for fourteen years.
3. Friends to love. Some who live miles away and yet have supported me and my family like none other.

So, while this has to be one of the hands-down hardest things to do (leave Elizabeth while she is just now coming out of the pain medicine and learning how to even just stand again), I know she will be well taken care of by John. ❤️ John and I switch places in three days, and I'll be with her for three weeks.

So love is a beautiful thing and yet can be quite painful. But ultimately if you have a chance to love, it is worth all the other feelings that may come with it. Happy Valentine's Day!

Jen saying goodbye to Lizzy after surgery before going home to Daniel and Hannah.

FEBRUARY 15, 2017 *(John)*

She's being challenged to do lots of physical therapy but it's all necessary for her to heal properly. Her leg looks wonderful!! I'm thrilled the tumor is out of her body!

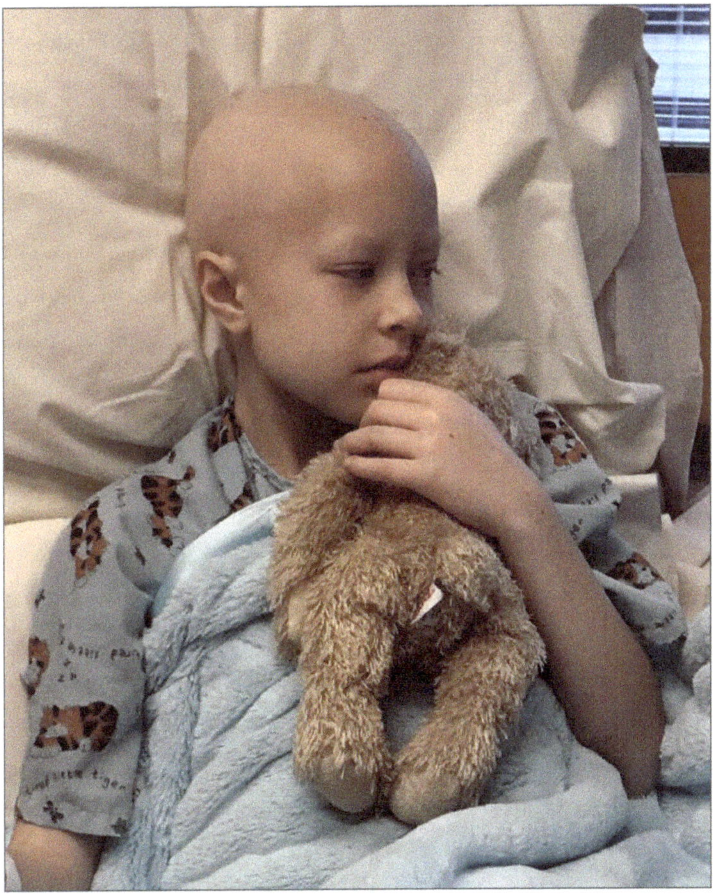

This picture of Lizzy hugging her teddy bear just melts my heart. It is a reminder of innocence and the simple joys of childhood during the battle against cancer. 🧡 #StJudeStrong

FEBRUARY 15, 2017

I know we all go through hard times and experience pain. The challenge is where do we let that pain take us? I've always thought Elizabeth was a blessing—filled with joy and peace this world needs. And now this. Why? She would have given herself to others before all of this. She would have gladly shared her joy with others. I know God didn't cause this, and yet this pain was allowed.

We all have pain, but what can we learn from Lizzy's current pain? How can we help others with this? How can she be completely healed? I pray God can turn our tears into joy and our ashes of mourning into beauty for dancing.

Oh, Lizzy, if only I could spare you from this pain. I love you my darling. I know this too shall pass and healing is yours.

FEBRUARY 17, 2017 *(John)*

The day after surgery, we immediately rocked physical therapy getting Lizzy up and moving. The past several days haven't been easy but we trudged through and have made progress. Lizzy turned her "can'ts" into "can-do's," "won'ts" into "wills," and "don'ts" into "do's." Sore today, but strong tomorrow! 👍👏👏

Pathology results will be ready next week to determine the effect of the chemo on the tumor. It is very important that there is no tumor in her surrounding bone. If they find a tumor, there will be more surgery or amputation. We are hoping for a miracle!!!

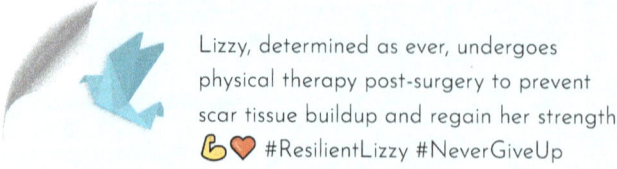

Lizzy, determined as ever, undergoes physical therapy post-surgery to prevent scar tissue buildup and regain her strength. 💪❤️ #ResilientLizzy #NeverGiveUp

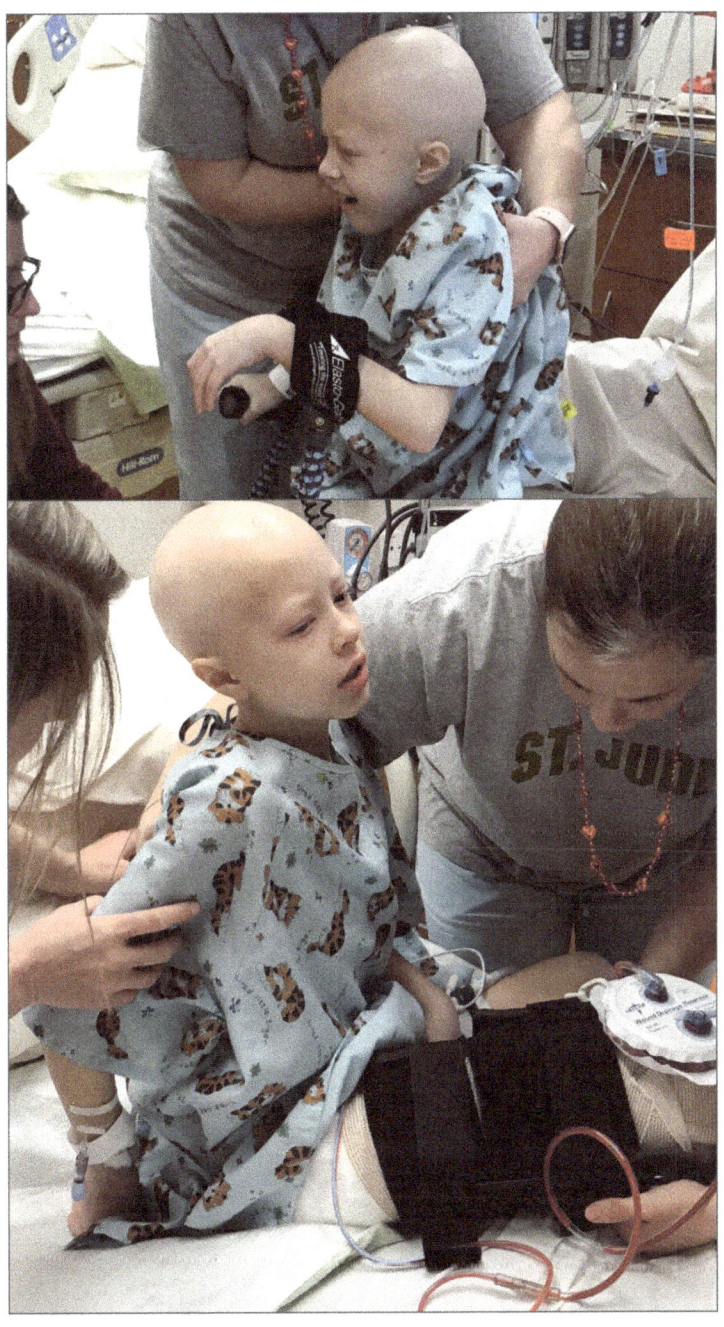

Lizzy's physical therapy the day after limb-sparing surgery.

FEBRUARY 21, 2017

She is experiencing nerve pain in the lower part of her leg. So, they are doubling her pain medicine. I have such an admiration for Elizabeth (and any cancer survivor or fighter). It is not easy to push through every day! Even small tasks like dressing, getting in bed, or going to the bathroom take a long time since she has to use her upper body to lift herself. I have to hold her leg at an angle while she maneuvers her clothes around the drainage tube in her leg while balancing herself on her other leg. She's amazing.

I videotaped her just getting out of the car and you can sense how hard it is for her. She still had the blood drainage thing from the surgery but that will come out tomorrow hopefully. We will let you know once we get her pathology results tomorrow how that went. Believing for a great report!

Some exciting news, we are being moved to the Target House! I will have to move all of our stuff over tomorrow, 😄 but that will give us more room when the whole family is here and more privacy as far as the kitchen area goes.

Lizzy getting out of the car a few days after limb-sparing surgery.

FEBRUARY 22, 2017

After a long day of appointments and having her drainage tube removed, we got the results from the pathologist. They were able to remove the total tumor. The surrounding bone does not have cancer in it!!!!! The doctors say there is a possibility that some cancer was left in the tissue, but I'm choosing to focus on the fact there isn't any cancer in her bones and that the rest of her chemo will deal with anything else.

The tumor was only 25 percent dead, but they are going to stay on this path of chemo. The only other option would be to add two more chemos to her regimen and the studies show there wasn't any difference in patients who received just the two chemos she will be getting. I believe this is a good report. We will continue on her path of healing!

Reflecting on my response now, I realize how incredibly naive I was at that time. If I had been more aware of the implications of any cancer cells remaining in Lizzy's body and what that might entail for her, perhaps my perspective would have been different. In my desperation for Lizzy to be healed, for her to improve, I clung to any semblance of positive news I could grasp onto, even if it came intertwined with the possibility of less favorable outcomes.

FEBRUARY 28, 2017

Elizabeth is healing from her surgery, but she still experiences a lot of pain. It's been hard at times. She will cry in immense pain and needs strong medicine to help take it away. Then she feels loopy from the meds. Her vision is shaky and she hears things at night. It hasn't been easy to watch. But when I get weary, I know where to go! Thank you for your prayers and love.

MARCH 1, 2017

The doctors want her to get back on the chemo train. We are going in tonight for fluids and then start her next round of methotrexate. So looking at the thirty-two weeks of treatments, even though it feels like we've already been here a long time, we are only on week nine. 🙁

We had been at St. Jude since the end of November. Four months had passed, yet hearing that we still had thirty-two more weeks of treatment ahead made it feel like an endless marathon—a journey you simultaneously wished would come to an end and found yourself utterly unable to enjoy.

MARCH 3, 2017

She's not eating much, but she's not throwing up. Hopefully her appetite will return soon.Evenings are especially challenging for us. As Lizzy and I return to our apartment at the Target House, there's a sense of relief that another day is behind us. I try my best to cook something, hoping to create a sense of "home" or normalcy, but Lizzy often doesn't feel like eating, leaving me to dine alone. Instead, she retreats to her room with twin beds, where she rarely gets the chance to simply play—a fact that weighs heavily on my heart. I yearn for her to experience the simple joys of childhood—going to school, attending parties, feeling normal—but instead, she faces pain, medications, and endless medical procedures. However, as I hear her chatting with her dolls while listening to Kari Jobe and worship music, I find comfort in the belief that God is here, comforting her—and us—through these tough times.

MARCH 5, 2017

It has been a rough day. It started at 4 a.m. when I had to wake her to give her meds. She awoke at 7 and 8 a.m. with loud anxious groaning.

There was lots of nausea. I was barely able to convince her to take oral meds. Then, a two-hour hospital checkup turned into five hours.

She is dealing with lots of pain and anxiety. To be honest, it is exhausting to help her with it. The doctors have prescribed anxiety medicine that also helps with nerve pain, but it takes a week to know if it is working. I sure hope it does. She just needs a break from pain, and her anxiety is making it worse. I'm glad she is resting now. Praying for a more peaceful afternoon. ♥

MARCH 8, 2017

We are back for another round of methotrexate! I literally just unpacked her last bag yesterday from our last hospital stay! Elizabeth hasn't eaten a real meal since Thursday. There is lots of nausea and pain. The good news is that her leg pain is somewhat going away and her pain team reduced her medication!!

MARCH 13, 2017

John went through an hour training on how to feed Elizabeth through her double Hickman line until she starts eating again. He will have a couple more training sessions as well! He packed everything from our six-day hospital stay. And guess what? She gets to start another round of chemo Wednesday. Which means packing everything and heading back to the hospital to do it all again. We can do this and are not alone. God is with us. By His grace.

Each week, Lizzy underwent the meticulous process of changing the dressing on her Hickman line, a vital lifeline connecting directly to her heart. These sterile coverings were indispensable for her treatment, serving as the conduit for chemotherapy infusion and sustenance when she was too unwell to eat, relying on Total Parenteral Nutrition

(TPN) for nourishment. TPN is the medical term for infusing food intravenously through a vein to prevent malnutrition. Lizzy's anxiety was palpable during these procedures, a reminder of the relentless challenges she faced on her medical journey.

MARCH 15, 2017 *(John)*

Tonight, Lizzy will receive her toughest chemo treatments—doxorubicin and cisplatin. She'll be an inpatient for the next few days. Nausea and vomiting are the common side effects that we'll be fighting. It breaks my heart to see her go through this.

MARCH 19, 2017

Lizzy is throwing up. It's real. It's horrible, and it's what is happening to our child. My hope is that one day we will stand on the other side of this terrible season and shout the high praises of victory! So, when we get there, may we never forget where we came from. We believe we will get through this season, with the help of your prayers and the grace of God, one day at a time.

MARCH 24, 2017

Elizabeth's counts have been low, and she has had to wear the mask for a day and a half. The kids and I were headed to Memphis tomorrow to switch and enjoy being together as a family. John just called and said Elizabeth has a fever of 102 degrees, and he needs to take her to the hospital because she is neutropenic. This is normal with chemo, but we've never dealt with it until now.

I am a little disappointed we all can't be together at Target House, but we will make this work. We will find a way to still enjoy our short time together as a family. Praying for her absolute neutrophil count (ANC) to go up and her fever to go down.

CHAPTER 6

Racing to a No More Chemo Party

FIGHTING CANCER WITH DETERMINATION

MARCH 29, 2017 (John)

Heading to Columbia for a long weekend stay. ♥ The nurses and doctors were all happy for Elizabeth to get to go home. It's the best medicine for her!

APRIL 2, 2017

Lizzy enjoyed her time with friends and family. Plenty of fun, laughter, and fellowship. So thankful and grateful she was able to come home for a few days!

APRIL 4, 2017

Heading back to Memphis. Tomorrow she will be inpatient in the hospital for her next round of chemo. Enjoyed sleeping in my bed while it lasted!!

APRIL 6, 2017

Elizabeth and I checked in last night to do Week 16 of methotrexate. They just started it this morning, and we've almost gone through our room's barf bag supply.

APRIL 10, 2017

No doctors' appointments today!! We relaxed all day. One appointment tomorrow, a ton on Wednesday, and then back to the hospital Wednesday evening. Thankful for days like these!

APRIL 12, 2017

Lots of physical therapy! Elizabeth is doing amazing. When I think of all the nerve pain she used to have, I know she has come a long way! Thank you God!! We are back at the hospital as an inpatient for another round of methotrexate. I am hoping it will go well, and we can go back to Target House for Easter.

APRIL 16, 2017

Happy Easter!! Elizabeth's head and lungs were really bothering her, so we stayed in the medicine room for four hours. She goes in for scans tomorrow.

APRIL 17, 2017

Elizabeth had all kinds of testing, scans, and X-rays done today. We weren't expecting news until Wednesday. Dr. Bishop came out right after we left D Clinic and wanted to tell Lizzy himself that her scans all looked clear!!!!! The spots in her lungs are gone! Nothing showed up anywhere including the other leg!!!! We are just thrilled!!!!! She was experiencing lung pain and headaches all day. They said it was a side effect of the methotrexate, so they are giving her steroids. Elizabeth will have her ears checked tomorrow as she is having trouble hearing. Hopefully that won't be an issue.

APRIL 18, 2017

Cisplatin, one of the chemos she has taken four times during her protocol, is known to cause hearing difficulties. That is why St. Jude does consistent hearing tests throughout their treatment. Apparently what happens is the follicles in the cochlear nerve can get damaged from cisplatin. The good news is that they are currently doing a lot of research at St. Jude about this. Apparently, they don't regrow in humans but do in chickens and fish! So they are testing these findings. Hopefully, in the future, they will have solutions for chemo patients who have experienced hearing loss.

Elizabeth has lost some hearing. Mostly with high-pitched sounds. It is difficult for her to hear the sounds "s" and "f" in words. Background noise also makes it difficult for her to hear. She has only one more cisplatin round left, so we are hoping for no more damage! Maybe like the fish and the chickens, the hair follicles in her cochlear nerve can regrow! 😊

APRIL 20, 2017

Thank you for standing with us. We are praying for no more damage to her hearing or to her heart. They checked her heart Monday, and it's fine. However, they continue to monitor her heart closely to make sure there are no changes. I want it to do its job and be done!

APRIL 25, 2017

Quick update on Lizzy. The past two days have been nothing short of awesomeness! Lizzy has a 2.5 week break before her next round of chemo. Her counts are good, and she is making progress.

APRIL 28, 2017

Her ANC is zero. It should be 2,000 so it can help her fight any infection. They had to cancel her physical therapy, and she is now in the medicine room ready to get platelets. She has also developed mouth sores under her tongue, and it hurts to swallow. We have avoided those pesky sores until now. John and Elizabeth are off to the hospital! Elizabeth has a fever of over 100 degrees, so she needs to be an inpatient awhile.

MAY 2, 2017

Elizabeth was able to get discharged from the hospital yesterday, and her ANC is rising!! John said it was at 600 today, but they want her platelets to rise as well. There is a possibility she may be able to come home for a long weekend so we can celebrate her and Daniel's birthdays together!! It was a rough ride for Lizzy this past week. I'm so grateful she is coming back to her normal Lizzy self.

MAY 4, 2017

Lizzy is on her way home for the weekend! At first they were concerned because her platelets were really low. Platelets stop any bleeding internally or externally. But they decided to give her a platelet transfusion and let her come home! Yay! We will just need to get her labs done in Columbia Sunday to make sure things are still looking good!

We were hoping to have a birthday lunch and invite everyone to come see her. She broke down and told John that she just wanted to spend time as a family. I think she is very emotionally drained. She hasn't been around a lot of her friends for a while, and I think it may be too much for her now. We just want to make her happy, and so we will save all that for the future!! She has many bright days ahead.

MAY 11, 2017

Elizabeth got the sweetest surprise in D Clinic when Dr. Bishop (her main doctor), Jess (her nurse practitioner), along with several nurses, and her friend Rylee (who happened to be in D Clinic at the time), all walked in with balloons and confetti while singing Happy Birthday to her.

John

DURING ONE OF Lizzy's inpatient stays, amid the routine of chemotherapy, I found myself in the parent room adjacent to Lizzy's, separated only by a small bathroom. It was during one of my mornings, as I stepped out of the shower, that I was greeted by the delightful sound of Lizzy's laughter echoing from her room. Curious, I quickly dressed and made my way to her bedside to discover the source of her joy.

To my surprise, I found Lizzy and Nicki, one of the nurses, engaged in an impromptu dance party, laughing and sharing moments of pure happiness. Witnessing their bond in that moment, I realized the depth of connection Lizzy had formed with Nicki, who, despite her role often involving less glamorous tasks like cleaning and odd jobs, approached her duties with unwavering dedication and compassion.

Later that same day, as Nicki and I crossed paths in the hallway, she confided in me, her voice filled with emotion. She expressed how, in her eight years of service at St. Jude, Lizzy was the first to consistently inquire about her well-being and genuinely take interest in her daily life. Nicki's tears mirrored the depth of her gratitude for Lizzy's genuine care and attention. Reflecting on that moment, I am reminded of the profound impact Lizzy had on those around her.

Lizzy showed me the power of encouraging others, despite what she was going through. I was continually amazed by the way she seemed to build her own strength and courage by encouraging others.

Even the cafeteria workers at St. Jude offer patients love and support. There were always volunteers helping patients and families get their food and find places to sit. I often think about the day the pizza chef gave Lizzy a chef's hat and helped her make a pizza. I can still almost see her smile radiating across the room. I can't tell you how many times Lizzy was in pain or distress and staff members dropped everything to help her. St. Jude always took care of Lizzy and our family. They never gave up on her; she was never treated as a lost cause. There were just so many people who gave so much love to our family during the most challenging time of our life. For that we will be forever grateful.

When Lizzy realized how much the staff was doing to make her feel comfortable, she wanted to return the favor and bless them. So the two of us created a little game together. During our visits to the hospital, we would go into the gift shop and buy little bags of popcorn or other things to give to the nurses and staff working with her that day. We both loved seeing their faces light up whenever they received their little surprises.

MAY 13, 2017

Lizzy knocked out some methotrexate like a champ!! We had a scare for an hour with her lungs, but the doctors were on top of it. She does have to take a steroid every time she takes methotrexate since she has an allergic reaction in her lungs. Her levels are great, so she is on fluids to keep flushing her kidneys. We will go back for a lab check tomorrow.

MAY 16, 2017

Elizabeth is doing great in PT!! Her therapist is so encouraging. Lizzy can bend her leg with the prosthetic in it to 92 degrees on her own. Once we have our next set of X-rays, Doctor Neal, her surgeon, will tell us when she can start putting weight on that leg. She may be free of braces and crutches in a month!!! Her other leg has grown longer than the other already, so they will have to get her some shoe lifts until she's ready for leg lengthening surgery. I don't think they planned on her growing so much so quickly!

MAY 17, 2017

Lizzy is going to knock out another round of methotrexate!! I was so happy she had almost no bad side effects!! I am hoping this round will be the same.

She bent her knee to 102 degrees today on her own!! We are so happy for her. I can tell she is gaining confidence and feeling hopeful about her healing. She zooms around on her crutches, is constantly wanting to make her nurses laugh, and is being joyful like her normal self. We only have eleven more weeks of this routine!!! I am so grateful. I am just amazed how we got this far!! I don't want to be boastful, but I feel like we escaped a fire. I don't really know how to explain it. I know we have scans ahead of us and more chemo, but, inside, I just feel so grateful.

MAY 19, 2017

Lizzy is doing well. She has a urinary tract infection. They said it's not serious, but they are working to make sure her kidneys don't get infected.

MAY 24, 2017

Elizabeth is ready to do her first outpatient chemo!! Instead of packing up for four days, we will come into the medicine room at St. Jude where they will administer her chemo and fluids. After a few hours of receiving doxorubicin, we can go back to the Target House. They have been monitoring her heart diligently and think she is doing great.

MAY 31, 2017

Today was Lizzy's first time to walk and bear weight on her leg since last Thanksgiving!! We are thanking and praising God! The ortho on-cologist doctor gave her the green light to no longer wear her brace and begin weaning off her crutches. Her leg will need to be lengthened since it is over a centimeter shorter than her other leg. This procedure will be done every three to four months until she is fourteen. We went straight to PT, and Lizzy rode a stationary bike! We are still on cloud nine and thrilled for her progress!

JUNE 7, 2017

John just noticed a mole on Lizzy's head. It wasn't there before. She says it hurts. It could be nothing. When John told me about it, my heart just hit my stomach. I don't want to worry about it.

JUNE 14, 2017

Elizabeth had to have an X-ray today because her ankle on the leg with the prosthetic has been swollen. They believe the swelling is be-cause she hasn't used that leg in several months. It's going to take a while to get used to walking again.

John noticed Lizzy getting tired today and had to carry her. Then, when he went to check on her after a nap, she had a fever. So no chemo tonight. Right now, they are headed to the medicine room. I'm praying it doesn't push her schedule back too much. As of now, she is scheduled to come home before school begins in Columbia. Before school!! How wonderful to have time to get organized and settled before she starts school again. So I'm hoping her fever goes away quickly.

John sent me a picture of Lizzy crying for me tonight as they put in her IV. My mother's heart is so sad, yet I know I need to be here for Daniel who has been battling a viral infection in his lymph nodes. Thank you for praying.

JUNE 16, 2017 *(John)*

All settled in and ready to rock this next round of chemo! Fluids all night and methotrexate in the morning. Only five more treatments to go!

JUNE 24, 2017

Lizzy got to be in some brochure or magazine for all of the Chili's restaurants earlier this month. Chili's heavily supports St. Jude. Lizzy will be in the St. Jude winter catalog, so this was a pretty fun day for her! We both got a few fun warm clothes for doing the shoot for them! Be on the lookout for their winter line and support St. Jude through your purchases! I hope Lizzy is OK with the fact that there may not be as many cameras following her once we get home! 😂

Lizzy loved St. Jude and wanted to give back to them however she could. So when ALSAC, the fundraising and marketing organization of St. Jude, asked Lizzy to be involved in their commercial promotions, she enthusiastically volunteered. The people for ALSAC loved Lizzy, so they started using her in a number of promotions for the hospital. She starred in numerous commercials and catalogs for St. Jude.

One fun opportunity Lizzy had through the hospital was being featured on the tables of more than 3,500 Chili's restaurants nationwide. Chili's has been an incredible supporter of St. Jude, with one of the medical buildings even named the "Chili's Care Center." Every year during their fundraiser for the hospital, Chili's creates standup cards to sit on the tables in each of their restaurants, featuring various patients and their stories, including Lizzy's. The photo shoot for this opportunity produced one of my favorite pictures of her. I can't tell you how many people sent me photos of themselves sitting at a table with Lizzie's picture beside them, tagged with messages like, "We went out to dinner and guess who we saw?" The widespread presence of Lizzy's picture in every Chili's restaurant across America was something we could never have imagined. Not only did it bring joy to our family, but it also helped raise awareness about pediatric cancer and the need for a cure.

JUNE 27, 2017

Busy day. Got discharged around noon and began appointments to prepare for her first leg lengthening surgery!! It's a twenty-minute, noninvasive surgery under anesthesia. During the surgery, they place her leg with the prosthesis into a box with a magnet circle in it that heats up. Inside the prosthesis, the metal expands, allowing the prosthesis to expand as a plastic piece loosens. They will need to do this procedure several times as she grows, lengthening it only one or two cm at a time. The final surgery will be when she is fourteen. Then, they will remove her child-sized prosthesis and replace it with an adult prosthesis. It is a lot to take in, but I believe it will all go smoothly. Surgery is at 7:30 a.m. tomorrow morning.

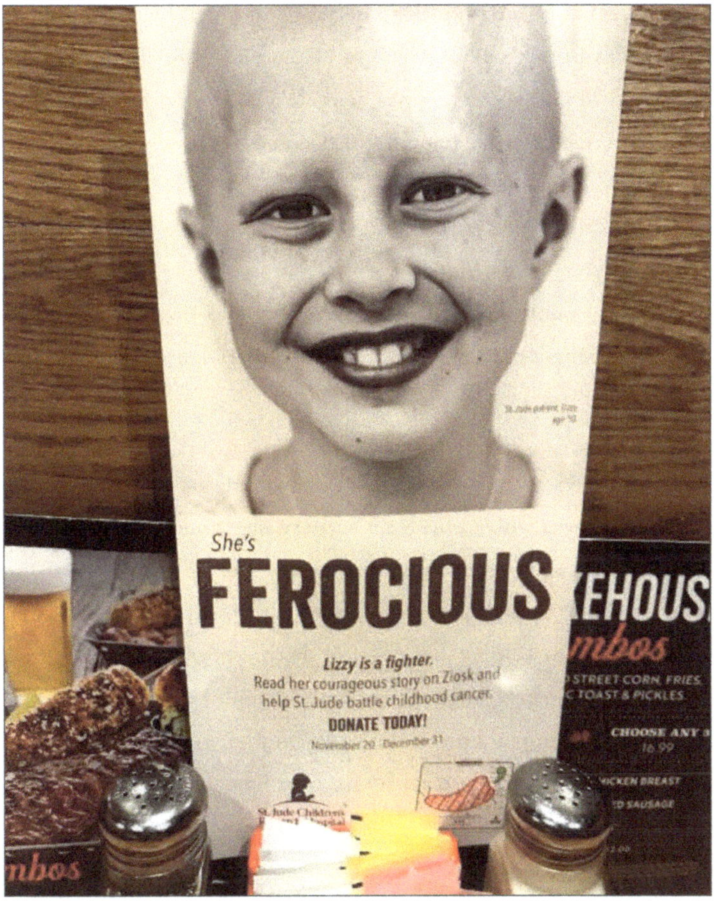

Meet the fierce fighter, Lizzy, whose strength and courage inspire us all. 🌟 This stand-up card, gracing tables in over 3,500 Chili's restaurants nationwide, embodies her ferocity and determination. It is one of our favorite photos of her! #LizzysStrength #Fighter

Some friends have asked again about the mole on her head. We think it is from Elizabeth picking at her head when she gets bored or anxious. It's become a habit we are helping her with. Right now, she has about ten little picks on her head. We are trying to ensure they don't get infected by keeping her distracted and covering them with Band-Aids. This too will pass!

JUNE 28, 2017

The surgery went well! Dr. Neal said sometimes they are only able to lengthen the leg .5 cm, but they were able to lengthen her leg 1.5 cm!! I'm grateful!

JUNE 30, 2017

When Lizzy was waking up from surgery, she couldn't feel or move her leg. Worried it might stay like that, she started crying under the anesthesia and said, "I've worked so hard in physical therapy. I've been working for years!" Janet, her physical therapist, was very happy that she didn't lose much range of motion. She said it was because Lizzy had been working so hard before her lengthening. We were happy with the results and are glad future lengthenings aren't something she will need to dread!

JULY 1, 2017

Last round of doxorubicin ever!! Only two more methotrexates to go.

JULY 6, 2017

Getting Lizzy ready for life at home and ready for school. I actually bought her some school clothes! I'm hoping she can go home at least a few days before school starts to give us a chance to get situated. Only two more chemos left and then some scans, and she is done! 🧡🧡

JULY 7, 2017

Lizzy's counts are low. John will continue to monitor her this weekend to ensure she doesn't get a fever. She may need a blood transfusion Sunday.

JULY 19, 2017

Lizzy is ready for her next to last round of chemo. She is ready to knock this out and is taking this stay like a champ. Fluids all night and then methotrexate in the morning. We're wiped!

JULY 20, 2017

Lizzy has been complaining about pain in her other leg and taking pain meds for it. John and I have been very concerned. The doctors ordered X-rays of her leg. They didn't see anything, so her surgeon thinks it is a stress fracture. She continues to be in a lot of pain. We will need to make sure she doesn't push herself too hard once she gets home.

John and Lizzy were at the hospital all day doing appointments, X-rays, and MRIs. Then John raced back to Target House and packed for her next round of chemo. I'll be there tomorrow to trade places.

JULY 22, 2017

This is our last "changing of the guards!!" The kids and I drove to Memphis yesterday to change places with John. Daniel is going to stay in Memphis with us for her final three weeks. Lizzy is tired, moving slowly and staying more in the wheelchair. We are working to find a new pace to allow both of her legs to get strong again. One more methotrexate to knock out and Lizzy is done with chemo!!!

JULY 26, 2017

Lizzy's last chemo has been postponed until Friday. She has mucositis that needs to heal up from the last methotrexate before she does another round. Praying it will heal before Friday so we can stay on track to get home before school!! We had a lot of testing done to prepare her for school. They want to make sure she has what she needs when she goes back.

Having Daniel here has been fun! We've been reading, folding origami, and playing with fidget spinners. We even watched some fun movies. We will keep you posted on her last chemo. We are ready to get it done!

JULY 28, 2017

Lizzy's last chemo ever!!!!! She will get fluids tonight to keep her kidneys flushing things out, and methotrexate will be given around 10 a.m. tomorrow morning. We will say prayers tonight and enjoy our last chemo stay in the hospital. Lizzy has spent over seventy days in the hospital since last December. Wow!! We are ready for a new healthy season! We are very thankful to be ending this part of her journey. Thank you all for staying with us and lifting our family up in prayer. We have needed it!

JULY 29, 2017

The last chemo bag was taken off around 2:30 p.m. today!! Wahoo!!! I'm not quite sure how to respond. Of course I'm excited!! It just hasn't sunk in that it is over. Maybe it won't ever sink in. From the day we learned of her life-threatening disease until now, I honestly don't know if it ever sunk in. I think I just went into autopilot and started setting the course for my child to get better and live.

I am tremendously grateful to God. He is my source of strength and the one who gave me hope I needed when facing this situation. As for now, I am on a mission to get chicken wings for the kids—and I'll sneak some fresh fruit in as well.

JULY 31, 2017

Happy Monday!! Today we said goodbye to things Elizabeth will no longer miss:

- Being attached to fluids! All those fun late-night trips to the bathroom. Today we said goodbye to her final fluids bag. 🎉🎉🎉🎉🎉
- The loud sound of the pump as it flushed fluids in her all night and day.
- Late-night fluid bags needing to be changed.
- Waking up at 2 a.m. because the alarm needs a new battery.
- Early morning meds at 4 a.m. (leucovorin) to flush out the methotrexate.

Lizzy has been sore walking, so she has been using the wheelchair. She practiced walking today without her crutch and she said it didn't hurt! We will take it slowly, but I love seeing her walk. Her final scans will be next week, and then we will head home. I'm enjoying watching this season start to end. We have a lot of wonderful memories, but we can't wait to make new ones on the other side.

AUGUST 1, 2017

I am packing all of Elizabeth's stuff at the Target House. John and Hannah will meet me on Saturday at a halfway point. He will take some of our things back so when we leave next week our car won't be so full.

I find my heart is so full. I'm re-reading all of the cards that have been sent to Lizzy during the past eight months. The love they carry cannot be denied. We cherish each gift. We were able to endure this journey because so many people supported us in love and prayer. We will never forget each act of love.

AUGUST 2, 2017

We found out today that Lizzy will need hearing aids because of the side effects of cisplatin. The hearing aids will help ensure her speech isn't affected by her hearing difficulties. We should get them this Friday.

We took a quick picture with Lizzy's favorite wound nurse, Irma! Irma can't make it next week to the No More Chemo Party, so I grabbed a quick picture. Irma is very patient and helped Lizzy so much during each wound dressing change. I love nurses like Irma who do such an amazing job taking care of the kids!

AUGUST 3, 2017

Elizabeth's last pentamidine treatment. Like all chemo patients at St. Jude, she will take some oral meds when she goes home to prevent a lung infection. She has been walking more today and hasn't complained of any pain.

AUGUST 4, 2017

Our sweet girl is rocking her brand-new pink and green hearing aids compliments of St. Jude! They will provide hearing aids for her every five years. I'm hoping she won't always need them! One of the first sounds she noticed after putting them on was a sheet of paper on her lap. She moved it and said, "Wow! That has a sound!" As the day progressed, she continued to hear all the sounds she had been missing. Daniel told her she looks like a singer wearing an earpiece. Sound check 1,2,3!!

As we edge closer to her final week, I talked to her oncologist to gather as much information as possible before we leave. St. Jude is a protective little bubble with answers to questions right at your fingertips. I want to get everything we need before we take her back home. I have considered wrapping her in bubble wrap, but I'm pretty sure it's not practical.

Lizzy will have a No More Chemo Party next Wednesday in the D Clinic. It will be a special time for us to celebrate the end of her treatments. If you are one of her nurses or friends at St. Jude, please message me for more info. We would love for you to be there!!

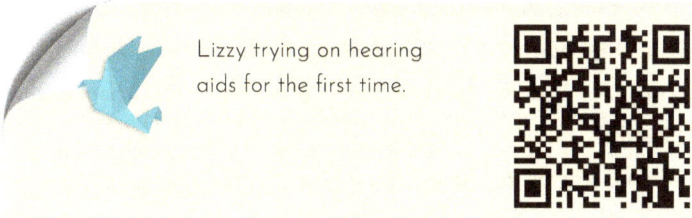

Lizzy trying on hearing aids for the first time.

A No More Chemo Party is a celebration held at the end of a patient's treatment at St. Jude. It is really pretty simple—just confetti, balloons, and food. But since Lizzy had done so many promotions for St. Jude already, they selected her for a commercial promotion highlighting the party. The production team at St. Jude had already prerecorded several different segments about the party, so we were gearing up for a huge celebration. We had prepared handcrafted thank-you cards and batches of brownies as tokens of our appreciation to the doctors and nurses. All five of us eagerly anticipated this milestone and the significance of the moment.

AUGUST 8, 2017

Dr. Bishop called to tell me the radiologist saw something on Lizzy's PET scan. The No More Chemo Party is postponed. We are devastated but not without hope.

AUGUST 8, 2017

We made a special trip back to St. Jude to meet with Dr. Bishop and the child life specialist. They said her left hip lit up in the PET body scan along with two spots above her right leg (the one with the prosthetic in it). Their concern was that Lizzy's hip pain hasn't been getting better. So they plan to do two separate MRI's—one tomorrow and one Thursday. We both had some tough questions for Dr. Bishop. He isn't ruling out hope, and I'm definitely not ruling it out. Hope is what has held us together up to this point. Hope holds me together as I pass kids in uniforms at the grocery store and realize Lizzy's school clothes will need to wait a little longer.

I am devastated. I have shed a lot of tears. I don't want to have Lizzy go through anything else. I just want to go home. I don't want to be away from my other kids anymore. I want to see John more than once a month. I have to believe the best and hope for the best. I'm holding on to the chance that this is nothing. I know this will be alright only because we have our hope in Him.

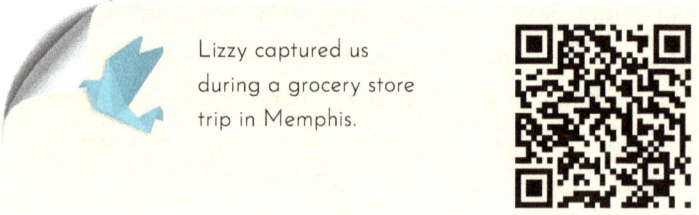

Lizzy captured us during a grocery store trip in Memphis.

AUGUST 9, 2017

It has been a long day, and I am drained. It started with an X-ray of her pelvis then progressed to an ultrasound of her leg with the prosthesis. Finally, we had an MRI of her left pelvis. Before her MRI,

I was called to the clinic. They told me they weren't going to do an MRI of her right leg tomorrow as scheduled because they already saw what they needed in her leg. They have scheduled a biopsy on Friday.

Unless they have this wrong, it will mean some form of further treatment. I literally cried silent tears after this news and prayed for God to let this be nothing. Surprisingly those tears helped. I do believe in miracles. I absolutely do. I'm just weary. I want my little girl to have her hair grow back. I want to see her sparkling clear blue eyes and not the eyes dilated from medicine. I want to see her walk without crutches, running and playing like other kids. These things may take longer than I want. Or perhaps a quick miracle could take place. I am not going to limit God. I am grateful for St. Jude for everything, but right now we need God.

Lizzy is so amazing. She understands what is going on. Today, during the ultrasound, she reached over and took my hand and said, "I'm just sad." I don't blame her. That's when I have the hardest time with this. She hardly ever complains. I have been amazed at the grace she has shown during the last eight months. So when she looks at me with hurting eyes, it's just too much. Yet I feel strength rising. I know the pieces will fall into place. We are tremendously loved, and I believe that a miracle, one no doctor can deny, will come. I know it will!

CHAPTER 7

Holding on to Hope

LIZZY'S CANCER RETURNS

AUGUST 11, 2017

Today, we surrounded Lizzy with love as she underwent a biopsy of the tissue above her right femur and in her left hip bone. Lizzy's oncologist broke the news that they believe she may have an aggressive form of osteosarcoma in her left hip. They also think the tumor has recurred in the tissue above her right femur. The results of the biopsy to tell us for certain will come in three to five days.

When we asked the doctor how we should tell Lizzy this news, he responded, "We have to be brave like Lizzy." Moving forward, we will continue to fight and be brave like Lizzy. As a family, we trust, rely, and hope in God. With God, all things are possible. 👍 🙏 🙏 🙏 🙏

Thank you for standing with us during this tough season!

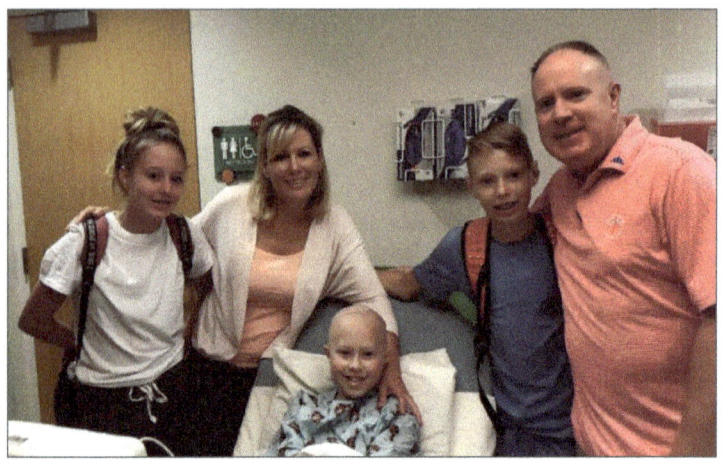

Gathering around Lizzy with love and hope before her biopsy on her right femur and left hip bone. 💗 Our family, including Hannah and Daniel, stands strong with Lizzy in this moment of uncertainty. The doctors suspect a return of her cancer, but our love and support remain unwavering. #FamilyLove #LizzysStrength

AUGUST 14, 2017

We appreciate your prayers and support. Emotionally, I am doing better. One of our dear friends said, "It is like running a marathon and getting right to the end only to find the finish line has moved—and then being told you have to keep running." That is exactly how it felt.

We will find the results of the biopsies this week. If they show osteosarcoma, then they will start her on a new chemo Wednesday evening to try to shrink the tumor. There is talk of surgery. I'm hoping the tumor will radically shrink and surgery won't be as intensive. We are praying for the pain to decrease in both legs as the tumor shrinks to give her relief. She has a hard time getting dressed.

AUGUST 15, 2017

Big day tomorrow with Lizzy's oncologist and ortho doctors to discuss their findings on Lizzy's biopsy.

AUGUST 16, 2017

The doctors believe the pain in her right leg (the one from the initial tumor) was inflammation rather than a recurrence of osteosarcoma! This means no amputation for this leg as the doctors had once told us. Praise God! However, they do believe there is osteosarcoma in her left hip. They have given us a new protocol to follow with two very strong chemos that have worked amazingly well for this type of cancer. There may be surgery in September if needed.

We are held together by the grace of God. He has given John and me scriptures to stand on and faith to hold steady through this horrible storm. His hope is ever radiant in our hearts.

Lizzy is pressing through. I talked to her today on the phone and she said, "Today I was supposed to start my new life back at school. I'm sad I'm not there." This is a reality for her, but she continues to trust God and give Him all her feelings. She knows she is loved, and we are with her every step of the way. And, in true Lizzy fashion, she continues to laugh and smile when given the opportunity. She is very brave.

- Please pray for strength and joy for Elizabeth.
- Please pray for complete protection. We ask that these new chemos will kill the cancer, the tumor will shrink quickly, and Lizzy has no side effects in her body.

- Please pray we have the wisdom to give her the proper food and supplements to keep her strong. There are so many lovely people presenting us with options. We need to know which ones will help her and not interfere with the chemo.
- Please pray for God's continual grace for our family to get through these next few months.
- Please pray for continual grace in our job situations as we have both gone from full-time to part-time.

There is a possibility we can do some of her treatments at St. Jude's Springfield (Missouri) affiliate. She will go inpatient tonight to start these new chemos. Her stay will be longer than before. It's never easy to stay long periods of time in any hospital. John will be with her for this first round.

AFTER ENDURING NINE months of grueling treatment, the crushing blow of a recurrence struck with unforgiving force. It even seemed to be more devastating than her first diagnosis. To describe it as a sucker punch would be an understatement. The realization that Lizzy couldn't return home yet, that more treatment loomed ahead, cast a shadow of uncertainty over our already fragile existence. In this protocol, there was no clear finish line; the path ahead was riddled with unknowns, leaving us adrift in a sea of fear and doubt.

This news not only shattered my heart and John's, but it also weighed heavily on our other two children. They longed for their sister's comforting presence, and we all just wanted our lives to return to normal. The pain we endured was overwhelming and relentless, especially knowing that with osteosarcoma treatment, if the initial protocol fails and the cancer spreads, the survival rate can plummet from 75 percent to a mere 20 percent.

Yet, despite the darkness threatening to engulf us, we clung to the flickering flame of hope. It was fragile, but it sustained us as we navigated the treacherous terrain ahead, uncertain of what lay beyond the horizon.

AUGUST 22, 2017 (JOHN)

There is a "thankful" board at our favorite coffee shop in Memphis. Lizzy surprised me by writing, "Thankful that I am alive and a cancer survivor. Lizzy, age 10. Still fighting." I know what I am thankful for.

Grateful moments at Muddy's Bake Shop in Memphis—a cherished escape from hospital life. Lizzy and I loved to explore Memphis any chance we could. #StillFighting #Gratitude 🧡

God raised up some amazing people to hold our hands and believe with us for our daughter. Throughout Lizzy's journey, we continually felt the love, prayers, and moral support sent our way by our community. We are givers and always want to work hard, but in these moments we had to allow others to bless us. As we made changes in both of our jobs, our finances dwindled, yet we trusted God. He provided.

Money was donated to help offset the expenses of our travel and lost wages during Lizzy's treatment. Cards, letters, and packages were sent to keep Lizzy's spirits high—she read them all! The power of all the people surrounding us literally carried us through this difficult time. There were constantly friends bringing dinner and groceries for our family to help keep a semi-normal pace for Daniel and Hannah. We are so tremendously grateful.

While our other two children are kind of in the background of this story, they really should be on the forefront as they endured so much during the fifteen months. This was not easy on anyone. We don't know what we would have done without their love and support carrying us through those difficult days.

AUGUST 24, 2017

She finished her first round of these two new chemos Monday. Right now we are in limbo. They have to wait two to three weeks before giving her more chemo. We want to bring her home and have her treated at the St. Jude affiliate in Springfield. Once we have a clear plan, we will let you know.

I wake up every day in high faith alert. Each day I hope for a miracle. I am grateful for God's courage and strength that holds me up during these difficult moments. At times I feel discouraged when

I walk past her empty bedroom. I write these things down so I won't forget and will remember to be thankful in the future.

AUGUST 25, 2017

Wonderful news! Lizzy has been accepted to the St. Jude affiliate in Springfield. According to her treatment plan, she should be finished in December. She will receive the rest of her chemo treatments at Mercy Hospital so she can be close to friends and family. All major scans and possible surgeries will be done in Memphis.

AUGUST 27, 2017

John and Lizzy wanted to come home to Columbia last week. However, the doctors felt we needed to wait because her ANC (white blood cells) would drop after chemo. Sure enough they did (zero on Friday). We were disappointed but assumed her numbers would rebound by this week. Well, they are in the medicine room at St. Jude now waiting to be admitted. This morning Lizzy woke up in pain with a high fever. She crawled into bed with John crying. He woke up from a sound sleep and quickly got them ready for the hospital. Since they didn't have a wheelchair anymore, he had to carry her all the way downstairs.

AUGUST 29, 2017

The doctors need insight and wisdom to understand why her right leg (the one with the prosthetic) is swollen. She isn't able to bend it at all and is in severe pain.

AUGUST 29, 2017 *(John)*

Lizzy was rushed to ICU due to swelling in her right leg. An infection, pain, and ICU team are helping her since an infection could be life-threatening. Her blood pressure and heart rate are high, and her oxygen is low. We are waiting on ortho to see if they will get all the fluids that are in her leg out.

AUGUST 30, 2017 *(John)*

This is John with the latest from ICU. Jen and I feel hopeful and have some direction! This morning, the swelling in Lizzy's leg has gone down. She will be in the operating room late morning to drain and clean up the area around her prosthetic. Once the fluid and infection have been cleared, the doctors believe her pain will be reduced. Thank you for your support and prayers.

AUGUST 30, 2017

Lizzy just texted saying she is ready to get out of the hospital. I bet she is! Her surgery went well. They used a four-inch incision to drain her leg and put antibiotic beads on her prosthetic to kill any infection. We pray that the incision heals quickly, her fever goes down, the tumor in her hip shrinks, and we can keep on the chemo schedule so we can get her home. One answered prayer at a time. ❤️

SEPTEMBER 1, 2017

John had a busy morning meeting with the infectious disease, wound care, pain, and ortho teams. The pain team is looking into some different pain meds to help Lizzy sleep at night. The staph infection team is reviewing the results of the surgery. Dr. Neal likes the way her leg is healing and believes her wound vac will be removed early next week. The doctors also want to do a chest X-ray to make sure she doesn't have pneumonia. Wound care will come in later to help with the places on her scalp that have been picked but aren't healing quickly. I'm praying her pain diminishes, her oxygen levels rise, her fever is reduced, and her wounds heal quickly.

SEPTEMBER 5, 2017

Lizzy has been without fever for over two days. She did have a staph infection, but apparently it responds to many antibiotics and makes the options of treatment easier. We will take it! Her heart rate is up, and her oxygen levels are back to normal. The swelling in her leg has gone down tremendously. They will take her drain tube out surgically tomorrow. Yay! The wounds on her head are healing nicely too. This was her ninth day in the hospital. Today was the first day she was able to get some fresh air. We checked mail and got to talk to a friend or two. Such a treat.

After having such a serious infection last week and with all of the teams we are now a part of (infection team, pain team, ortho team, etc.), the doctors decided it would be best to keep her here for a while versus moving her to Springfield. We were disappointed at first but agree that we need to do what is best for Elizabeth. We are grateful for a day with no bad news and celebrate each prayer request that gets answered. Miracles can happen all at once or little by little. I'll take either. 🧡

SEPTEMBER 10, 2017

Lizzy was discharged on Thursday after twelve straight days in the hospital! She had the tube removed from her leg while she was awake. She was so brave. She did scream a bit, but I told her to go for it. I've never had a tube pulled out of me, and this was her second time to have this done. If she needs to scream, go for it!

SEPTEMBER 14, 2017

They started chemo again last night. This is a five-day, hospital-based chemo. We pray it will target any cancer cell in her body, kill it, and leave no bad side effects.

An update from Jen and Lizzy before starting round two of chemo.

SEPTEMBER 16, 2017

Lizzy's surgery went well. They drained four ounces of "stuff" from her right knee. I asked what causes this to swell up again even on antibiotics. They aren't sure. I'm praying this does not keep reoccurring and we can move on to healing. Hoping for clear answers soon.

SEPTEMBER 19, 2017

Praying for doctors to have some answers for us tomorrow regarding her right leg. Her breathing has been strenuous. She's been very nauseous today and has hardly eaten. Thank you for standing with us. We love you all!

SEPTEMBER 20, 2017

I talked to her oncologist about her lung pain. After some quick breathing tests, he concluded it may be due to stress or anxiety. He decided she needed a blood transfusion. Her hemoglobin was low and her energy has been lacking, so I'm hoping this will be a good pick me up for her!

SEPTEMBER 23, 2017 *(John)*

We're enjoying a peaceful time in the Amy Grant Music Room at The Target House. Lizzy taught herself how to play, "Joy to the World" on the piano. It's a simple, quiet day here but I'm enjoying my time with my girl. 🧡 🤍

We will forever cherish the profound impact of the music therapy department at St. Jude on Lizzy's life. Among her favorite moments were the sessions spent immersed in music, where she found solace and growth beyond words. These special therapists nurtured Lizzy's musical talents, encouraging her to sing and even teaching her to play the ukulele. With their guidance, Lizzy blossomed into a confident performer, sharing her beautiful voice with others.

Songs like Kari Jobe's "The Garden" and "The Lost Boy" from Peter Pan became her anthems, offering comfort and strength during challenging times. We want to share a song with you that Lizzy wrote during her journey. We hope that reading these words shows you a glimpse of that spunky, strong girl that is our Lizzy!

Recordings made at St. Jude of Lizzy singing.

I Can Fight Through

By Elizabeth Wampler

When I was 9 years old I had to stop my life to fight
I wanted to run around, do cartwheels on the ground
I couldn't do that so we had a little chat, I had to fight
 my way through a little path
I wanted to run away from the doctor, But they said
 sadly to stay a little longer.

I didn't want to fight, I didn't want to fight, But I
 said, I said
I can fight through, yeah, I said, I said
I can fight through, yeah, I said, I said
I can fight through, yeah, I said, I said
I can fight through, yeah, Whoo, yeah, Whoo, yeah

I couldn't find my way through it all alone, yeah
I wanted to run away and go home, yeah
I just couldn't, I just couldn't
I just wouldn't, I just wouldn't
I just have to fight no matter what

I found a really bright spot up in the sky, I climbed up
 there to see what going on
I found Jesus healing people from the war, I turned
 and saw a line there was a lot more
I had a big relief and walked up to the people, Then
 Jesus said to come up right now
I fell on my knees and wept on the ground, Then I
 heard him say it's okay

SEPTEMBER 25, 2017 (John)

This might be my first selfish Facebook rant! Moving forward, I will continue to be so positive and optimistic that Joel Osteen will have to tell me to chill out. 🙂

Yesterday, Lizzy and I spent the day crafting friendship bracelets together, enjoying the tranquility of making slime and watching a movie together. However, as night fell, the atmosphere shifted dramatically. By Lizzy's bedside, I stood, gripping her hand tightly as she writhed in agony, her cries piercing the air, pleading for her mom. Watching my daughter in such unbearable pain almost tore my heart in two. Holding her hand, I felt the weight of her torment and suffering. Man, it hurt everything within me.

I realize this is not about me. As a father, I will do what I have to do to stand, fight, and support my daughter and family through this journey. I debated whether or not to post this, but I wanted to give you a picture of what Lizzy is going through. My intention is not to seek sympathy but to offer a glimpse into the reality she faces. Despite it all, Lizzy maintains a remarkable attitude and continues to radiate with her beautiful smile. —feeling fed up at St. Jude Children's Research Hospital.

SEPTEMBER 26, 2017 (John)

Took Lizzy out on the town and celebrated her pushing past the pain. Her counts are up, her right leg looks better, and we MIGHT get to come home on Friday (been away from home for over four months).

Lizzy is gearing up for a full schedule of appointments in the next two days—MRIs, PET body scan, X-rays and whatever else they throw at us. These tests and scans will be critical in determining how her tumor is responding to the new treatment. We are praying and believing for the best!

SEPTEMBER 28, 2017

Tonight, Lizzy was totally surprised by two Ballet Memphis dancers who gave her a private performance.

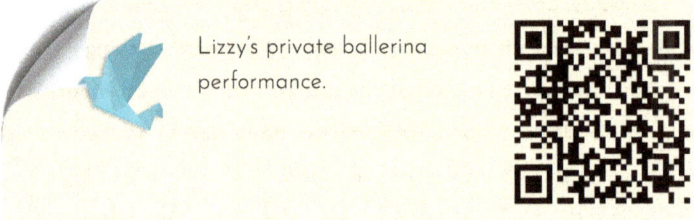

Lizzy's private ballerina performance.

Meeting these ballet dancers was a dream come true for Lizzy since she had always wanted to become a dancer. A few months later she got to reconnect with these two special ladies when she was invited to tour the Ballet Memphis. They showed her how the dance costumes were made, and she even got to sit in for a private dress rehearsal.

SEPTEMBER 29, 2017

We got some exciting news!! Lizzy gets to come home for a six-day break! She hasn't been home for close to five months, so we're thrilled to be together as a family. The first thing she wants to do is to pet and snuggle with our two cats. 🐱 Her scans and tests show that there are some improvements and a decrease in activity in her left hip. According to her diagnostic imaging notes, there is a "slightly improved appearance of the left posterior ischial bone metastatic disease." Bottom line, the chemo is working and her treatment plan will continue on with four more courses (three to four months) of chemotherapy. Radiation therapy is also an option the doctors will consider down the road. They will look at new scans after two more rounds of chemo to determine surgery potential in her hip as well. The doctors are also closely monitoring some spots in her right femur.

OCTOBER 5, 2017

Lizzy enjoyed her six-day vacation in her own home with her family. We did normal everyday things but enjoyed doing them "together." She also got to see some of her friends. Lizzy enjoyed playing with her cats, sleeping in her own bed, swinging on our tire swing, talking with her sister, and playing 2K18 with her brother.

Chemo starts tomorrow, so we are enjoying our last bit of freedom out of the hospital while we can. We are praying for these next two rounds of chemo to shrink and kill the cancer cells in the tumor on her left hip. Miracles still happen!

OCTOBER 6, 2017

Lizzy is learning how to walk again. It's the second time she's had to learn how to walk this year! It has been painful, but she pushed through like she always does. Her right knee has not been able to straighten since her staph Infection, so this is helping her.

OCTOBER 6, 2017

Getting ready for her next round of chemo!! She will be there five days and four nights! The tumor is in her left ischium and part of the pubis of her left side. This is a hard area to surgically remove. Her surgeon has some concerns about completely removing the tumor without any margin being left behind. So these next two rounds of chemo are very important to shrink the tumor. Each round is one week with three weeks in between for her body to recover. In about seven weeks, she will be going through more scans to see how this is progressing to help determine all of these major decisions.

CHAPTER 8

Celebrity Smiles and Compassionate Hearts

FINDING JOY AMID THE PAIN

THROUGHOUT OUR JOURNEY at St. Jude, we were blessed to meet a myriad of amazing individuals. Lizzy's vibrant personality, coupled with the unique environment of a children's hospital funded by donations, created a perfect breeding ground for these encounters. These interactions became lifelines for Lizzy providing much-needed strength and encouragement in the middle of her battles with pain and suffering. Each meeting, whether with a celebrity or fellow patient, felt like gentle hugs and kisses from God, giving her a breather from the pain.

Throughout Lizzy's months at St. Jude, I found comfort in sharing her journey on Facebook. With so many challenges, it was heartening to sprinkle some positivity and light into our updates, offering a glimpse of the amazing people she met. People followed her encounters, eagerly anticipating who she would meet next, and each interaction became a cause for celebration. In a time filled with darkness and uncertainty, it was a joy to witness Lizzy finding moments of happiness and connection, and it seemed the entire community celebrated alongside us. Who wouldn't want to uplift a little girl during her darkest moments?

While these experiences would have been fun and exciting under different circumstances, the weight of Lizzy's cancer seemed to intensify their impact, transforming ordinary moments into extraordinary ones. Meeting these individuals provided a welcome respite from our sorrow, infusing challenging days with joy and significance. This is certainly not the path I would have chosen for Lizzy, no parent would. Yet, with God walking alongside us, He was able to create beauty from the ashes—even in our darkest times.

OCTOBER 10, 2017

This has been a tough chemo—lots of nausea and plenty of tears. One more night to go. Ready to get out of the hospital.

The exciting news? The Houston Rockets totally made her day, maybe even her whole week!! 🏀 🏀 When James Harden and Chris Paul take selfies with you, well it's hard not to smile! She even missed a nausea med and never even noticed!! Thank you Houston Rockets!! The Rockets are Daniel's favorite team, so when I texted him saying Chris Paul was getting an autograph from James Harden just for him, I'm pretty sure he nearly fainted. 😄 Such a great way to finish one more night of chemo. #houstonrockets #jamesharden

Lizzy had the incredible opportunity to meet numerous sports personalities including the Harlem Globetrotters and some Olympic medalists. She attended the FedEx PGA golf tournament as well as met dancers from the Memphis ballet. Although she met players

An unforgettable moment with James Harden from the Houston Rockets! 🏀 Grateful for his kindness and support during our family's journey. #Gratitude #KindnessMatters

from several basketball teams, including the Detroit Pistons and the Memphis Grizzlies, her all-time favorite was meeting James Harden and Chris Paul from the Houston Rockets. When James Harden arrived, knowing how much her brother loved him, Lizzy exclaimed, "Oh my gosh, I can't wait to tell Daniel." In a heartwarming gesture, James grabbed my phone and took a selfie with Lizzy. Though it may seem small, that extra effort meant the world to us.

Later we received a handmade "Houston Rockets bear" from the wife of the Rockets' General Manager. She originally made them for the children of the team but made an extra one for Lizzy. It meant so much to Lizzy to have a special gift just like the Rocket kids (aka Chris Paul's kids) did. She was amazed! Another special gift that came to Lizzy during that time was from Miss Elementary Tennessee, Makayla Murphy. Makayla had worked hard to earn her crown. Yet when her mom asked her what she wanted for Christmas, she told her she wanted to give the crown to Lizzy because she felt she deserved it.

OCTOBER 16, 2017

Our life truly balances on taking temperatures! Lizzy's ANC is 0 so her temp can not get to 100.7 degrees, or we head to the hospital. We snuggled all night, and I could feel her temperature rising. At 9 p.m. it was 100.4. I waited an hour as they instructed me to do, and it went down to 99.7.

OCTOBER 18, 2017

Her ANC is 2,000!! Wahoo!! So great. She hasn't had a fever since yesterday. They are still checking for some other viruses, but we will get out of the hospital today. Sometimes I just stare blankly at the doctor or nurse when they ask me about her pain. I have to think about which part of her body we are talking about—head, stomach, lower back, pelvis, leg, foot. This journey can be daunting at times.

OCTOBER 24, 2017

We loved having Lizzy at home! To be together under the same roof for three nights in a row was complete joy. We are a normal family with sibling fights, chores, homework, after school events, friends, sleepovers, driving lessons, and all the other beautiful/stressful crazy stuff that makes a family. Lizzy's eleven-month journey has touched every aspect of all of our lives. It's absolutely the hardest on Lizzy, but it has been difficult for our other two children also. This weekend my heart filled up as I watched all three of them interact with one another and call each other names. It was so fun to watch Lizzy laugh as they called her a name. In true Lizzy fashion, she held her own and dished it back at them. The strength that comes from being the youngest!

OCTOBER 25, 2017 *(John)*

I was given the highest compliment from Lizzy recently. In our conversation, she stopped me and out of the blue told me I sounded like Paul Blart from Mall Cop. 😂 😂 😂

Lizzy is gearing up for her fourth treatment on the solid tumor unit at St. Jude. We will be cooped up in this hospital room for the next five days. Oh, not to worry! There will be plenty of things to do to stay busy and have fun. 😁 Before being admitted, we had a knockdown, drag out, get at it tickle fight. This was smack-dab in the middle of the busiest part of the hospital. 😊 Lizzy just laughed and yelled as we laid down on the couch waiting for her next appointment.

John and Lizzy went live on Facebook from the hospital to share an update, which unexpectedly turned into a tickle fight.

NOVEMBER 6, 2017

So many things. First, Lizzy's ANC is up to 900, and we got to escape the hospital! That's always great! Second, Lizzy has been working on a piece with *The Today Show* for St. Jude to air during the week of Thanksgiving. *The Today Show* always gives St. Jude time every day during the week of Thanksgiving to highlight what they are doing as a hospital. Lizzy was chosen to be in one of those segments. It will be about her and Ashley's relationship. Ashley was her first nurse here at St. Jude. She had osteosarcoma as a child—just like Lizzy.

I am humbled to have Lizzy in their show. I know no one wants their child in a show for cancer, but I'm thankful that God has allowed her these fun opportunities to help fill her days with some exciting things.

She let her light shine. One of the questions Sheinelle Jones asked her was, "How do you stay positive all the time? You just seem to radiate positivity." Lizzy told her no matter how dark things get, she always focuses on the bright side. Then she said she has faith in God. ♥

As we finished our day, we made a stop at Kroger to gather groceries for the Target House. It was amazing to watch her excitement as she carefully selected apples for our applesauce, scooting herself in the wheelchair to pick out each one. Later I asked her if being in a wheelchair ever made her feel sad. Her response was: "No, if I do get sad, I just remind myself that one day I will be able to sing, dance, and do the normal stuff again like I used to do." Yes, Elizabeth, I believe that too. I do!

NOVEMBER 8, 2017

I think Lizzy has had one of the best days of her life. 💜 She absolutely adores Chip and Joanna. (Who doesn't?) They came to Target House to remodel their cafeteria. Lizzy was chosen to be the first one they revealed it to. 🤯 We got to personally meet Chip and Joanna with all of their camera crew. They spent a lot of time with Lizzy. (I didn't have my phone!) It should be in some upcoming Target video coming up. Joanna gave Lizzy her necklace and told her they would be praying for her. 💜 💜 Then Chip got his hair cut, and they donated $200,000 towards St. Jude! 💜

When we first arrived at St. Jude with Lizzy, our days were often spent in the hotel room. Initially, there wasn't a room available for us in the long-term housing, so we stayed in a hotel room at the Ronald McDonald House. It was there that Lizzy discovered the HGTV station, a channel we didn't have access to back home. Almost immediately she started watching Chip and Joanna Gaines on their show, *Fixer Upper*. It is unusual for a nine-year-old girl to be so drawn to a home renovation program, but Lizzy was entranced by Chip's playful humor and Joanna's practical expertise. Perhaps their dynamic reminded her of the relationship between me and John, I'm not sure. Nevertheless, she formed a deep connection with the show and continued to be a fan as she went through her chemotherapy protocol at the hospital.

So when Chip and Joanna collaborated with St. Jude for the first time in 2017, this partnership led to the renovation of the dining and kitchen area of the Target House, where we were living at the time. The Target House serves as long-term accommodation for families, providing a home away from home for those who may need to stay in Memphis for extended periods while their child receives treatment at St. Jude. Although each apartment has its own kitchen, the communal dining area was primarily used by organizations bringing dinner for the residents.

The renovation Chip and Joanna undertook was truly stunning. Using pieces from their new Target collection, they transformed the space into a warm and inviting dining area. Featuring wooden tables, a coffee bar, inspiring artwork, and a white subway tile backsplash, the design refresh created a cozy atmosphere for families to gather and share meals. Joanna even went on record saying it was her all-time favorite renovation.

Before our meeting with them, we had recorded a video featuring interviews from both Lizzy and me, sharing our story. This video was sent to them ahead of time. We were unsure how much time we would actually get to spend with them or if they would even see the video. When the moment finally arrived, we met Chip and Joanna in the newly remodeled dining area where the producers staged our encounter for the commercial shoot. As they walked into the room, Lizzy, standing in front of me and leaning on her crutches, was visibly overwhelmed. She just physically leaned back, and I thought she was going to faint. It was as if she couldn't believe they were standing right in front of her.

There was an undeniable presence to both Chip and Joanna. I was struck by how tall they both were in person, and Joanna's beauty was even more striking in real life than it appears on television. Their magnetic personalities and evident talents shone through effortlessly.

During our meeting they presented Lizzy with a signed copy of one of their books. But what truly touched Lizzy was when Joanna removed her gold chain necklace and placed it around Lizzy's neck. It was such a gesture of genuine kindness and compassion.

Joanna expressed how moved they were by our story and Lizzy's journey. Lizzy was absolutely speechless! Then, after we recorded the video, they allowed all the other families to come in to meet them. Among the families there was Lizzy's good friend, Bailey, who had the same type of cancer as she did. Since his family lived locally in Memphis, they sometimes missed out on events because they weren't staying at the Target House. Like Lizzy, Bailey also developed a relationship with the Gaines family, and it has endured over the years.

Everyone gathered for some food in the newly renovated dining room, and then we later adjourned to the patio to witness an unforgettable moment: Chip getting his head shaved. This was part of his "Operation Haircut" campaign, where Chip pledged to buzz his hair if his social media followers raised $25,000 for the hospital. Remarkably, they exceeded expectations, raising a total of $230,000. Chip made Lizzy feel so special by engaging with her throughout the shaving process. With a playful spirit, he repeatedly exclaimed, "I want my head to look like Lizzy's!"

It's hard to imagine meeting anyone else who would have left such a profound impact on Lizzy as Chip and Joanna Gaines did. Their warmth and kindness were truly exceptional. We took pictures with them and have been fortunate to maintain a connection ever since. After their visit, Joanna even took to her Instagram account to share their experience, expressing, "We are leaving Memphis changed…we go with your faces on our minds and your stories in our hearts" (Joanna Gaines, Instagram, 8 November 2017). Their genuine care and empathy continue to resonate deeply with us.

All of this affirmed to us that our child was truly seen and that her story left a lasting impact. A 2019 *People* magazine article about Chip and Joanna noted that a life-changing moment for them was

When Lizzy met Chip Gaines at St. Jude, magic happened! 💝 Chip shaved his head, raising $230,000 to fight childhood cancer! 🎗 His heartfelt gesture left Lizzy speechless. #OperationHaircut #StJudeHeroes #ChipAndJo #ChildhoodCancerAwareness 💥

Chip Gaines on Instagram, 2019:

When @joannagaines and I visited St. Jude two years ago, those kids changed us—their joy, their hope, and playfulness in the face of their battle against cancer, there's no way it couldn't have. But you know that feeling you get when you meet someone who you feel connected to right away, like you've known them forever? For me, one of those people was Lizzy. She was magnetic: her curiosity, the way she talked and moved, the way she laughed. It was angelic! She was absolutely captivating....The #ChipinChallenge is for the brave kids just like Lizzy. Because I believe when we join together and ALL chip-in, even just a few bucks, we can save lives. If this just saves one life, if we just get one kid home to live happily ever after, it will all be worth it. Think about chipping in—and head to the link in my profile to see how you can help. Every one of these kids are worth it, and together we can change the world meeting Lizzy Joy Wampler which "inspired Chip to raise $1.5 million for cancer." ("We're Better Together." *People*, 18 November 2019, p. 48). Reflecting on their experience, Chip shared in a 2022 article on a St. Jude website, "Jo and I are kind of all-inners. When we went to St. Jude in Memphis, Tennessee, we came back, and we were like, 'For the rest of our lives, we're going to do whatever we can to support that beautiful organization.'"(Karina Bland. "The moments that cemented Chip and Joanna Gaines' steadfast support of St. Jude Children's Research Hospital." stjude.org, 17 November 2022). Since then, they have become St. Jude Ambassadors and have raised over $11 million through various fundraising events and partnerships. Continuing their commitment, Joanna later painted several watercolor pictures of flowers, one of which was named in honor of Lizzy. Joanna described it as a fitting tribute to Lizzy's "unique strength, resilience, and radiance."

NOVEMBER 16, 2017

X-ray of her femur and MRI of her pelvis today. PET body scans tomorrow morning. We will talk to Dr. Bishop tomorrow.

- Praying for God's highest and perfect plan for Lizzy to unfold.
- Always standing for her complete healing.
- Wisdom for the doctors for every decision.
- Grace and strength for all of our family.

NOVEMBER 17, 2017

We don't have all the answers. Dr. Bishop has concerns, but so many things are still unclear. Her right leg has been hurting. It has more activity that lit up in the PET scan. They did a biopsy on this area in August, and it did not show up as osteosarcoma then. They will do a

CT scan of just that area on Monday or Tuesday of next week. Her spot on her pelvis is confusing as well. In the MRI, it looked like it was shrinking, but on the PET scan it looked like it may have grown. They will let us go home for Thanksgiving. Dr. Bishop will meet with a board of doctors to discuss a new plan and will call us with their findings on Wednesday before Thanksgiving.

I asked many questions. What stage is her cancer? They don't stage osteosarcoma. It's either localized (in one area) or it has spread. Hers has spread. So if it were staged, it would be stage 4. This is not what we wanted to hear, but I do have peace. I know God will see us through. I know you all have been praying, and I feel greedy asking you to keep going. There are so many others that need prayer. If you do say a prayer for her, please pray for the doctors to decide the best plan. God knows what this sweet girl needs.

So here we are again. Last year we were waiting for her results the day before Thanksgiving. We are doing about the same this year. Strange how things have happened. We have so much to be thankful for, and I am grateful for all of your prayers and support. Lizzy is doing well. She said she has a lump in her throat, and I assured her that if she felt the need to cry, go right ahead. She's such a sweetheart.

NOVEMBER 22, 2017

Guess who is headed to New York City? We are very excited and humbled for this unexpected opportunity. Lizzy will be on *The Today Show* Friday morning to pass out gifts for the audience with Marlo Thomas on behalf of St. Jude! Praying for a safe and pain-free trip for Lizzy. Very grateful and thankful. 🧡 🧡 🧡

Thank you everyone for celebrating these fun opportunities for Lizzy. Our hearts are full from all your wonderful comments and prayers. God bless each one of you. See you in New York!

NOVEMBER 24, 2017

Getting prepped and ready to go live on *The Today Show* around 8:30!!

Lizzy's story was featured on *The Today Show.*

Another very special promotion opportunity provided by St. Jude was when Lizzy got to appear on *The Today Show* in November 2017 for their "Thanks and Giving" holiday fundraising and awareness campaign. It was during a very difficult time for us. It was after Lizzy had relapsed and was receiving a new chemotherapy treatment. She also had an infection in her leg near her titanium rod. We were having to stay in the hospital more, and she was in a lot of pain. She was also very anxious and started picking the top of her head, so it was covered with open scabs. So it was just a really hard time.

Every year, around the week before Thanksgiving, *The Today Show* collaborates with St. Jude, and Marlo Thomas often appears on the show to highlight stories about patients at the hospital. In 2017, they chose Lizzy's story. During the segment, they focused on Ashley, one of Lizzy's nurses, who was also an osteosarcoma survivor treated at St. Jude. They captured touching moments of Lizzy and Ashley walking down the hall together, showcasing their bond. The interview with Ashley and Lizzy was unscripted; we didn't prepare Lizzy or tell her what to say. We simply let her lead the conversation. What struck me most was Lizzy's boldness in sharing her faith during the interview. She spoke with confidence, making me immensely proud of her. Additionally, Lizzy sang during the segment, showcasing her courage and talent. After the interview, *The Today Show* graciously invited us to New York to appear live on the show as well.

The day before Thanksgiving, our entire family flew to New York for the appearance on *The Today Show*. Upon landing, John received a message from Dr. Bishop with the results of Lizzy's latest scans. It was disheartening news—the chemotherapy protocol we had been hoping would work had failed. At that moment, amidst the excitement of being in New York with our family, reality hit hard. We realized there was little hope left for Lizzy's recovery. So once again, it was a conflicting mixture of emotions. We were excited to be in New York with our entire family for the first time, however, we just found out that the chemotherapy was ineffective.

Despite the challenges and mishaps, we pressed on. The airline lost my luggage, adding to the chaos of our trip. Navigating Lizzy through the busy streets of New York in a wheelchair on Black Friday was quite the adventure. It was almost comical, really. We garnered curious looks from passersby, likely wondering why we would bring a child battling cancer to such a hectic place. My response was always the same: "We're here for St. Jude." Despite it all, we eventually arrived at the set.

The Today Show arranged for an outdoor shot featuring Marlo Thomas alongside Lizzy and another young boy—a truly memorable experience for us all. Being chosen to participate in such a significant event was incredibly special. While we hadn't met Marlo Thomas prior to this, we were immediately struck by her warmth

An unforgettable moment on *The Today
Show* set with Marlo Thomas, National
Outreach Director for St. Jude. ✺ Grateful
for the opportunity to visit NYC courtesy
of St. Jude, where Marlo's kindness and
grace shone brightly upon Lizzy. 🙏
#StJude #MarloThomas #Gratitude

and compassion, especially towards Lizzy. During an interview, Marlo's honesty stood out. When asked about Lizzy's condition, instead of painting a rosy picture, she candidly shared that Lizzy had relapsed and that the medical team was doing everything possible for her. Her truthful approach resonated deeply with us.

After *The Today Show* event, we were treated to a wonderful Thanksgiving dinner, offering a much-needed respite from the hospital environment and a chance to briefly feel normal again. I seized the opportunity to take both of my daughters shopping at Macy's. Yet, with the hustle and bustle of retail therapy, nothing felt normal. How does one shop for a child confined to a wheelchair, with a swollen leg, and uncertain days ahead? The emotions were overwhelming. I was also conscious of trying to create a semblance of normalcy for my sixteen-year-old daughter Hannah, who undoubtedly felt the weight of her sister's illness. Despite her love for Lizzy, navigating a hospital environment can be exhausting for a teenager. I grappled with the realization of the intense pain Lizzy was experiencing. She relied on the medication Ativan to manage her anxiety and pain. At Macy's she requested her medication, but I hesitated. I didn't want her to be overly-medicated during our time together, yet I couldn't bear to see her in pain either. It was a delicate balance, fraught with conflicting emotions.

Despite the challenges we faced, I remain profoundly grateful for all St. Jude did for our family. They didn't have to arrange for us to travel to New York or host us for a lovely dinner. I only hope that our participation somehow benefitted St. Jude's mission. While it was a sacrifice for our family to undertake such an endeavor, particularly with a sick child, it was our way of contributing; a small gesture of appreciation for the remarkable care and support we had received.

NOVEMBER 27, 2017

We loved New York! It was an exciting trip for all of us. We are very grateful to have the whole family together for Thanksgiving. We enjoyed seeing the sights of New York City. Lizzy did amazingly well on *The Today Show* and was so blessed to meet Marlo Thomas! I have to admit, pushing a wheelchair around Times Square during Thanksgiving weekend is not for the faint of heart. There were some hard times, but we paced ourselves and stopped for breaks when needed.

John is with Lizzy for the next two weeks. The pain in her right leg and left hip has increased. They have a biopsy of two areas in her right femur scheduled on Wednesday. Truthfully, the information I have gathered from the doctors is kind of bleak. We are standing on God's Word of Hope. To watch her be in pain, even on such an amazing trip like New York, is taxing on the whole family.

NOVEMBER 28, 2017—*A Letter from Lizzy*

Dear Dad,

I am very blessed that our whole family got to go to NYC!!! We had so much fun!!! Tomorrow I have a biopsy. I am having H-E-L-L pain every day. It's so annoying. I could just scream right now. Today we have an ultrasound on my leg. I wish we didn't have to do it. You are the best dad ever like Philis said. 😊 I'm lucky I have a dad like you.

To: John Christian Wampler
Love: Elizabeth Joy Wampler

NOVEMBER 29, 2017

This is a crucial time for Lizzy. She needs a miracle. We are talking about more chemos, possible radiation, surgeries, even possible amputations. We just don't have all the answers yet. But when I turn around and see how faithful God has been to us, I know He is behind us, beside us, and before us. Thank you for your fervent prayers.

It's always incredible to see how even in the pain, God weaves moments of beauty into our journey. John and Lizzy received a special invitation to attend a Christmas party at the Cannon Center for the Performing Arts hosted by the Visual Music College. Dr. Ken Steorts asked John if Lizzy knew any Christmas songs to play on her ukulele for the event. Lizzy didn't, but she quickly taught herself "Silver Bells" and bravely agreed to perform for them.

She was frightened and in pain. She told me she was worried the pain meds would make her fall asleep while playing. John encouraged her to push through the fear, and she did. With trembling hands, she sang her song, fearing the worst. Amazed, the audience rose to their feet in applause. They weren't focused on her lack of experience; instead, they saw a remarkably brave girl who dared to be courageous.

I truly believe this was yet another "setup" from God. In the midst of Lizzy's brokenness, God allowed His light of Hope to shine through. It's a powerful reminder that our pain does have purpose. He never abandons us in our pain; rather, He is always there, guiding and comforting us. Somehow, even in our darkest moments, He manages to reach beyond us and touch others, meeting them in their pain. I'm deeply humbled by His boundless love and grace.

DECEMBER 2, 2017 *(John)*

Today was an emotional day as Lizzy and I watched close to 20,000 runners in the St. Jude Marathon. They were all running to support friends or family that are currently fighting cancer or have lost the battle. We just received news from Lizzy's doctor that two spots on her right femur and one spot on her left hip came back positive for an aggressive form of osteosarcoma. The doctors believe this cancer will not be treatable and surgery will not be an option. Without getting into details, Lizzy has increasing pain in both legs and no amount of pain medicine has worked so far. The doctors are working to concoct the right mix of meds to get her pain under control.

On Monday, we will meet with Lizzy's doctor and "quality of life" team to discuss the new treatment plan moving forward. We want to set some goals and decide what is best for Lizzy. The doctor will allow Lizzy to be at home with her family increasingly in the coming months.

As I am posting this, Lizzy is crying uncontrollably in the next room on FaceTime with Jennifer. As expected, she is taking this very hard. She told me that she is "done and ready to live a normal ten-year-old life—playing LEGOs, Barbies, and being with family." I held her in my arms on the couch as she punched her pillow pet and let her emotions out. Last night, I walked into her room and saw her on all fours on the bed crying out to God in tears asking Him, "Why is this happening to me?!?!"

Despite everything that Lizzy is battling, she continues to think of others rather than herself. Her kindness and thoughtfulness towards others shines and inspires others everywhere she goes. Lizzy's second and third grade teacher, Becky Bond, is here in Memphis to support her husband as he ran in the marathon. She just had surgery in her back and wasn't able to run. Lizzy was very concerned for her well-being and offered to give the teacher her wheelchair. Then Lizzy pulled out a $20 bill given to her by a runner and tried to give it to her teacher to help pay for dinner. This is just one example of Lizzy's kindness and heart towards others.

You BEAT CANCER BY HOW YOU *live,*

WHY YOU *live,* AND THE MANNER IN WHICH YOU *live.*

—STUART SCOTT.

When I broke the news to Lizzy, I looked at her and told her that she is not alone and will not battle this cancer by herself. She is surrounded by many people that are praying, supporting, and cheering her on. A good friend of ours reminded me that there is ALWAYS hope! Hope will shine the brightest when the hour is darkest. Jen and I hold onto the God kind of hope and know that God is good and in complete control. We will fight for our daughter and never give up! We invite you to fight and stand with us!!

DECEMBER 3, 2017

By now I know most of you have read John's last post. I wanted him to share, but I knew I would want to share as well. This page has been very helpful for me personally. I know if I share from my heart, I will have peace and connect with one of you dear friends. Even if I don't personally know you, if you have been reading, sharing, praying for our sweet Lizzy in any way, believe me, you are my friend. Thank you.

I don't have a lot more to say right now. I am not shaken from my faith in her healing, I am just feeling a saddened peace. No matter how my prayers get answered, I know the truth. God loves me. He cares for my whole family and has not forgotten us. He will be faithful to us. When you absolutely know those things, you gain the strength to pick yourself up and continue forward no matter what kind of hell you are walking through. I want you to know, I am not trying to convince myself of these things, I really believe them and His provision for healing. A dear friend told me when I pray and ask for healing for Lizzy, the Lord looks at that as an act of worship. He will honor all of my prayers. He will. They are not in vain. He will honor every single prayer each one of you has taken the time to pray on behalf of Lizzy and our family. I want you to know that. Your time and act of love will not go unnoticed.

After talking to Lizzy tonight, this girl wants to live with every fiber of her being. She would be willing to have both legs amputated if it meant she could live. What do you say to that? She has mourned over all the things she has already had to lose: her beautiful hair, her friends, going to school, time with her brother and sister, the ability to dance, do any sports, and just being a normal kid.

I don't know how this will look going forward. We want to be together as a family and offer Lizzy everything we can to help her live every day the Lord has given her. There isn't a person reading this page who can confidently say they know how much time they have left on this earth. Our days are numbered and none of us is promised tomorrow. Lizzy has blazed through this life so genuinely, brightly, passionately, and sweetly. I don't know the number of her days, but I want this girl to live. Every. Last. One. The world needs her light. The world needs all of our lights. So there it is. If I must hope against hope for the very necessity of her miracle to come to pass, then so be it. I will cry unto God with my voice against this Goliath of osteosarcoma until I see the crack in its helmet and believe our prayer "rocks" can beat it down. As a mother having watched her daughter suffer for a year now, I will trust in God's comfort and knowledge of how her miracle needs to come to pass. There is so much to take in. We will bravely take one day at a time by the complete grace of God.

I am in a group of over 3,000 members for osteosarcoma. I have asked some hard questions about alternative health options, what has truly worked, different protocols of other hospitals, and more. At first, I didn't want to know about osteo. I just didn't. I knew enough to get us through day-by-day. I didn't want to "receive" any of it. Now I just want to know what this ugly giant looks like. It's ugly. We not only need miracles, but cures. Lizzy was devastated when I told her they only spend 4 percent of all the funds given to cancer research on pediatric cancer. Of the 4 percent, only a small, small percent is being used for osteosarcoma. That's just the truth. This need not be. She simply said, "But we haven't had a chance to live yet." I said, "I know, I know."

St. Jude is following the same course of action of other hospitals. Had we amputated her leg in the very beginning, it does not guarantee she would not have had a relapse. I have seen your messages about different natural health ideas. If we haven't tried it and it's doable, we are open. This is a very aggressive cancer. Our biggest prayer is for wisdom. Right now we are following peace day-by-day.

I pray a gust of faith would pick us all back up and continue to raise up others to join us to pray for Lizzy. We are so humbled and grateful for each of you. We do believe in miracles. God bless each and every one of you.

DECEMBER 4, 2017

Lizzy receives a round of chemo today. She broke down when they told her Friday that she could lose her voice with this chemo. That broke her heart because she wants to keep singing. I am believing this chemo won't do this. They also discussed putting her hands in ice water as many kids get burns on their hands. Yes, this is what we in 2017 have to treat our kids with for osteosarcoma.

Lizzy called me yesterday just floating on a cloud. She went to church with John at the Life Church in Memphis. One of the pastors who ran for Lizzy in the St. Jude marathon this weekend had the entire church pray for her. She said she just felt flooded with peace and God's presence. This gives me such hope. He sees our sweet Lizzy. He hears her desperate cries of help. He loves her and will be with her every step of the way.

DECEMBER 7, 2017

Lizzy woke up with intense "sword-like" pain in her lungs and had trouble breathing. Any effort to blow her nose, breathe, or move gave her pain. Preliminary findings are that this is fluid buildup in her lungs. Osteosarcoma gravitates towards the lungs, so we are watching this closely. Lizzy was scheduled to go home but now is required to stick close to St. Jude because of the seriousness. Hoping she will be home for Christmas!

DECEMBER 10, 2017

I had my 20 percent off coupon for Ulta and was able to take Lizzy shopping for makeup yesterday when I got here. John says he tried to get her some makeup, but she kept saying she wanted to wait for Mommy. 💗 The only reason she is wearing makeup at ten is because of her situation. Being bald is not the easiest thing for a ten-year-old beautiful girl. Lizzy said she looks forward to waking up and putting on her makeup. That's reason enough for me. (:

Lizzy is struggling. If you notice dots on her face or head, it is due to her picking because of anxiety. There are many tears. She desperately wants to be healed and is tired of being bald and in pain. She is on morphine twice a day and that is still sometimes not enough. It's a humble place to be in to watch your daughter climb in and out of a car into her wheelchair like an elderly lady. She's only ten. She should be running, leaping, dancing and twirling. Right now she is crying in pain.

I have been scouring the Internet looking for answers. It is like trying to eat an elephant with a spoon. We have many unanswered questions right now. How far and how long do we look for other options? We are relying on God each step of the way.

In the Bible, Jesus healed everyone who came to Him. Even if someone was unsure and asked, He was always willing. After being here at St. Jude for a year, this is not what we have seen. We have met the most beautiful, faith-filled people who have had their children pass on to heaven and receive healing on the other side of this life. One year ago our family walked into this war zone. We have literally hidden in the verses of Psalm 91. I can't account for all the families I have met, but I know we believe God that healing has been provided for us. We have to believe without seeing, isn't that what faith is all about?

At St. Jude I have met some of the strongest families I have ever known. We want to embrace everything we have gone through and become stronger for it. We want to be better people. We want our lives to help other people and for God to use this all for good. But our main focus is for our ten-year-old little girl to live every one of the days the Lord has numbered for her. I believe she has so much to accomplish in this life. Miracles, miracles.

Please pray for her pain to decrease and for her doctors to have wisdom for her every step of the way. Please pray Lizzy will live out all the days the Lord has planned for her and be completely healed of osteosarcoma.

The extensive team at St. Jude—doctors, nurses, therapists, and receptionists—consistently stood behind Lizzy during her journey. Among them was Lizzy's oncologist, Dr. Michael Bishop. As Lizzy neared the end of her treatment, she encountered a distressing development: her fingers began to blister and a rash appeared on her face, making it impossible for her to wear makeup. This was particularly challenging for Lizzy, who, at ten years old, was at an age when some of her peers were just beginning to experiment with cosmetics. Despite being bald for about a year and losing her eyelashes and eyebrows, Lizzy still viewed makeup as a source of empowerment and confidence. So when we brought the issue to Dr. Bishop's attention during a visit to his office, his unexpected response left us bewildered. Without a word of explanation, Dr. Bishop abruptly left the room, leaving Lizzy confused and on the verge of tears.

About that time, Dr. Bishop walked back into the room and saw Lizzy crying. He was taken aback by her distress and immediately sat beside her on the bed. With a playful grin, he removed his doctor's cap to reveal a silly wig underneath. It was clear that he had donned the wig beforehand, intending to bring a smile to Lizzy's face. As Lizzy's tears turned into laughter, Dr. Bishop engaged her in a "serious" conversation, all the while sporting the goofy wig. They even took a few selfies together, capturing the moment of joy. This simple, yet heartfelt gesture exemplified the dedication of the doctors at St. Jude, who consistently went above and beyond to ensure Lizzy felt loved and cared for, even in the midst of challenging circumstances.

DECEMBER 11, 2017

The doctors feel they have methods to prolong Lizzy's life but, at this point, not completely cure her. They will continue to use these methods as long as we can maintain Lizzy's quality of life. Doing these procedures can help prolong her life and give us time to see if there is a trial or study that could cure her. The psychologist assured me they will walk us through each step of the way. This conversation brought me

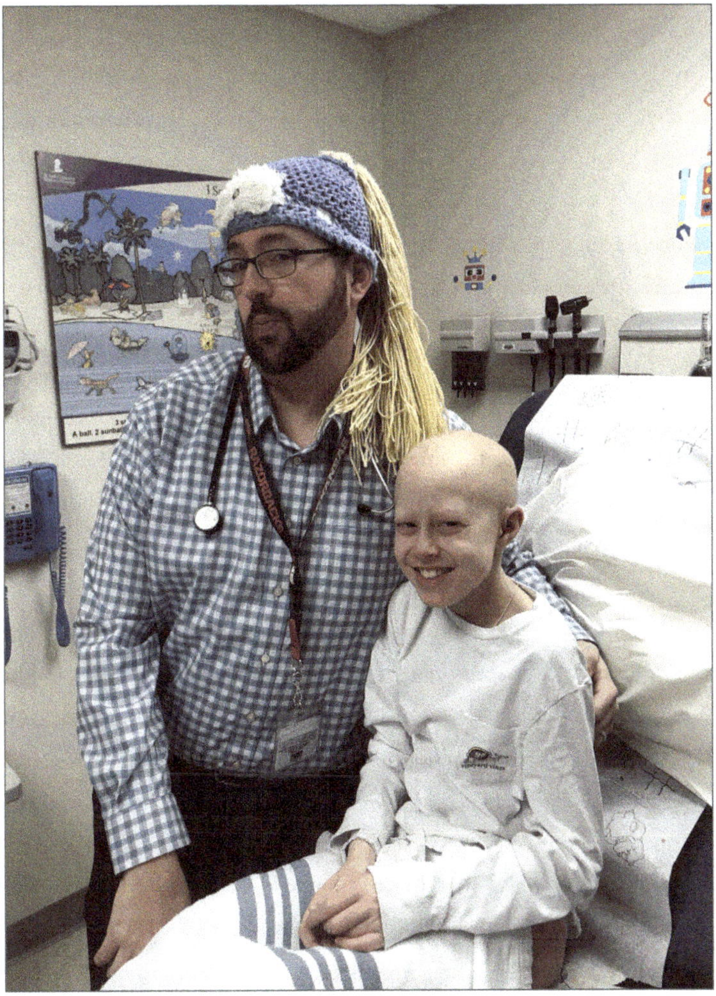

Dr. Michael Bishop, our hero at St. Jude! 🌟
His silly wig brought smiles during tough days.
Grateful for the amazing care and support.
🧡 #StJudeHeroes #BrightenOurDay

peace. I felt God's reassurance that He is with us each step of the way. Lizzy has such a strong will to live, and I had peace knowing we didn't have to make all these decisions today. I understand the importance of chemo to stabilize, shrink, and keep the tumors from spreading.

DECEMBER 18, 2017

Quick update since Lizzy has been home. 🎄 😊 One of the goals of Lizzy's doctors is for her to be home more often in between treatments. We are now under St. Jude's "quality of life" team. This was very intimidating to me, but once I met this team, I felt much better. The team is made up of an oncologist, a nurse practitioner, a pain team, a psychologist for the parents, and much more. They all help communicate and bridge the gap between Lizzy and our hospitals here in Missouri. Lizzy can continue treatment through St. Jude but receives labs at home to make it more enjoyable.

We had our first visit today with the nurses, and it went well. We are waiting for her lab results since her nose has been bleeding today. She had a sore throat all week due to the chemo, so I'm hoping she can get some relief soon. We will go back to St. Jude after Christmas for another round of chemo and then scans in the beginning of January. Being with quality of life does not mean her treatments have stopped. They are still hopeful that the treatments will stabilize things for a long time until we find the right cure. Keep the faith! ❤️

Coming home has been wonderful and challenging at the same time. We are finding a new rhythm to our family. Lizzy has to go up and down stairs every day, so we have to ensure someone is in front or behind her each time so she doesn't fall. Her bed is too high, so we just put the mattress on the ground. Her siblings are very active and are always running around, wrestling with each other, and playing basketball. These are things Lizzy always enjoyed doing with them.

For now, she needs to just watch and find different ways to connect. Her siblings love her and try their best to accommodate. It really does take the whole family to help a cancer patient.

DECEMBER 19, 2017

Lizzy made it to her brother's basketball game last night, but she was wiped today! She is finally getting platelets, and it's her first medical experience here in Columbia. I'm so familiar with what to do while we are at St. Jude. Being here is going to take some getting used to. I'm hoping these platelets help her feel better so she can enjoy all the fun things she's been invited to this week.

DECEMBER 27, 2017

Before we left home for Christmas, someone prayed that Lizzy would be surrounded by family, friends, and love this Christmas. She really was and had so much fun being at home. It was bittersweet having to pack up and head back to Memphis yesterday. Daniel came with us. Today has been a long day of doctor's appointments. We've been here since 8:30 a.m. and probably won't leave until 5 p.m.

DECEMBER 31, 2017—*A Letter from Lizzy*

Dear Dad,

Thank you for being the sweetest dad you can ever be! You are kind, nice, thoughtful, & awesome! Tomorrow is New Years!! I can't believe it's going to be 2018 tomorrow. We have been through a lot this year. But guess what? We are _not_ giving up. My goal for next year is to read the whole entire bible until 2019. And that I will eat healthy every day and drink my special drink and not complain. I love you soooooo much.

Love: Elizabeth Joy Wampler

JANUARY 4, 2018

I would be lying if I posted, "quick update on Lizzy." I already know I'm not going to be able to "pen" what's in my heart down quickly. For the past few days I've been here in Columbia with Daniel and Hannah while John has been with Lizzy. I've been organizing Daniel's room to help him finish the school year strong and focused. We've been trying to make his small room feel bigger, and I believe we've accomplished it! I've enjoyed helping him. He told me last night he really likes his room now. That made me so happy.

Several years ago I ran an online consignment boutique. It was then that I discovered I loved luxury, pre-owned purses. I enjoy the quality of the rich leather, even if it's vintage. I recently came across a beautiful preloved purse at an amazing price. So, last night I tried to restore one of the handles on this purse. Since I'm not a master leather craftsman, I began getting frustrated as I was completely absorbed in restoring these handles to perfection. To a casual onlooker, the purse handles looked fine. But to me, I knew I could work harder to get them into an even better condition.

Then John sent me a text and told me to watch an old video of Lizzy and him dancing. He told me it made Lizzy cry watching it. My heart felt that lump in it that I am constantly trying to push down. I didn't want to watch it. I busied myself with other things, knowing of course that I was going to end up watching it.

It's a long video, but it reveals so much. First, it shows our humble and cluttered downstairs. I saw bags of clothes I was going through to keep or to sell. But it also reveals the gentleness and love John has always displayed when playing with our kids. He had a way of making our girls feel like princesses when they were young. Finally, it most beautifully reveals the spirit of sweet Lizzy. Her zest. Her goofiness. Her desire to dance, twirl and be lifted up and spun around like a little ballerina. You even see her spunkiness at the very end when she runs to the camera to get a chance to see herself dance.

Lizzy and John dancing during happier times.

That lump in my throat and my heart revealed to me why I had allowed my mind to become so focused on restoring the purse's handle last night. With all my cleaning, rubbing, sanding and soaking, I was trying to do to that purse what I so desperately want to do for Lizzy. I so desperately want to reach down and grab away all that gross, tormenting cancer. I want to see my hands throw it as far away from her as I could. I want to scrub clean all of her little organs from the harshness left behind from chemo that has been pumped into her body during this past year. I want to restore each eyelash I've watched fall out and grow back, just to fall off again from her eyelids. I want to feel her soft, beautiful blonde hair where there is nothing but baldness now.

I want to restore my daughter. How much more does God want to see her restoration? It is hard to watch the little girl in this video dance around without a care in the world knowing her body has been trapped in a wheelchair for the past year unable to dance. But there is a beautiful part to this story. Cancer may have tried to trap Lizzy's body in that wheelchair, but she didn't let it trap "her." I've seen her spirit push through the barricade cancer had set before her and run it over and free herself. I've seen her laughter shove cancer out of the way over and over again. I've watched her spunkiness and radiant light tear through every cloth of darkness cancer has tried to strangle her with and shine brilliantly to hundreds if not thousands of people. She has led many others who were in the darkness themselves out into the light. And she's not done.

Cancer is tough. It comes to steal, kill, and destroy. But it doesn't have the final say.

By the grace of God, His promises and all of our faith, her body will one day rise up and shatter the sentence cancer has tried to put on her once and for all. I'm ready for that day. I'm not giving up. I will use all the tools God has given me, and I will help in any way I can to bring her restoration. We love you all and appreciate all your prayers for Lizzy's miracle. God's power is at work in her body, and we aren't giving up.

CHAPTER 9

Brave Like Lizzy
THROUGH TEARS AND TRIUMPH

JANUARY 9, 2018

Lizzy finished the first of five cycles of chemo last Friday in Memphis. She was able to come home Sunday and should be here for a week. She will have labs done through hospice, and if she needs more care, she will head to Women's and Children's MU Hospital here in Columbia. I obviously love having her home so she can do normal things like go to her brother's and sister's basketball games. She is feeling well, although she must take morphine and some other meds every day. She continues to have pain on and off in her right leg in the area of the tumor. Although she does have a few mouth sores from the chemo, I'm hoping they will stop before going down her throat like they did last time. Her hands are very raw and chapped from the chemo as well. Otherwise, she is a strong girl. She believes she will be healed. She doesn't want to even consider her Make-a-Wish until she is able to swim and walk. How can I argue with such faith?

I will be taking her to Memphis for scans next week. They will determine more of her future treatments. Thank you for praying for a healing miracle—however it manifests. I'm praying she will live all of her days that the Lord has created her for. ❤️

JANUARY 10, 2018

Lizzy's hands from the chemo are burned, raw, and blistered. 😞 She isn't miserable, but they cause discomfort. She is very self-conscious about them. It makes me sad that she has to endure this.

JANUARY 13, 2018

Lizzy has been home for almost a week. It's been so nice for us to all be together. She said she felt like she was at home. ❤️ Until now, she has felt like a visitor since she's been in Memphis more this past year than here with us. Hospice helps take her labs. They are a kind staff, and I'm grateful for the convenience.

Lizzy's right leg has become very swollen. We had to take her to University Hospital for an ultrasound because her doctor from St. Jude wanted to make sure it wasn't a blood clot. Thankfully, it wasn't since that would have meant some kind of surgery this weekend.

Why is it swollen? We don't know. I will take Lizzy back to Memphis on Monday to have more scans. These scans will show the doctors if the chemo is working or if we need a plan...D??

I need your prayers. As I've watched her hands become burned by the chemo and her right leg swell, there have been moments when my breath caught in my throat and my heart skipped a beat. It's tremendously hard at times. I have a deep trust in God and know her days are in His hands. I just want to stop seeing this sickness attack her body. Please pray for a healing miracle—that any cancer in her right leg and left pelvis will die and leave her body. Pray for wisdom for the doctors to make the best decisions. Help them be aware of any trials she could be in or considered for. Pray for our entire family to continue to walk this journey in the grace of God. We covet your prayers!

JANUARY 17, 2018

We have received the results of her scans. The cancer has spread. The tumors in her right leg and pelvis have grown. Osteosarcoma has spread to her lungs and possibly her rib cage. Dr. Bishop broke the news to us and comforted Lizzy once the tears started falling.

Throughout these past months, Lizzy and I have had some heart-to-heart talks. As a mother, I need to be there for her in all areas of life to help her understand healing, miracles, and possible death. As I type the word "death," I have not given up hope. God knows my heart and my trust is in Him. But I need to make sure my daughter isn't afraid and understands what she is facing. We started to talk on Sunday after she broke down and cried, "I don't want to die." That's when I told her about the beauty and peace we have to look forward to in heaven. This was more than a cute Bible story before bed. This was the truth to soothe her very soul and spirit. Afterwards, she said it was the best talk she ever had in her life. It seemed a burden was lifted from her. She has remained so strong through all of this, but I wanted her to know that there will be peace—either here on earth or in the presence of the Lord.

For three hours during my drive back to Memphis, I listened to miracle stories. This strengthened my faith that our lives are in God's hands. If Lizzy is meant to live another thirty or more years, God is mighty enough to see to it. I don't know how long she will live. But I knew in my heart that now is the time to have these conversations with her.

During our conversation with the child life specialist today, we discussed Lizzy's "quality of life." To my surprise, Lizzy interjected, proclaiming, "I love my life. Even though I have cancer right now, I love it." Her words struck a chord within me. How often do we complain about our circumstances, while here is a young girl, stuck in a wheelchair, enduring almost constant pain, missing out on school, and burdened with numerous medications, yet finding joy in life. I find myself praying for those who enjoy physical health yet hate their lives. May they discover the beauty and purpose that lies within each day. Life, indeed, is a precious gift, one that should be treasured and used wisely.

While we were finishing our day today, I asked Lizzy how she was doing. She said, "I know I should be sad, but I just have peace." I told her that is because we are walking close to the Prince of Peace. Our hearts ache with the thought of this #*@! cancer sitting in Lizzy's body. But we are not without Hope. It is not a fake hope as in, "I hope I win a million dollars." Instead, we know that though this world will try its hardest to take this away, it just can't. Our hope is, and will forever be, in God. He is a God of miracles, and nothing is impossible with Him.

JANUARY 17, 2018

Lizzy really wanted to post something today. I haven't edited it for her, but I thought it was a sweet glimpse into her heart. ♥

> Hi!
>
> This is lizzy, I know we got some bad news but for some reason I have peace. I know it's weird that I found out that I don't have a high percent chance to live but I just know if I go off to heaven one day, I will not have any pain and any sorrow.
>
> When I'm in heaven I will be doing flips, cartwheels, and playing with a white fluffy dog and cat. But most

importantly I will be telling God to do something awesome to all the people that prayed for me and supported me. I want to give back to all the people that blessed me. I told my mom that when I go to heaven to give all my toys, makeup, stuffed animals and other stuff to the orphanage and homeless so they can have blankets to keep warm, and clothes, toys, and jewelry. I want to give to the poor and make them happy. Cause everybody needs joy in there life, right? 😁

I know it might sound that I'm not positive and I think I'm going to go to heaven soon but I am positive that I will live and survive. And next thing you know I'm in collage and am working at St. Jude. I'am 100 percent sure that I am going to survive!! 🎉 🎉 🎊 😁 Thank you for all your prayers and support, you have been a huge help to are family!

—Elizabeth Joy Wampler 😊 😊

JANUARY 17, 2018—*Lizzy's Text to a Friend*

The doctors found cancer in my lungs......I have a 20 percent I could live. I don't know why cancer keeps coming in my body. But when I die, please know that I will be safe in heaven and when you die I will be waiting for you to come, and then we can live in a mansion together. 😊 I hate cancer soooooooooooo much!!!! It destroyed our friendship so that we can't see each other, and cancer made me not go to school, so I can't spend time with you. Cancer did a lot of things but when I die I will still remember you and always watch you and think about you. 😊 I want to see you before I go off to heaven. Next time I go home I want to visit you. Thank you for being a great friend to me! Please pray! 🙏

JANUARY 21, 2018

Lizzy and I have had some long days at the hospital. We were glad when Saturday came, and she had no more appointments. She spent the day with some new friends and had the best time making slime and loving on their dog! Wednesday evening we were blessed when some of the Life Church staff came to pray over Lizzy. It was a sweet time in the presence of the Lord. We know we have a lot of churches standing with us, and it means so much. Here is where we are with her treatment:

The doctors have decided that radiation treatment to her leg and pelvis, starting the week after next, would help alleviate some of her pain. She will be fitted for a mold this week. Radiation will last ten days. In many cases, radiation can help with osteosarcoma pain for up to a year. She has been on morphine for too long. This will help give her a better quality of life.

Dr. Bishop and I are going to go over a few trials for which Lizzy may qualify. Otherwise, she may take an oral chemo every day at home to help stabilize the tumors. I haven't read the best results with this option. We want Lizzy to have the best quality of life possible, but, of course, we want quantity as well. The doctors say if we choose to do nothing, she may have less than a year with us. We know God holds her days in His hands.

We need His grace now more than ever. Spending long days in the hospital just focusing on these issues can feel so overpowering. I do better to focus on the moment before me and soak in my time with her. There is so much for which to be thankful. Today I walked outside on the back patio of Target House and remembered grilling in the summer and spending time with other families there. We all had so much hope that we would be able to take our children home soon. I recognize that hope deferred does indeed make the heart sick. But I don't let my heart stay there. I know I can't. I just feel the pain and trust that a better day is coming. Then I allow God's peace to flood my soul.

I do read all the articles you send me and have gained some knowledge about osteosarcoma. This is not like adult cancer and doesn't respond to many things that are used to treat adult cancers. I have had her drink as many veggie juices as she would tolerate. I had her taking turmeric in between her chemo treatments. (So much so that her palms were orange at one time.) She has been drinking a healthy herb from Japan three times a day that costs $300 a month. (A dear lady has been paying for it for her.) I've rubbed essential oils all over her body for months as well. When she isn't too nauseous, she has taken tons of vitamins. But I can only ask a ten-year-old to do so much. She's gone through a year of chemo and takes a handful of medicine three times a day. I will continue to search for the miracle answer, but at times it's so overwhelming. I feel like it's my job to find a cure for osteosarcoma. That is a hard cross to bear. We ask for your prayers to know what is the best plan for Lizzy. Please continue to pray for the cancer to die in her body.

John

THE PASTORS AT Life Church loved Lizzy and provided huge support of prayer, friendship, and encouragement to us during our time in Memphis. Among them, Joe and Kelli Carson stood out as our cherished friends. Today, they serve on the Board of Directors for Lizzy's Foundation.

JANUARY 28, 2018 *(John)*

We are having fun, joking around, and relaxing today before Lizzy rides the radiation train. Lizzy will undergo radiation for ten days to reduce her pain level. Also, she will be taking an oral chemo twice a day for a month. Dr. Bishop is confident in this treatment plan as we move forward expecting and anticipating the best outcome for Lizzy.

At the same time, Lizzy will be taking fentanyl along with her increased dose of hydromorphone to manage the pain. In the past, there have been many sleepless nights, tossing and turning in agonizing pain. This morning, I watched her rock back and forth in pain. As a father who wants the best for his daughter, it was very hard to watch.

Jen and I went out last night on a dinner date and caught up on everything. It seems we are "like ships passing in the night." It was hard to say goodbye as Jen left to go back to Columbia.

With open hearts, Joe and Kelli Carson, together with Life Church, embraced Lizzy and our family while we were in Memphis. Kelli welcomed us into their home with countless homemade meals, offering Lizzy the warmth and comfort of a home-cooked dinner that made her feel loved and secure.

JANUARY 30, 2018

It's been a rough day for Lizzy. Her eyes were examined today as she has had some issues with her eyesight. Her eyes are extremely dry and have a slight scratch on the cornea, most likely due to the chemo and opium drugs she takes for pain. She has been experiencing a lot of pain from the chemo and is scheduled to have her first radiation treatment today. However, she is neutropenic and has a fever of 104 degrees. As I type this, they are trying to find a vein in her arm to do an IV. There have been lots of tears because she hates that with a passion.

I've been thanking God for all the prayers you have offered on her behalf. We appreciate you adding your faith and walking this hard season with us. It has taken everything we have to watch our daughter endure so much pain. We have dug deep into the depths of our faith, grasping to access every life raft for our daughter as we watch cancer drowning the life out of her. I know God has already provided for her healing.

FEBRUARY 1, 2018

The past two days we have seen a breakthrough in managing Lizzy's pain. We are grateful to the team of nurses and doctors at St. Jude for helping to get this under control. Lizzy is about to undergo her third radiation treatment (out of ten). She gets to choose the music she listens to while being treated. She always selects her favorite music from Kari Jobe. 🧡 🧡

FEBRUARY 5, 2018 (John)

Today, Lizzy will undergo her fifth radiation therapy treatment. Only five more to go! The treatments cause her to be tired and her skin to look like it's been sunburned. Hopefully radiation will slow down the cancer to help her pain. She has been feeling better after the treatments. When radiation is finished, we hope to move out of the St. Jude Target House and bring Lizzy home. She will go back to Memphis for scans at the end of the month. We will miss the friendships we have made while in Memphis but look forward to having our family together under the same roof in Columbia.

FEBRUARY 6, 2018

Our journey often feels like a roller coaster. Today is no different. This morning, Lizzy was all smiles. This afternoon, she is in D Clinic as doctors and nurses scratch their heads as to how to treat her current condition. They keep starting and stopping medicines. You can imagine how frustrating that can be.

Her hands and feet are blistering from the oral chemo and causing her intense pain. She can't dress herself. It hurts to wash her hands, and she can barely hold a book. It's a miserable quality of life. So, we have stopped the oral chemo and taken her off methadone. She has intense swelling, sunburn redness, and burning down her right leg and left pelvis area where she had radiation. The radiation doctor has only seen this side effect once before. They believe it is a culmination of her chemo reacting to the radiation. The doctors need wisdom.

When I FaceTimed with John and Lizzy, I encouraged Lizzy to be strong. She broke down in tears. She misses whichever one of us is not with her. Most of the time she is smiling but that doesn't mean she's not hurting on the inside.

I know at times that believing our daughter will be healed is almost laughable. Although no one would actually laugh at us, I feel like we are climbing upstream. Yet, as her parents, we are committed to believe for our daughter. We've got nothing else. We don't have the doctors' reassurance that they can help our daughter anymore.

We don't have a natural cure out there (as of yet) that has proven to heal recurrent osteosarcoma. All we can do is to stand on the promises that God does want her healed and will provide for her. Join us in trusting in healing and miracles for complete recovery. We won't give up as long as she has life and wants to live. We can't. We don't know many parents who would.

FEBRUARY 11, 2018

Tonight, Lizzy and John will be moving out of the St. Jude Target House and into the Tri Delta House. The rule at the Target House is if patients are away for more than seven days, then they lose their housing. Because Lizzy will be back home in Missouri, we will be moving out. Lizzy is projected to come back to St. Jude two or three times a month for scans, tests, and follow-up appointments. We have a lot of great memories at the Target House and will be forever thankful for a wonderful place to stay! It has allowed our family of five to be together whenever Jen and I switch places every two weeks.

The Tri Delta House is where it all started for us. This was the first place we stayed when we arrived in 2016 and were blindsided by Lizzy's diagnosis. My sister and cousin were in the Tri Delta sorority at Southern Methodist University in Dallas.

FEBRUARY 12, 2018

Lizzy went downhill this morning. They are doing a CT now after noticing she is having trouble breathing.

FEBRUARY 12, 2018

She is doing better. She's in ICU but may be moved to the solid tumor floor soon. They did a reverse drug to counteract all of her pain meds because they didn't know why she was so lethargic. John said it was difficult to watch her because she convulsed and shook as the drug took effect. They are putting her on a pain pump as we speak.

FEBRUARY 12, 2018

It's been a long day. The CT scan of her lungs was normal, but she is extremely exhausted. All her vitals and labs are good. When the nurse goes in to wake her, she answers all the questions.

I've been debating whether I should get down there. I am not in a good state of mind to drive for six hours, so I decided to wait. Thank you for continued prayers. She remembers everything from this morning and was aware of getting the reverse drug. She said she was in so much pain at that moment she wanted to die.

My prayers have been for God to have mercy on us all. We are doing our best to walk through this. I love God and am thankful as He holds my hand through all of this. I pray my other two children can sense Him with us.

FEBRUARY 13, 2018

She's doing better and was released from ICU. She went back to Tri Delta housing. She's a little nauseous but compared to how she was yesterday, that's an amazing improvement. Her right ear seems plugged, but we're hoping that will heal quickly. We are still shaken from yesterday's event. We want the best for Lizzy and continue to seek God's help. Hoping Lizzy can come home soon. She finished her last radiation treatment yesterday. They gave her balloons to celebrate. We are humbled and so very grateful for your prayers. She needs a miracle, and our family needs a lot of grace.

Lizzy continues to amaze us. Last night during a FaceTime call, she said, "Can we just stop and thank God I'm alive?" ❤️ Yes, sweetie, yes we can.

FEBRUARY 14, 2018

A year ago today, Lizzy got off of pain meds from her limb-sparing surgery. This year has brought so much pain and tears. The heart has such great capacity to love—even while it's been broken over and over. Happy Valentine's Day 🧡 💜

FEBRUARY 22, 2018

Lizzy left the hospital scene behind her and spent a wonderful week in Orlando, Florida, for her Make-a-Wish at Disney World. Make-a-Wish sent our entire family for a six-night stay at "Give Kids the World Resort." They gave us passes to Disney World, Universal Studios, and SeaWorld. Our entire family will never forget their amazing generosity.

It was a miracle in itself that Lizzy felt well enough to enjoy the entire trip. Although there were plenty of painful and emotionally hard moments, she came through with a smile. I think one of my favorite moments was hearing Lizzy say she felt like a kid again. Lizzy has had to face so much and had to mature so quickly that it sometimes feels her childhood is slipping through her fingertips. This trip allowed her to dream and believe again like a child. John and I often caught ourselves tearing up as she got lost in the moment of Disney. She didn't worry about pain or the giants she has faced this year. We needed this break so much. Daniel and Hannah also enjoyed their time. Although it made me very nervous, Lizzy rode every ride with them except for one. They all had a blast!

Unfortunately, Lizzy and I will head back to Memphis (and to reality) on Sunday. We need wisdom about the future. The doctors suggest putting her back on the oral chemo. But, after watching her endure the side effects, we are uncertain that's the best option. Unfortunately, it may be the only option to keep the cancer at bay. Her fuzzy, blonde hair has started to come back in. Her hands and

Magical moments at Disney World's
Magic Kingdom with Lizzy and Hannah,
courtesy of Make-A-Wish Missouri. ✨
Grateful for the chance to create cherished
memories together as a family. 🏰🎠
#MakeAWish #DisneyMagic #FamilyTime

face aren't burning and peeling. She looks and feels so much better without the chemo.

Our current walk is very challenging. We are trying to let our children know we still have faith that she can be healed, but we are also preparing them, with comfort and love, for the eternal life we get to look forward to in heaven. We are eagerly expecting a miracle every day. Yet we have already been pushed so close to the border of this life on earth with Lizzy that we must do all we can to keep them feeling safe. Lizzy asks hard questions for which I don't always have answers. We appreciate your continuous prayers for healing, wisdom, and divine guidance. We treasure your prayers more than you could ever know.

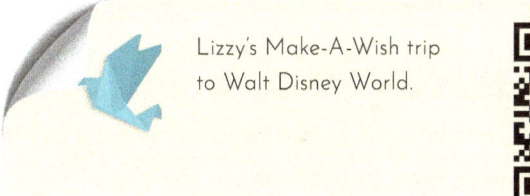

Lizzy's Make-A-Wish trip to Walt Disney World.

MARCH 2, 2018

When I packed for Memphis Monday, I really didn't know what to expect. We've been walking this non scripted journey for a while, so I went ahead and packed for a week. Before leaving, we had a powerful prayer time with some seasoned prayer warriors. Lizzy is seeking peace and is tired of the pain. Yesterday, she discovered a new lump by pressing in between her rib cage. Her breathing is becoming strenuous. As much as she wants to live, she believes her life here on earth is coming to a close.

I'm sure you can understand how difficult it is for me to even write those words. There isn't a guide to tell parents how to be faithful when facing these types of challenges. I just want peace in my heart to help Lizzy live out her days here on earth. We've talked about what is in her heart. She has more things she wants to do, and I want to help her accomplish them. So, after a meeting with the doctors and with Lizzy's approval, we agreed to try a low dosage of oral chemo one more time. We aren't ready yet to just do "nothing," and we wanted something to slow down the process of the tumors.

I'm so grateful we have hope and a promise of eternal life with God. I told Lizzy I have peace knowing God will take care of her. She doesn't want to leave our family and make us sad. I told her, we want her to be healed. It would be amazing if her healing happens on earth. But if it takes place in the presence of our God, then how glorious that will be.

I'm sorry if you aren't prepared for this update. Things have progressed quickly. No one knows the amount of days they have been given. The doctors guess Lizzy has only months left—with or without chemo. We will go home for three or four weeks before returning to Memphis for checkups and scans. At any point, we can stop her chemo and bring her back to St. Jude. But, right now, Lizzy wants to be with family as much as possible.

Yesterday Lizzy met with her music child life therapist, Amy, who had her sit in the massage chair and listen to some peaceful music. This helped ease Lizzy's pain and breathlessness. The employees at St. Jude care so much about each patient. Everyone wants to do more for her. This disease has progressed to a point that even if we find a trial somewhere that could help, it may be too late for her. We would love your continuous prayers to guide us through this walk of faith with Lizzy. We stand on all of God's promises for her. We believe in miracles and know God loves her and wants her healing.

CHAPTER 10

The Strength of Samson and Fragility of Tinkerbell

LIZZY'S FINAL WALK HOME

MARCH 4, 2018

I drove home from Memphis Friday with Lizzy. We were told she may have a few months left to live. Unfortunately, things have changed. Once we got home, we noticed rapid deterioration in Lizzy's health. Her pain increased, and she seemed to fly through her pain meds. She has struggled to breathe, and I wondered how our family could endure this for several months.

This morning at 6 a.m., I gave her some meds and frantically realized we were almost out. I quickly called "quality of life" at St. Jude, and they sent Lizzy's hospice nurse. After her assessment, she told us Lizzy is entering the transition phase. She believes Lizzy may have about fourteen days left. So we are making preparations. We have oxygen and are trying to make things as comfortable as possible. We have discussed this with all three kids. There have been many tears. Yet God has proven His faithfulness and confirmed His presence in our hearts. John and I take turns being the strong one, supporting each other while the other grieves. Truth be told, this year has initiated a grieving process in all of us.

As I went outside to retrieve the book about dying that is referred to by hospice as *The Little Blue Book*, I had a meaningful discussion with Lizzy's nurse. She complimented me on our parenting. She mentioned she can sense the preparation we have done and can feel a sense of peace within Lizzy. I expressed gratitude to her and admitted I feel absolutely clueless about how to get through this. Yet I realized our faith is guiding us. As believers, our lives are a preparation for this very moment. We put our faith in Jesus, recognizing that life on earth is not the end.

I asked about the experience of those without faith, and she conveyed a sense of heaviness, emptiness, and fear prevalent in homes where individuals are nearing death without hope. She mentioned that often, in those moments, the person cries out for solace. That is why hospice has a chaplain who can provide prayer and guide individuals in the prayer of salvation to find peace with God. That's our hope. What a glorious blessing of living in the present moment, knowing where our hope is anchored. This enables us to avoid carrying the despair and fear of the unknown that lies beyond this fragile world.

I took the time to write this because even amid our grief, I want to share a beautiful glimpse of hope with those who may not have it. I want to let you know that peace can be found in the Son of God. Lizzy will be fine. Her little body has just endured so much and is in need of relief. Her hope transcends our understanding and lies in a greater place.

We will keep you updated in the days ahead and will let you know how you can help our family. Right now your prayers of strength and grace are so much appreciated.

IT WAS OUR oldest daughter, Hannah, who bore the weight of this revelation most heavily. To Hannah, the nurse's prediction seemed unfathomable, shrouded in a veil of disbelief and denial. "How can she possibly know it's going to be fourteen days?" she pleaded, her voice trembling with anguish. It was a stark reminder that time was no longer measured in months, but in the fleeting moments we had left to prepare Lizzy for her journey to heaven.

Watching a ten-year-old child face the end of their life and preparing her for heaven is an unimaginably difficult task. It forced us to confront the concept of heaven in a tangible, concrete way, rather than as an abstract notion. As Christians, we often think of heaven as a far-off destination reserved for the distant future. But for Lizzy, heaven was imminent—she was going there soon. We had to lean on our faith and believe in God's plan, accepting the certainty of life after death.

Our faith demanded more than mere belief; it required a profound trust. We had to really trust Him to take our child from us with the certainty that she would be alright. We had to cling to the assurance provided by scripture—that those who mourn will be comforted, and that God will ultimately turn our mourning into dancing. Though the prospect of living without our daughter seemed unfathomable, we had to surrender to God's will, trusting in His unwavering faithfulness.

MARCH 8, 2018

Even in our darkest days, the light of Jesus continues to shine brightly.

John's father has also been seriously ill following open-heart surgery. We recorded this intimate video of Lizzy FaceTiming her Pop Pop. It's a special moment between a granddaughter and her grandfather saying, "Goodbye for now." ❤️ Both of my in-laws are such great grandparents, and they are very important to Lizzy. This moment shows the pure love of a grandparent, coupled with Lizzy's gentleness, as she struggles through the pain to show love.

I reached out to my mom last night to see if she wanted to talk to Lizzy. With tears in her voice, she expressed that she couldn't bring herself to say goodbye. She mentioned that she would only do so if Lizzy wanted to, and although Lizzy agreed, the emotional difficulty made it too challenging for them both. Despite the difficulty in saying goodbye, we hold onto the belief that this is not truly farewell but a "see you later." We find comfort in the understanding that Lizzy will soon be in a better place.

There were many family members who wanted to say goodbye. Initially, we thought we would include Lizzy's friends. We started with her good friend, Aria, and her mother. Unfortunately, the emotional weight of bidding goodbye proved too difficult for both Aria and Lizzy. After that first friend, we realized that confronting mortality was too heavy a burden for ten-year-old children. So after that we only allowed family and a few handpicked friends to come say their final farewells.

Numerous dear friends found themselves unable to face the prospect of seeing Lizzy for the final time. Even my mother, residing in Wisconsin and battling her own health challenges, was among those who chose not to say goodbye. Despite having frequently conversed with Lizzy throughout her journey, the finality was overwhelming. I remember her expressing, "I just can't bring myself to say goodbye to her." Lizzy, understanding as ever, accepted her decision with grace. The thought of never seeing Grandma again was too much for her to bear as well.

There was a sacredness to those moments. One instance that stands out in particular was when Lizzy was speaking to her grandfather, Pop Pop, over video chat shortly before her death. Despite his recent open-heart surgery rendering him unable to physically be with her, both of them knew the conversation might be their last. Neither of them was able to speak at first until Lizzy finally broke the silence saying, "I'm going to miss you." Tearfully, Pop Pop responded, "I'm going to miss you too. But I'll see you again. I will see you in heaven." It was a moving exchange captured on video—a moment of profound farewell, as John's dad reassured her of their reunion in heaven. I wanted to make sure we captured that moment on video because, as difficult as it was, it was very important to her faith journey.

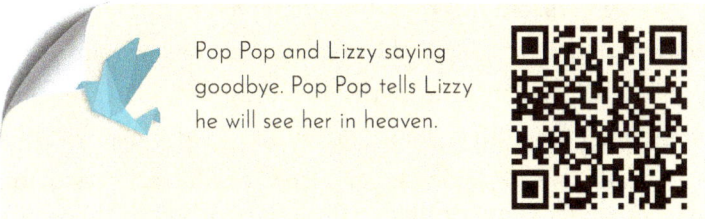

Pop Pop and Lizzy saying goodbye. Pop Pop tells Lizzy he will see her in heaven.

On Tuesday, Lizzy mustered the strength to go out to lunch with me. She specifically requested to go to Jina Yoo's, her favorite restaurant. Jina has been a family friend for years.

In her sweet and innocent voice, Lizzy posed a tremendously difficult question to Jina. She asked for advice on how to prepare for heaven and not miss her mom and family. Jina was visibly moved and emotionally impacted by the weight of Lizzy's question.

Today, I read her a book a friend gave me on heaven. The peace is becoming more and more evident in Lizzy's heart. We continue to pray for a miracle in the midnight hour. She loves it when we pray but then says, "I understand why you keep praying, but I'm fine. I just want to go on. I don't want to keep hurting."

I am so honored to walk these days by her side. I have grown so much on the inside. I have experienced such sorrow mixed with glimpses of such eminence and beauty it's so hard to explain. Her life is so bright. Thank you for your continued prayers for glorious days for Lizzy.

More than anything, Lizzy wanted to keep on living. The prospect of leaving our family behind and making the journey to heaven without us weighed heavily on her heart. I recall a heartrending moment during our final lunch out at Lizzy's favorite restaurant, just days before she passed, when she posed a profound question to our close friend, Jina Yoo.

As we gathered together, Jina attempted to engage in light conversation, remarking on Lizzy's cute attire and her pink backpack. Yet when Lizzy revealed that the backpack held her attached morphine pump, Jina's demeanor shifted, confronted with the stark reality of Lizzy's intense pain. Undeterred, Lizzy pressed on, seeking guidance from Jina.

But when Lizzy asked her question, Jina found herself at a loss of words, tears welling in her eyes. "How do I not miss my mom and my family so much when I get to heaven?" Lizzy's inquiry hung heavily in the air, a testament to the profound depth of her longing

Watching Lizzy say her goodbyes to Aunt Allison, Uncle Mark, and her cousins was a heart-wrenching moment. The depth of her love for them was undeniable, and we are profoundly grateful they came to bid her farewell. Lizzy's bond with her family was something truly special, and their presence meant the world to her. 🧡 #CherishedMemories #Family

for us. How does one answer such a heartfelt question from a child who is preparing to go to heaven?

Since she was the baby of our little family, Lizzy didn't have much experience with infants. However, she was fascinated with babies and had always longed to cradle one in her arms. When I shared her desire on Facebook, a mother of one of Lizzy's friends responded, mentioning that her sister had recently welcomed a baby boy. So on the appointed day the newborn arrived at our home.

Lizzy's tenderness with the infant was heartwarming. She approached him with the utmost care, gently asking him if he was going to open his puppy dog eyes or go back to sleep. She marveled at his tiny features, from his delicate hands to his cute bald head, which almost matched her own, except his head, she said, was much more beautiful. Despite her friend's mother's comment about Lizzy looking like a seasoned pro, Lizzy confided that this was her first time holding a baby.

I anticipated a positive reaction to the video of Lizzy tenderly holding the baby. However, what I didn't expect were the responses I received after sharing it. Several sweet mothers reached out to me privately, sending pictures and names of their babies who were already in heaven. They all said they would be honored to have Lizzy hold their little one for them when she got to heaven until they could cradle their babies themselves. How precious is that? I showed Lizzy pictures of all the babies she was supposed to find in heaven to hold. She took that request very seriously and said, "Gosh, I'm going to be very busy." ❤️ Lizzy would have been such a good little mommy. It comforts me to think of her in heaven with those sweet little ones.

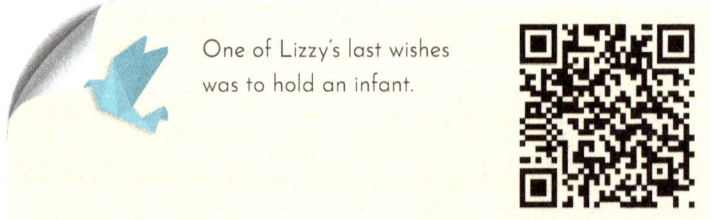

One of Lizzy's last wishes was to hold an infant.

MARCH 9, 2018

While reading a book about heaven to Lizzy, she expressed concern for a friend who doesn't want to know Jesus. Despite her own challenges, Lizzy deeply wants someone to help her friend. Her love and concern for others, even in her darkest moments, is very moving and just deepens my love for her.

We had the privilege of having Shay Roush from The Crossing Church come over to water baptize Lizzy, fulfilling a desire she had expressed for a while. Despite initial nervousness, particularly due to medication, Shay assured her these feelings were normal for a ten-year-old. After the baptism, Lizzy mentioned that her eyes, and everything around her, seemed to sparkle.

We have so many pictures of Lizzy, but her struggle is becoming greater. We aim to honor her by not sharing too many pictures of her during difficult times. But moments like these, reflecting such beautiful memories and strong faith, are ones Lizzy would want others to see. Faith has always been such an important part of her life.

Lizzy's body is starting to shut down. Although she has pain in her right leg and upper hip occasionally, it is really her lungs and heart that hurt the most. The tumors are starting to press on her lungs. The hospice nurse told me Lizzy is now only able to get breath from the upper part of her lungs, resulting in very shallow breathing. Mobility has become significantly challenging for her. She has been experiencing heart pain in the past few days, requiring 12 mg of morphine every five minutes, with additional pumps needed. It's a sobering and difficult situation to witness. I am amazed at the strength displayed by Daniel and Hannah throughout this challenging journey. Their resilience is truly commendable.

I told Lizzy the analogy that her life is like a candle that chose to burn so brightly that the wick is now coming to an end. While it might

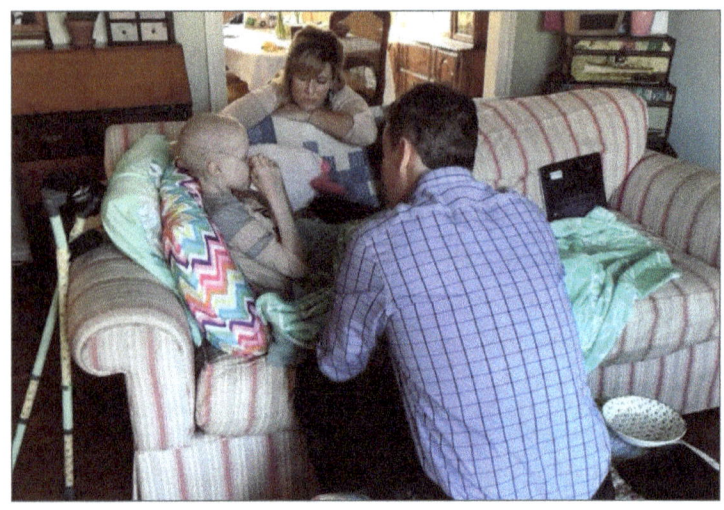

Grateful for the visit from Minister Shay Rousch of The Crossing Church, who baptized Lizzy in our home. ✨ After this sacred moment, Lizzy said the world looked "sparkly." #Blessed #FaithJourney

not be a perfect comparison, each day feels like watching a beautiful flower slowly dropping its petals. Each day and each breath are a gift, as emphasized by Lecrae in his video to her. The other night she sat up in bed and said, "I'm still alive! I'm still alive!" She told her teacher, Mrs. Bond, during a recent visit, how glad we were she was alive when she awoke to see another day.

I know I often share too much information, but I feel in some way that sharing the challenges and faith that sustain us may bring comfort to others. Journaling these moments has helped me navigate this journey. Thank you for allowing me to share with you these gentle peaceful moments from our family's treasure. I pray you find some kind of comfort by seeing sorrow being walked out with the faith of God holding us through each moment. Matthew 5:4 tells us that those who grieve will find comfort! He is always present in these moments, and He will be there for you as well.

"Let us give thanks to the God and Father of our Lord Jesus Christ, the merciful Father, the God from whom all help comes! He helps us in all our troubles, so that we are able to help others who have all kinds of troubles, using the same help that we ourselves have received from God" (2 Corinthians 1:3-4, GNT).

As Lizzy delved deeper into her understanding of heaven, she asked to be baptized. As parents, we left the decision of getting baptized up to our children, believing they would discern the appropriate timing for that significant act. John and I held our own baptisms in high regard and wanted our children to have that same meaningful experience. Our minister, Shay Rousch, baptized her in the comfort of our living room, engaging Lizzy in a conversation about her faith that was profoundly moving for all involved. A few nights later, Lizzy abruptly sat up and motioned with her arms. Since I was sleeping nearby, I immediately inquired what was wrong. She surprised me when she said, "Did I miss it? Did I miss the communion?" This occurrence inspired our family to share the precious sacrament together later that evening.

Throughout the early months of 2018, our church community at The Crossing in Columbia had been documenting Lizzy's steadfast faith through a series of videos. These recordings, culminating during the final days of her life, serve as a testament to her lasting devotion. I will always be thankful that they captured her, with oxygen tubes tethered to her frail form, reciting her favorite scripture, Psalm 91.

MARCH 10, 2018

What a surprise for Lizzy to receive a wonderful video from one of her favorite recording artists, Kari Jobe!! Lizzy always requested music while receiving radiation, and she almost always chose to listen to Kari. I often remember walking into Lizzy's room and sensing the peace and presence of God as the music flowed. Kari heard Lizzy singing her song, "The Garden," and responded by sending a special video.

It was such a blessing to receive a personal video from contemporary music singer and songwriter Kari Jobe and her husband Cody Carnes. Lizzy looked up to Kari so much and consistently listened to her songs. Every time she underwent radiation treatment, she would ask for Kari's music to be played. The music was such a source of healing for Lizzy, providing her with needed strength and a comforting presence during some of her darkest moments. A family friend had forwarded a recording of Lizzy playing the ukulele and singing one of Kari's songs to Kari herself. In response, Kari and Cody sent a heartfelt video directly to Lizzy, assuring her of their prayers. Kari expressed that she believed Lizzy was one of God's favorite people. It brought immense comfort to Lizzy to hear Kari's voice singing lyrics like "I believe you're my healer" and "I am not alone, you will never leave me," welcoming her into heaven as she lay dying. Knowing that Lizzy connected so deeply with Kari Jobe and her songs brings me comfort, knowing she found peace in God through her journey.

MARCH 10, 2018

Mizzou's freshman basketball player, Michael Porter, Jr., is the real deal! He came to our house to meet Lizzy. During his visit, he took time and prayed with her. Lizzy was brave enough to pray for him as

Lizzy watching the video sent by Kari Jobe.

well. He was so kind to get on her level and talk about heaven. He is a true class act and a gentleman! While gifts may open doors, it is a person's character that sustains and defines them. Michael has a great character that speaks volumes about his integrity, values, and the way he navigates through life. Lizzy asked him how he overcomes obstacles and challenges in his life. He told her it's all about perspective. Setbacks and disappointments are only a moment of time in light of eternity and heaven. Thank you Michael Porter Jr.!!

We allowed only a handful of people to come say their goodbyes—aunts, uncles, cousins, a beloved teacher (whom she cherished dearly), and notably, Michael Porter Jr. (MPJ), a freshman basketball player at Mizzou. His presence among those permitted to say their goodbyes held great significance. Lizzy was an avid Mizzou fan. It was big news in our hometown that Michael's father, Michael Porter Sr., had left his coaching job at the University of Washington to become the assistant basketball coach at Mizzou, bringing along his two sons, Michael and Jontay. Michael was one of the top basketball prospects for the class of 2017. Unfortunately, during the opening game of the 2017-2018 season, he was hurt in the first half of the game against Iowa State with an injury requiring back surgery. But by February 22, 2018, he had finally been cleared to practice with the team; he had returned to the court on March 8, two days before he came to our house.

Mizzou has a longstanding tradition of supporting pediatric cancer, stemming from the journey of Brad Loos, a former Mizzou assistant men's basketball coach, whose daughter, Rhyan, was diagnosed with neuroblastoma at the age of five. This tradition began three years prior, when Mizzou hosted a game benefiting the Loos family's "Rally for Rhyan" charity. During this special game, Mizzou players proudly wear the names of children with cancer on the back of their jerseys. In anticipation of this 2018 game, Michael Porter Jr. wore Lizzy's name on his T-shirt. Since he was so inspired to connect with her, Brad reached out and arranged for Michael to meet Lizzy at our house at 5:00 that evening.

When he arrived at our door, we were expecting to see an entire group of people. Instead, it was only nineteen-year-old Michael, standing six feet ten inches and holding a pair of size fourteen blue and gold basketball shoes. Michael entered the room and found Lizzy nestled under a stack of quilts, connected to oxygen, resting on the couch in our living room. Without hesitation, he pulled up a chair by her side, positioning himself to meet her gaze. Their interaction unfolded as if the two of them were in their own little world, oblivious to everything else around them. Their conversation flowed seamlessly, touching on a multitude of topics with Michael displaying a remarkable presence and genuine engagement throughout their interaction. They talked about basketball, and Lizzy asked about his back injury.

Lizzy was so excited at the prospect of meeting this young man. It was an extraordinary opportunity for her to engage in conversation with someone she admired deeply. This encounter meant the world to her, and it brought a radiant smile to her face. But after about twenty to twenty-five minutes, Lizzy's energy was beginning to fade. So Michael gave Lizzy the shoes and took photos

Lizzy with the incredible Michael J. Porter Jr., former Mizzou basketball star, now a pro player. 🏀 Genuine and kind, Michael is the real deal! Forever fans of MJP Jr.! #BasketballStar #Kindness

with us. Then he went outside and talked with fourteen-year-old Daniel who was shooting hoops on the driveway. He didn't have to do that. His willingness to spend time with Daniel as well was huge. It showed Michael's understanding of how deeply cancer had impacted our entire family, not just Lizzy.

Despite his hectic schedule, MJP proved to be a class act. His character demonstrated that he was a gentle giant who towered above us all, yet he remained remarkably grounded and relatable.

He texted us several times afterward asking about Lizzy. While he initially came to our home to uplift Lizzy, she ended up encouraging him instead. Later, we came across his post on Instagram where he described Lizzy as one of the most amazing people he had ever encountered. He reflected on how Lizzy reminded him of the fleeting nature of life, emphasizing the importance of preparing oneself for God during our time on earth. He said of Lizzy that she "only has hours left in this world, but she's excited because she knows she gets to spend eternity in heaven with God."

We later talked to Michael's mother, Lisa, who revealed that talking to Lizzy that day deeply humbled him and provided him with a newfound sense of gratitude and purpose. Later that year, Michael was drafted by the Denver Nuggets. Since then, we have seen countless stories detailing his visits with other cancer patients and the profound impact he has had on them. It's pretty awesome. That moment was a gift, an incredibly meaningful and holy moment for our entire family.

MARCH 12, 2018—
A Text Thread Between John and Lizzy

JOHN: How is your breathing??

LIZZY: It is soooooooo hard to breathe. I feel like it's going to be soon for me to go to heaven. :(

> **LIZZY:** Goodnight. I love you sooooooooooooooooo much! I can't wait to see you soon!!!!

> **JOHN:** I love you too honey!! Daddy is here anytime you need me!

MARCH 13, 2018

Moments with Lizzy having her eyes wide open for pictures are few and far between. Her morphine continues to go up. I'm cutting food into smaller and smaller pieces, yet not much is being eaten from each plate. Despite having two books, her phone, and a few stuffed animals that follow her from room to room, Lizzy is too tired to engage with them. She finds it difficult to open her eyes, and her texts to friends have become fewer. She waits and smiles when Daddy, Daniel, and Hannah come home. She sometimes calls for "Mommy" like she did when she was a little baby. 🧡 Occasionally, forgetting her situation, out of the blue, she asks me to take her to Panera or Target. I gently tell her we aren't going anywhere, and she slowly lays back down. At this point, her body is like a delicate China doll.

One night she sat up in bed. When I asked what she was doing, she said she was waiting for communion and hoped she didn't miss it. John served us all communion that night.

She wants to go to heaven and to be freed from pain. I laid prayer cloths on her and earnestly prayed, laying her little body at the foot of Jesus. I know God hears my cries and is closer than I even realize.

Yet we are not like those who have no hope. Right now we are in the midst of a waiting pattern where life moves very slowly. People come and go leaving behind love and food. We are so honored by each act of kindness. We will continue to keep you updated and are so grateful for your love.

I distinctly remember another conversation shortly before her passing when I had to tell her she didn't have to fight anymore; she didn't have to try so hard. During her fifteen months of treatment, we had asked her to do so much—to lie motionless in an MRI tube for long periods of time, to withstand countless IVs, and to undergo a multitude of surgeries. We had urged her to be strong and to keep going.

But as we approached the end of our journey, I realized it was time to release her from this burden. With tears in my eyes, I told Lizzy that there was nothing more we could do for her, and she was going to pass away and go to heaven. She understood. She just said, "Mom, you're asking me to do a very hard thing right now. You're asking me to go somewhere you've never been before." I affirmed this and reassured her that while it was a journey into the unknown, she had the strength and courage to make it. She would be going to heaven to be in the presence of God.

Jennifer holding Lizzy close during her final days, captured by the compassionate Kelly Scott, NP. ♥ Kelly's kindness extended to bringing Lizzy a smoothie, seen here, and sharing a book about heaven. We treasure this photo of our last moments together. #TenderMoments #CompassionateCare

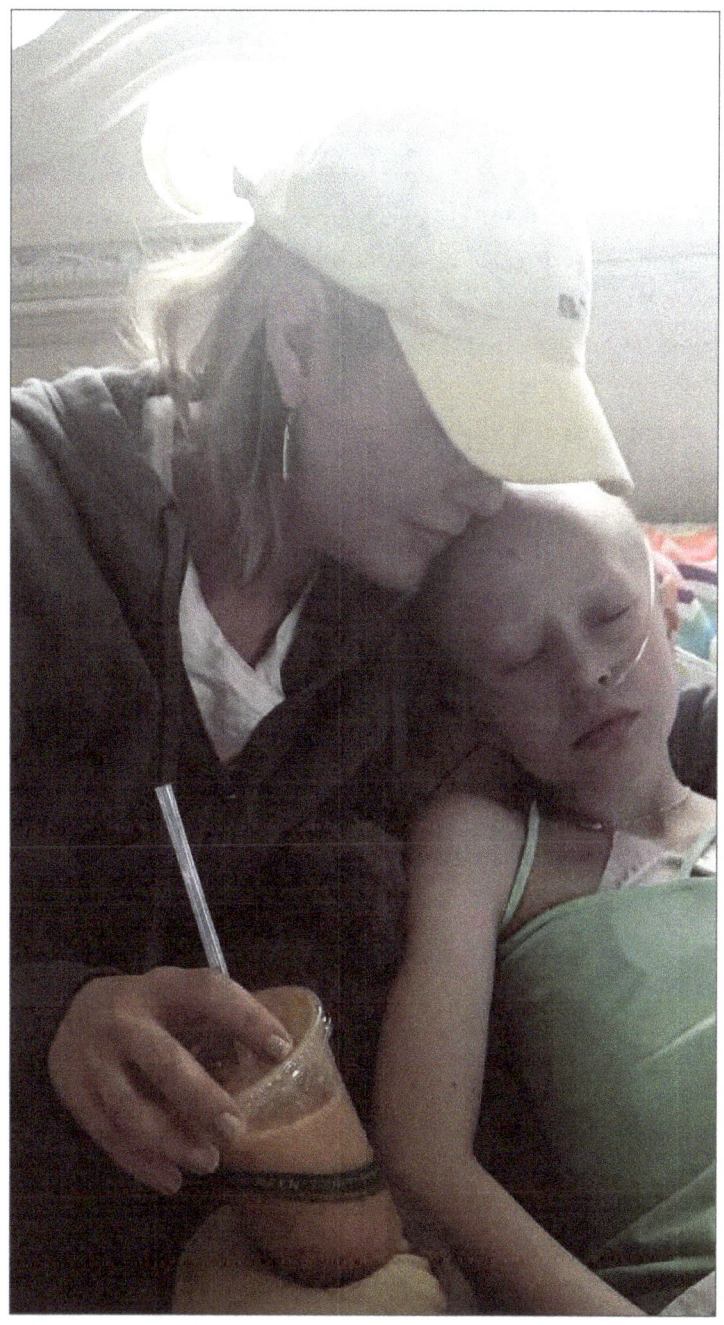

MARCH 15, 2018 *(John)*

Lizzy has bravely and courageously run and finished her race here on earth. She was in the arms of her mother at 3:30 a.m. when God called her home. We are in total peace that she no longer has to suffer. Thank you for all the love, support, and prayers during Lizzy's walk of faith. Please respect our privacy as we prepare for the coming days. We will keep everyone posted on the funeral arrangements. Lizzy's legacy lives on!! #bravelikelizzy

Looking back and recalling Lizzy's passing, a flood of emotions rushes through me, words tumbling in my mind, each struggling to convey the depth of this moment. The night stretched endlessly as we gathered the children to bid their farewells, sensing the impending goodbye. Lizzy's morphine drip reached its highest level, oxygen turned up, a testament to her struggle. Exhaustion weighed heavily on me, having been awake for twenty-four hours. Finally, I yielded to John, allowing him to take over while I stole a moment of rest, the hospice nurse by our side.

In the dead of night, John reached out to St. Jude, desperate for guidance as Lizzy battled fiercely. Their advice led him to a pharmacy in Jefferson City, racing against time for the medication. With a brief hour of sleep, I awoke, urging John to rest as I resumed care of Lizzy. At one point, I remember her sitting up, struggling for breath. Gasping, she repeated, "I can't do this. I can't do this anymore!"

I whispered, "It's alright honey. That's a great place to be because that's when God takes over." Those words brought her comfort as she settled back, allowing me to cradle her in my arms.

Nestling beside her, I held her fragile form, feeling her gradually relax into my embrace. In a tender moment of serenity, she delicately removed the breathing tube, a gesture both unexpected and poignant. Then Lizzy, as she often did, gave me gentle kisses on the arm before resting her head to sleep. In that moment of silence, I realized that I was the first person to hold my daughter when she was born. Now, I was the last one to hold her as she passed away. It was there, amid the softness of her growing hair, free from the grasp of chemotherapy for the first time in fifteen months, that she found peace at last.

After John and I had our quiet moments with Lizzy, we gently roused the children. It was a difficult decision, but we knew they needed the opportunity to bid their final farewells to their beloved sister before the funeral home arrived to take her away. Waking them in the early hours of the morning must have been incredibly challenging for them, grappling with the heaviness of saying goodbye to their little sister. Once we were all prepared, we contacted the funeral home. As they tenderly lifted our precious girl, a soul-stirring moment unfolded. The funeral home staff remarked to John that they could hear the muffled crying of our children as they passed by Daniel's room. It was a sound that would forever linger in their memories, a testament to the depth of sorrow felt by our family.

MARCH 20, 2018

So much has happened during the past two days that we will never forget. During this time, Jesus has been lifted up, our family has felt comfort and love, and Lizzy has been honored.

Please read what Colin's mom, Brenda, our dear friend and one of Daniel's best friends wrote. Colin was a pallbearer for Lizzy. It was a holy moment under the tent yesterday in the rain, when we buried our sweet Lizzy's earthly body. These young men were there for that very moment. Brenda Eggers Bruggeman wrote:

My final thought of the day as I rested my head on the pillow was of six remarkable men. Jerry was asked to shepherd Colin and five other boys ages eleven through seventeen through the honor of being pallbearers. Today, they stepped up and carried a physical and emotional load and did the job of men, walking alongside a friend on his hardest day carrying sweet Lizzy. These boys might shoot gummy bears across the room, laugh at a toot, or forget to take out the trash, but when it really matters, they step up. What a beautiful picture of love! Thank you for trusting them with this honor John and Jennifer Wampler.

Lizzy's final journey, carried by some of those who held her dear. ♥ Among them, her devoted brother Daniel is standing strong in the foreground. Her cousin, Luke Steiner, was also among them. Their bravery spoke volumes. #FinalGoodbye #ForeverInOurHearts 💚

Lizzy's funeral unfolded as a moving tribute, a beautiful gift of love encompassing every moment. The entire service was filled with a profound affection for Lizzy, her untimely departure casting a rawness that pierced our hearts. The profound impact of Lizzy's life on the community was unmistakable as we gathered to honor her memory.

Friends from Fort Worth, long absent from our lives, traveled to attend her funeral, along with friends from Tennessee. Even the pediatric office where Lizzy was a patient and where John worked, closed its doors for the day to pay their respects. Dr. Wheeler, a pivotal figure in Lizzy's journey, also suspended his clinic to join us. Christian Fellowship School went above and beyond by live-streaming the funeral, allowing those unable to attend in person to be part of the commemoration. Despite our shattered hearts, this gathering served as a strong reminder of the unity found in honoring our beloved Lizzy, drawing us together in shared grief and love.

Among the many touching moments, Mrs. Bond, Lizzy's teacher, shared a heartfelt reflection that painted a vivid portrait of Lizzy's essence, capturing her beauty and spirit with grace. Frank, Lizzy's ten-year-old best friend, emerged as a beacon of strength, delivering a heartfelt tribute to their cherished friendship. My heart swelled with pride as my daughter Hannah bravely expressed her love for Lizzy, her words a testament to their bond. And then there was our sweet Daniel, Lizzy's courageous brother, walking alongside her coffin with his friends as pallbearers, a sight etched in my memory forever.

The graveside ceremony unfolded under cold rain and raw emotion, a stark reminder of the cruel reality that no parent should have to bury their precious child at the tender age of ten. It was a day shrouded in sorrow; the weight of grief palpable in the air. Yet even in the darkness, the love for Lizzy illuminated our hearts, a ray of hope amid the storm.

During Lizzy's funeral, I found comfort in expressing a fragment of my mother's heart, overwhelmed with gratitude for the privilege of being her mother. In that emotional moment, all I could focus on was the gift she had been to me and the honor it was to have been chosen to be Lizzy's mother. John's speech echoed in my mind as he shared tender memories of their daddy-daughter dates alongside the harsh realities of pediatric cancer. His words resonated deeply, a reminder that we must do more, that there is an urgent need for greater action. That moment stayed with me, imprinting a determination within me: we need to do more, we need to do more.

Obituary

Elizabeth Joy Wampler, age 10, bravely and courageously ran and finished her race here on earth on March 15, 2018, after a long battle with cancer.

Elizabeth "Lizzy" was born on May 8th, 2007, in Springfield, MO. She was welcomed into our family with great joy. She was a loving, joy-filled child from the very beginning. She was naturally considerate of other people from an early age. Lizzy naturally adored and looked up to her older brother, Daniel and sister, Hannah. She was a loving and affectionate daughter, granddaughter, niece and cousin. Lizzy was known as a faithful friend. She adored school and had a passion for science. Lizzy was in ballet for a few years and truly wanted dance to be in her future. During her treatment while at St. Jude, Lizzy was introduced to the ukulele and found playing a comforting distraction while spending hours on end in the hospital. With the help of her child life specialist, she discovered her voice to sing. Lizzy could be found alone in her room at the St. Jude Target House in Memphis where we stayed, singing along with Kari Jobe, one of her favorite worship singers. As a devout Christian, Lizzy had a child-like faith in God.

Elizabeth was featured on the NBC Today Show, honored at professional and college sporting events, aired in multiple St. Jude commercials, recorded three songs, featured in a promo video with Chip and Joanna Gaines for Target, and was featured in 3,500 Chili's restaurants nationwide. At the same time, Lizzy's greatest accomplishment was positively impacting and touching lives everywhere she went. Her last contribution was her desire to donate parts of her body to St. Jude for further research and help in finding a cure for osteosarcoma.

She is survived by her parents, John C. Wampler and Jennifer L. Wampler of Columbia, Missouri, sister Hannah G. Wampler, brother Daniel D. Wampler, grandparents Dee and Anne Wampler of Springfield, Missouri, and Larry and Bonnie Gayhart of Adell, Wisconsin, aunt and uncle Mark and Allison Steiner of Springfield, Missouri, and cousins, Olivia and Luke Steiner of Springfield, Missouri.

In honor of Lizzy who was a bright and colorful young lady, one of her requests was that everyone wear bright colors to celebrate her life.

Friends will be received from 3:00 p.m. to 7:00 p.m. Sunday, March 18th, 2018, at Parker-Millard Funeral Service. Celebration of Lizzy's Life will be held at 10:00 a.m. Monday, March 19th, 2018, at the Crossing Church. A private family interment will follow at Columbia Cemetery. In lieu of flowers, expressions of sympathy may be made to Lizzy Wampler's Walk of Faith Facebook page.

CHAPTER 11

A Father's Heart

NAVIGATING LOSS AND HEALING

John

LITTLE DID I know that the end was closer than I thought. In December of 2017, Lizzy was visiting with a group of Louisiana State Highway Patrolmen who were taking a tour of the St. Jude Target House apartments. She was entertaining the group, and everyone was cutting up and having fun. While Lizzy was clowning around with the patrolmen, I received a phone call from the doctor. It was one of many calls that no father should ever have to take. More unfortunate news that Lizzy's tumors were not responding to chemo and radiation. It was the first time the words "hospice" and "keeping her comfortable" were spoken. The doctor then clarified that they were not giving up on her but had exhausted treatment options. At that moment, it dawned on me that Lizzy would fulfill her Make-A-Wish and then return home for end-of-life care. My mind couldn't take it all in. How could my daughter be dying? It couldn't be true.

One of the patrolmen, Master Trooper Paul Toups, later told me they were "drawn to Lizzy." When the patrolmen saw me come back after the call, they could tell it was not good news. So they shifted and began focusing on me to provide support and encouragement.

St. Jude got us hooked up with Koala Care, "end-of-life" support for transitioning—either at St. Jude or at home with hospice. We wanted Lizzy to spend her final days in the comfort of her own bedroom surrounded by family. Yet we didn't know how it would look or how long it would take.

Lizzy's decline became evident after her Christmas at home and her Make-A-Wish experience. As her condition worsened, she bravely expressed her inability to endure further suffering. At some point, Lizzy told us, "I can't do this anymore. It hurts too much, and I can't breathe." Jen consoled and reassured her that it was okay to stop fighting. We went from fervently praying for her healing to asking that God take her and end her suffering. This was an unimaginably difficult journey, marked by a profound shift in trusting and resting in God's perfect will. I remember my prayer:

"God, not my will but Your will be done. I give you Lizzy. Here is her life. I'm going to just stop fighting and give it all to you."

After that prayer, I felt a whole different level of trust. I should have been trusting like that the entire time, but I just couldn't. I realized that although the lessons of trust that God sends us are often wrapped in difficulty, the benefits far outweigh the cost. Surrendering to God's will also brought an overwhelming sense of peace and relief, despite the agonizing decision to let go. It was like a huge weight had been lifted from my shoulders. It was the hardest prayer a father has to pray—to release and hand over your daughter to God. As the end drew close, witnessing her suffering became unbearable. It was so difficult to watch her endure such pain, leading to a heartfelt plea for God's mercy to end her anguish.

The night of her passing, our family surrounded Lizzy as she lay in bed. We reminisced about special memories together as a family. With a strong foreboding that this might be her last night, I felt a prompting to ask both of the children to tell Lizzy what she meant to them and how much they loved her. It was an intimate time of sharing that produced many tears from us all.

Lizzy's passing and the emotional toll of her funeral left me grappling with the daunting prospect of life without her. Unsure of how to navigate this new reality, I found myself at a loss, struggling to fill the void left by her absence. Despite my overwhelming grief, I made the decision to return to work just two days after Lizzy's Celebration of Life service. While it didn't signify a return to normalcy, work provided a much-needed distraction, allowing me to re-engage with life, move forward, and regain a sense of purpose.

The moment Lizzy took her last breath on earth, she took her first breath in heaven. She was finally home. The homecoming celebration began in heaven at the same moment our family was crushed by grief. Yet raised in a Midwestern town in Missouri, I learned that men were supposed to be the strong ones. I had to be tough and always push through—keeping my emotions at bay and not allowing them to surface. There was never room for weakness. When things became too much, I put my head down and fought harder. Men did not talk about their pain regardless of the severity. These rules, passed down from my grandfather, and likely generations before him, perpetuated a culture of silence about pain and suffering. Looking back, I now realize that substances like alcohol served as a makeshift salve, numbing the ache of unspoken pain.

In contrast, women had a completely different set of societal expectations, where emotional expression was not only accepted but often encouraged. They were the communicators, the ones who vocalized their pain and sought solace in shared experiences. While the men, strong and silent, learned to express grief physically by throwing themselves into work or projects around the house to keep themselves occupied and avoid dealing with emotions. They turned to physical activity, like playing basketball or going to the gym, to release anger. In navigating these coping mechanisms, men often inadvertently distanced themselves from the women in their lives, unsure of how to navigate their partner's emotional landscape alongside their own. This disconnect bred confusion and resentment, as each party operated under a different set of societal norms.

I've tried every strategy imaginable—throwing myself into work, drowning my sorrows in alcohol—but no matter how fervently I pursued these escapes, the pain never goes away. It is a constant ache that refuses to leave, a forever heartbreak, continuing days, months, and even years. My grief is not temporary, it is a permanent fixture etched in the very core of my being. Yet there is an ignorant misconception held by some that time can somehow heal all wounds, that after a few months or a year we should have moved on, as if grief has an expiration date. But those who have never experienced this degree of devastation will never understand. This soul-breaking loss is utterly devastating and will never completely go away.

One of the biggest turning points in my grief journey occurred when I realized I wasn't alone. As I allowed myself to be vulnerable, transparent, and authentic, I discovered a multitude of people willing to offer support without any ulterior motives. They simply wanted to alleviate the burden of grief that I carried as a father mourning the loss of his daughter. Instead of judgment or discomfort when tears flowed freely as I told my story, they embraced me and offered a listening ear. Rather than telling me to "toughen up" or "fight through it," they taught me to persevere and offered healthy coping mechanisms for handling loss. Their gift of compassion provided a safe space for me to release the pent-up pain, grief, depression, and despair—allowing healing to gradually unfold.

I learned to let it out—releasing every ounce of pain, even the darkest depths of sorrow, to pave the way for healing and growth after the loss. I lowered my defenses and allowed others to see the authentic me, freely expressing my thoughts and emotions, even on the toughest days. I embraced the fact that some days are harder than others, yet each new dawn brings with it the promise of a fresh start. Above all, I realized that Lizzy's wish for me is to embrace a life full of passion—smiling, laughing, and loving once again.

In my quest for healing, I started a men's grief support network for fathers who have experienced the devastating loss of a child called "Just For Dads." Once a month, we meet together to talk and build each other up. We are linked because we have all weathered unthinkable pain—drowning, car accidents, suicide, cancer. Our gatherings foster a profound sense of solidarity and strength, where grown men are encouraged to embrace vulnerability and authenticity. It is a remarkable sight to witness as these courageous fathers open up, allowing their emotions to surface unabashedly, tears freely flowing as they share their stories and support one another through the darkest times.

Society may mistakenly see expressing feelings and seeking help as signs of weakness and instability, particularly for men. However, in reality, such actions require immense strength and courage, essential for confronting life's challenges head-on. Fathers, in particular, should not attempt to navigate their journeys alone. By reaching out to support others, I have personally found both hope and healing. It has become clear to me that my deepest desire is to empower fathers with the necessary tools to move forward with vulnerability, transparency, and authenticity.

Finding support by reaching out to help other people, much like Lizzy did, has also been a cornerstone of my healing journey. It's a reminder that life is bigger than my own problems. By extending a hand to fellow fathers struggling through the unfathomable loss of a child, I have discovered a deep sense of purpose and contentment—one that transcends my own grief. The act of supporting them through their grief has helped me more than they will ever know.

To honor her memory, I sought out avenues for sharing—support groups, counseling sessions, cherished friends, and faith. Finding these outlets made all the difference to help me heal, grow, and move forward. I needed to give myself permission to tell her story and not be ashamed to "always be talking about her." Although my grief journey may look different than yours, I urge you to find whatever combination works best for you. Above all, remember that bottling emotions up inside just prolongs the pain. Embrace the power of releasing your emotions. By leaning on trusted friends or a supportive group, you will allow yourself the grace to heal.

What I've come to realize is that the fathers who are not merely surviving, but also thriving, amid their grief are the ones who have been able to find a purpose—a cause greater than themselves—on which to focus their energy and honor their child. Focusing on others seems to give them a sense of energy, meaning, and contentment. On the other hand, those who remain inwardly focused, consumed by their own sorrow, find themselves trapped in a cycle of their own grief, endlessly trying to make sense of it.

By summoning the courage to extend a lifeline to those drowning in despair, I've not only lifted their spirits but also experienced personal transformation.

Pain is what binds us together. We're all stuck in a broken world where terrible, painful things happen. If there's one thing that everyone can relate to, it's pain, so use it to find common ground. Reach out for help, realizing it is not a sign of "weakness," but rather a badge of courage and strength. Grieving is painful, hard, and scary. Although it is always with you, it is survivable; you can get through it although it will drain you physically, mentally, and emotionally. But you will come out on the other side of this very long and lonely tunnel as a different person. And when you do, there is no going back to the old you.

Today my definition of success has changed. I no longer feel like I'm rushing around trying to prove myself to the world. I'm no longer the "go-to" guy at work. Instead, I do my job but don't do it as if I want to run the company someday. I am constantly working towards a simpler way of life. The idea of helping others helps me. Material things don't have as much meaning now. Spending time with my wife, my other two kids, and our dog, Memphis, is much more satisfying than working long hours to acquire things that don't bring happiness.

I love my girl just as much as you love yours. The only difference is mine lives in heaven. Our culture doesn't cope well with hearing about children gone too soon. But that doesn't stop me from saying my daughter's name and sharing her love and light everywhere I go. Just because it might make you uncomfortable doesn't make her matter any less. I want Lizzy to know that I miss her dearly and haven't forgotten her. I want her to understand that while her life was cut irreversibly short, her love lives on forever.

I make a point to visit Lizzy's burial spot frequently. A stone adorned with her picture and a verse from Psalm 91 serves as a marker. Somehow, being in this sacred space brings me solace; it's where I can honor her memory and navigate my grief. On special occasions such as her birthday and Christmas, we bring flowers for Lizzy. When the weather is nice, I ride my bike to the local flower shop, My Secret Garden, to buy a beautiful bouquet. Then I hop on my bike and ride down Main Street with flowers in one arm and holding the handlebar with the other. The vibrant blooms seem to mirror Lizzy's essence—bright and beautiful. Visiting her grave is emotionally gut-wrenching, leaving me in a state of profound grief each time I walk away. I'm a mess! Yet we continue to go to share special moments with our beloved daughter.

Lizzy possessed a remarkable perspective. In the middle of her pain, suffering, and separation from family and friends, she was still able to see the bright side of life. The 2017 St. Jude Marathon was held shortly after we learned there was nothing more the doctors could do, and that Lizzy would be going home with hospice. Part of the route runs right through the St. Jude campus. Despite her own challenges, Lizzy was determined to uplift and inspire the marathon runners dedicated to fighting pediatric cancer.

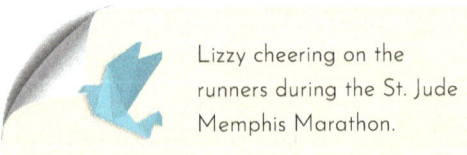

Lizzy cheering on the runners during the St. Jude Memphis Marathon.

Lizzy shines at the St. Jude Memphis Marathon, her spirit undaunted. 🌟 Beside her, Michael Albrough, a steadfast supporter from Arizona, joins her in spreading hope and love. #StJudeHeroes #InspirationEverywhere

There seemed to be a sea of runners along the marathon route passing through the St. Jude campus. On both sides of the route were kids with crutches and wheelchairs surrounded by cheering families. All of a sudden, out of the corner of my eye, I saw Lizzy wheel herself out into the middle of the road.

Turning around and facing the onslaught of runners, Lizzy extended both arms to give high fives to athletes on either side of her. In response to her gesture of courage and determination, swarms of runners stopped to offer hugs, gift cards, pats on the back, or a touch of the hand.

Witnessing her selfless act was a scene I will NEVER forget, as she urged the runners onward in their pursuit of a cure. Despite her own battle drawing to a close, Lizzy's message resounded clearly: the fight against pediatric cancer must persist until better treatments, and perhaps even a cure, are found. Inspired by her resilience, Jen and I remain committed to advancing research and treatment options for osteosarcoma and pediatric cancer, determined to honor Lizzy's spirit and legacy.

Osteosarcoma has changed the course of our lives, stripping away much of what we hold dear. I came across a poem written by an unknown author that still deeply resonates with me titled, "What Cancer Cannot Do." In moments of despair, these words offer solace and strength. "Cancer is so limited … It cannot cripple love. It cannot shatter hope. It cannot dissolve faith. It cannot destroy peace. It cannot kill friendship. It cannot suppress memories. It cannot silence courage. It cannot invade the soul. It cannot steal eternal life. It cannot conquer the spirit."

Lizzy's life didn't stop just because she was in the hospital facing a catastrophic, terminal disease. She lived her life to the fullest. She embraced each moment with an unmatched zest, acknowledging those around her and radiating warmth and positivity. Let's be clear, Lizzy wasn't immune to bad days or occasional bouts of frustration. She despised cancer and longed to be elsewhere surrounded by her friends. Her innate ability to see the bright side of life touched many hearts, and she refused to let cancer define her. Instead, she used the boundlessness of her spirit to confront the limitations of the disease head-on. Lizzy's resilience and positivity were a testament to her strength and unwavering determination to live life on her terms, despite the challenges she faced.

Upon hearing that Lizzy would be admitted to their ward, nurses eagerly sought to care for her, drawn to her contagious positivity. While she had every reason to succumb to negativity, Lizzy consciously opted for happiness—it was a deliberate choice. Despite her circumstances, she consistently chose to dwell on the bright side of life, leaving a lasting impact on those fortunate enough to encounter her sunny disposition.

We did our best to prepare Lizzy for her death while we struggled to accept it ourselves. I've met many parents who have experienced the sudden loss of their child, often without the opportunity to say goodbye. I deeply cherish the time we had with Lizzy, knowing it was a privilege denied to many. We had time to talk about heaven and help prepare her for death.

But, in the end, Lizzy was brave as she went on her journey to heaven, leaving behind a void in our hearts that can never fully be filled. We mourn her absence, grappling with the ache of her loss, yet finding solace in the belief that one day we will join her there. It is a bittersweet anticipation, knowing that while we must endure the sorrow of separation for now, there nears a time when we will be together again, free from suffering and united in eternal love.

As she faced her cancer head-on, Lizzy wrote about pain in the journal she kept while going through treatments. I want to share some of her words:

Don't waste that pain. God never said that we would understand everything that God has planned. Don't just go through it—grow through it. Every difficulty He is making me stronger. Difficulties are a part of life. There's a lesson through the pain. Nothing is a coincidence.

Lizzy understood that you can't quit living just because you are in a difficult season. During her toughest treatments, Lizzy never sat on the sidelines but stayed in the game and learned how to play in pain. She discovered that one of the most powerful antidotes to personal pain is helping someone else and becoming a blessing to them, diverting attention from her own struggles. Lizzy didn't just go through the pain of osteosarcoma—she grew from it.

There have been so many wonderful cards, notes, dinners, flowers, and well-wishes. So much love and support has helped us to push forward. Yet we sometimes struggle when others say, "We know what you're going through" or "She's in a better place." It doesn't take away our grief. Although those words are well-intentioned, we mostly just need space to grieve and grow closer in our walk with God. As our dear friend Brenda Schaeffer Jones wisely said, "You don't 'get over it' or 'move on;' instead, you keep moving forward and embracing each day to the fullest." That, my friends, is exactly what Lizzy would do, and it's what she would want for all of us. Bam, let's do it!

CHAPTER 12

Whispers of Love, Echoes of Loss

A MOTHER'S GRIEF THROUGH THE SEASONS

Jennifer

GRIEVING IS HARD. It hurts. It's painful. Yesterday I went for a run, as it's one of my tools to navigate through this season of grief. Perhaps to onlookers I might have seemed like the "crying runner." At times, a wave of grief would hit me. This grief was so tangible. I couldn't help but let out a loud sigh and silently shed tears as I ran. Fortunately, after my second mile, a sense of composure and strength washed over me, allowing me to finish my run without so much emotional pain.

The little things can be such profound triggers of grief. Going through Lizzy's belongings is filled with emotional weight. Each item holds a piece of her essence—the notes in her purse, the backpack filled with her essentials she carried with her to every inpatient appointment, the unfinished friendship bracelets, recently bought items like her new pink Adidas shoes she barely got to wear, the Archie comic books she never finished, and the list she made for me of the fruit she wanted from Hy-Vee. The little fuzzy green North Face® hat and gloves still smelling like her evoke a deep sense of connection. Encountering any of these special items feels like a punch in the gut, reopening a wound that's left exposed. The emotions tied to these tangible items are raw and bittersweet.

The most profound moment came when I held her books; it felt as though I cradled hours of her life in my arms. Each page turned held a piece of her, a fragment of the countless moments she spent immersed in their worlds, finding solace amid the chaos of doctor appointments and treatments. Those books were her sanctuary, offering respite from the relentless pain. As I held them close, I felt an indescribable closeness to her, reluctant to let go, for in that fleeting moment I was united with her in a world where her spirit soared freely through the pages.

It's undeniably difficult, but we allow ourselves to grieve—to face this pain together. John, Hannah, Daniel, and I, each in our own way, need this process. We understood it would come, and as a family we embraced it. Our love for her is enduring and everlasting. We will continue to love her; our connection is unbroken. Reflecting on the visitation, I am touched by the wonderful people who came, offering their support and condolences. Every card and message sent our way is read with gratitude. John, with a joyful heart, writes thank you cards whenever possible to express our appreciation for the flowers and support from the kind and generous individuals who have reached out to us.

These sentiments are just glimpses of the numerous people— literally tens, if not hundreds—who have communicated in various

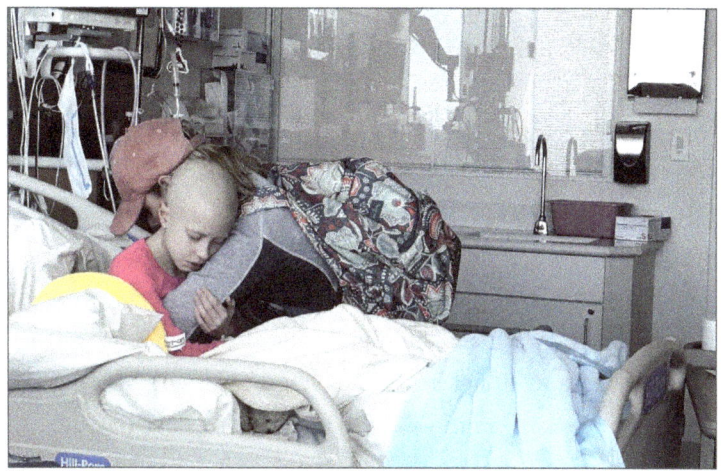

Saying goodbye never got easier. 🧡 Jennifer embraces Lizzy, torn between staying by her side and returning to care for her siblings in Columbia. #Heartache #FamilyLove

ways that Lizzy's life mattered, that her life was seen, and that she made a significant difference. Each card and message serve as a source of healing, as they narrate the life and hope Lizzy brought and continues to bring to others.

"She brought me out of a really dark place. I could only get out of bed and live another day because of Lizzy's smile, courage, and faith."

"If Lizzy could be brave, then I knew I could too."

"Lizzy's life and story being told opened my family who were closed off to the gospel for years into asking questions about heaven and Jesus. She is encouraging my nephew who has osteosarcoma and is facing his battle right now."

"Lizzy's smile brightened up any room."

"Lizzy brought me closer to God."

"Lizzy made me want to become an oncology nurse."

These powerful testimonies reflect the impact Lizzy had on the lives of those around her and the inspiration she continues to provide. We are aware that there are more stories yet untold, and we believe God's work is far from finished.

Lizzy was our precious gift. I know she brought immense joy to us when she was born, pulling us out of a sad and dark place. I believe that one of her missions here on earth was to bring joy, hope, and to share her unwavering faith and the love of God.

In the days after her death, the array of decisions to be made and preparations to be undertaken left little room to grieve. Thankfully, John took the initiative to make some significant decisions before Lizzy's passing. At that time, my attention was primarily dedicated to caring for Lizzy, and while I may not have been actively involved in the preplanning, John's foresight allowed us to concentrate on the present moments amid the flurry of tasks.

A few days after the funeral, I finally found the strength to visit her resting place. The contrast from the day we laid her earthly body to rest was striking. The day of her funeral held a holy hush for me. Despite the downpour of rain and the chilly air that enveloped us, there was a profound sense of peace. Under the tent at the burial site, the minister kept his words raw and basic. While he shared several thoughts, my mind retained two key messages. He emphasized, "In times like these, we all need to remember that God is good, and this is not where Lizzy really is. This is not Lizzy."

Visiting her graveside is a bittersweet reminder of the baby I held in my arms, now gone from this earthly realm. Though I can't dwell in that place of sorrow indefinitely, I allow myself moments to acknowledge and process these feelings. During my initial visits,

Jennifer's heartache is palpable as she looks at Lizzy's tombstone. A mother's love knows no bounds, even in grief. 💔 #ForeverInOurHearts #UnfathomableLoss

I felt an immense weight of sorrow and could only manage to say, "I'm so, so sorry, Lizzy. I'm so sorry." It was incredibly challenging to understand how, despite doing everything in our power to keep her alive, she was no longer with us. It was a tough reality to grasp, but with time I've found peace in letting go of those feelings of guilt.

Even though I am aware she is not physically present in this carefully chosen and tranquil burial place, a peaceful place thoughtfully picked by John, being here provides me with a small measure of comfort. I know that her earthly body, which held her spirit and soul for a decade, now rests in this sacred spot permanently. This place serves as a connection point for me, a space where I can find solace whenever needed. I'm confident that John and the kids can do the same. However, I hold onto the undeniable truth that she is more alive now than she has ever been in her entire life in heaven with Jesus.

I have found myself intermittently overwhelmed by grief. I knew it was coming, having experienced it at different times as I felt my daughter being pulled out of my hands by osteosarcoma. I know it will take time, but I will get through this stretch of mourning and someday emerge on the other side.

I am comforted by the thought of sharing pictures of her peaceful burial site and writing down a few words. There's a sense that putting all of this into words lifts a bit of the grief and allows healing to trickle in. It dawned on me how beneficial my Facebook posts have been for my own well-being.

This journey with Lizzy has transformed me. Having seen first-hand what truly matters in life, I'm inspired to run my race just as Lizzy taught me. I want to radiate my light as brightly as she did until I reach my final day.

The Monday night after Lizzy's celebration of life, as I lay down to sleep, I experienced a soft, warm wave of love gently enveloping me. This wasn't God's love; it was Lizzy's love—my daughter's love. I could feel her, and my mother's heart recognized the love was hers. I just knew. At that moment, I heard her soft voice repeating, "I'm so happy mom!" This brought immense comfort to me at that particular moment. I've tried to recreate that feeling since, but I can't. It remains a unique and precious gift from her—a moment allowed by God for me to sense her love. Knowing she was concerned about us and how we would miss her, I believe God granted her the opportunity to bring me some peace. I cherish that moment and eagerly anticipate more "heavenly encounters" in the days and years to come.

Our family has been navigating our new dynamics as a family of four, acknowledging that we will always be a family of five. Simple tasks, such as reserving a table at a restaurant, have taken on a different tone as I learn to say, "We need a table for four." The first instance of doing this was when I made a reservation over the phone for Easter lunch. I wasn't quite prepared to undertake the significant task of cooking for such an important day. As I spoke the words, "There will be only four of us now," during the phone call, the sound of the number four triggered an unexpected wave of emotions, and I had to hold back tears. The call ended abruptly, and John later had to apologize on my behalf for the sudden conclusion.

Another extremely challenging moment was going to Target for the first time after Lizzy's passing. It was a place she always loved, and I had shopped there for my kids for as far back as I could remember. While browsing through the women's clothing section, I heard a toddler crying out for their mother, striking a deep chord within my heart.

It was clear that the mother had momentarily stepped away, leaving the little one with their dad. The child's desperate cries for the mother resonated with me profoundly. It reminded me that I wouldn't be needed as a mother in the same way I had been. Lizzy's battle with cancer had created a unique dependency on me that I cherished. No one else needed me in that same way. The intensity of the moment overwhelmed me, and I sought solace in the women's dressing room. There, I allowed my tears to flow silently until the weight of grief lifted, even just a little.

It's these seemingly insignificant moments that act as subtle triggers, setting off an avalanche of tears. I'm beginning to understand more about how grief operates, though I am still in the early stages. Over the course of my life, I've faced numerous heartaches, and I've witnessed God carrying me through them enough times to discern a pattern. I've observed that when grief comes upon you, or perhaps opens up inside of you, the pain runs deep.

There was a day when I spent several hours in deep grief, and I feared it would never stop. Yet, it did. Afterwards, I went for over a week without shedding a tear, grateful that I had allowed myself to express those emotions on the day when I did.

I anticipated sadness but not tears. Then we met with dear friends from Memphis, who went out of their way to share lunch with John and me. The excitement of seeing them turned into an unexpected welling of deep grief. I thought I had already cried through those emotions, but it caught me off guard. That's when I realized that this might be how grief works—it's not a constant, but rather a wave that arises when triggered. We can't dwell in that grief daily; instead, we're designed to gain strength and move forward. Yet the human heart continues to love the person we grieve for, and when it needs to grieve, it will.

These friends triggered that response in me because our relationship over the past nine months or so has been deeply intertwined with Lizzy. When I saw them, I could feel their profound love for Lizzy, and that was enough to spark my own love for her, bringing forth grief.

I share this not to evoke emotions or solely for sadness. Instead, I want to highlight something beautiful. In these moments of grief, challenging as they may be, there is a profound reality. I have been blessed—blessed to have loved an amazing daughter, blessed to feel deeply and experience the true essence of being alive, to genuinely "feel" love. It's a gift, truly. I am striving to walk in that reality more and more. I want to share this in the hope that it will comfort someone else in their grief.

Grief is a poignant reminder of the depth of our past love. It is a tangible sign that our hearts have experienced the profound connection and affection that comes with loving someone. Not everyone has the chance to experience love. Some individuals, for various reasons, may not have been given the opportunity to feel the warmth and tenderness that love brings. There are those who, due to unique circumstances or personal challenges, may find it difficult to experience and reciprocate love. Grief is not just a response to loss; it is also a testament to the richness of the love that once existed. It underscores the profound impact that love has on our lives and the lasting impressions it leaves on our hearts.

A friend shared a touching encounter from the morning Lizzy passed away. She went to bed praying for us, only to wake up at 3:30 a.m.—the exact moment Lizzy was passing—and started praying for us. Another friend had a similar experience, waking up at the same time and hearing loud cheering and shouts of joy and celebration like never before. She believes God allowed her to hear the sounds of heaven as Lizzy walked through the pearly gates. I believe this with all my heart having heard similar accounts of those who have completed their life's journey. I believe God has revealed beautiful glimpses of Lizzy to comfort us. It assures us that He knows our sorrow and reassures us that Lizzy is now under His loving care.

In preparation for Hannah's recent birthday, I spent almost two hours one day going through old baby photos of Hannah and me. This reflective journey helped me focus on the blessings of motherhood. While the earthly journey of mothering Lizzy has ended, I hold onto the gratitude for the ongoing joy of being a mother to Daniel and Hannah. It's a reminder that even in the pain of loss, there is still a wellspring of love and connection in the present.

Among this morning's Facebook memories was a picture of Lizzy in the backseat of our car. In the photo, she was peacefully sleeping and holding onto her green barf bag. I remember that day, eagerly awaiting her awakening so we could explore the new side of Memphis I had just discovered.

However, revisiting such pictures is a complex experience for me. On one hand, I'm confronted with the memories of Lizzy's suffering, a stark reminder of the challenges she endured. Simultaneously, it brings me back to a time when my faith stood unshakable. During that period, I had no doubt that Lizzy would triumph over osteosarcoma, and our journey through it would leave us grateful and transformed. The notion of a relapse or the possibility of her passing never crossed my mind.

Yet, as the Bible aptly states, "Hope deferred makes the heart sick" (Proverbs 13:12). There's a profound sadness intertwined with those memories, not rooted in bitterness but in the realization of hopes and expectations that went unfulfilled. I don't dwell in that place of sorrow, but honesty compels me to acknowledge that I have often experienced it.

Moving past the gentle Facebook reminder, I found solace in a sweet picture of Lizzy with her first-grade class at Christian Fellowship School. It helped redirect my focus to cherished moments that bring warmth and joy, offering respite from the more somber aspects of our journey. It could not have been more perfect timing as I wanted to thank this now fifth-grade class for all the beautiful cards they sent us. Lizzy was blessed to have attended two exceptional schools, both of which showered her with love. The heartfelt sentiments from Christian Fellowship School and the recent batch of cards from Cedar Ridge Elementary, where Lizzy attended second and third grade, brought us so much comfort. It dawned on me that the teachers at both schools have been a pillar of strength, guiding grieving hearts through this challenging time. The empathy and love for Lizzy have not gone unnoticed, and we are profoundly grateful for the unwavering support provided to our family.

This morning brought a sweet message from a fellow St. Jude mom, someone I have never formally met. Over the past two months, I've received numerous encouraging messages from strangers, all sharing how Lizzy has made a positive impact on their lives in some meaningful way. However, today's message carried a special significance, prompting me to discern a lesson within it that I'm eager to share. Here is a portion of her message, and then I'll explain what I have learned:

I know we don't personally know each other, and I'm sure you have many messages piling in daily, but after last night, I had to reach out. My little boy was diagnosed with neuroblastoma in June 2017. He gained his wings January 13th, 2018. We saw Lizzy many times throughout our clinic visits.

The first time I saw her though was days after we found out about Kaden's diagnosis. They were having a dance type event in front of the cafeteria. I was getting coffee, only half awake, and happened to look over right when she started dancing. It brought me so much joy and hope at such a rough spot.

Once in the clinic, Kaden's nose started bleeding. She looked at me and asked if I was okay. Me. This young lady with such a big battle was asking me if I was okay. I was instantly humbled and calmed. There is no doubt she is a child of God.

Last night I took my younger son out to eat at Chili's. Lizzy's picture was on the back of the menu. He saw it and said, "Look,

KK is eating with us!" All he recognized was the bald head and assumed it was his brother, despite the glaring differences. It brought a tear to my eye but also some joy. They may not be physically here, but God still has a way of having them show up right at the exact moment.

I remember well the day this mother mentioned. It was in June when Sherri Laffey Sarrouf's dance team visited St. Jude. Lizzy, captivated by their passion and kindness, couldn't contain her excitement watching them dance. Despite experiencing pain and lacking clearance for dancing activities, Lizzy, yearning for a moment of normalcy, took a courageous step and joined in their dance.

For about fifteen precious minutes, she immersed herself in the joy of dancing with their team, a snippet of which I captured on video. While the joy was evident, what remained unseen was the underlying pain. The lesson from that day was profound: Lizzy chose to follow her heart, stepping out of her pain, current struggles, and discomfort to embrace a chance for joy. That choice made all the difference. Lizzy's pursuit of joy not only brought happiness to her but also inspired hope in another person.

Our lives and choices make such a difference to others. People are always watching us. Lizzy could have opted for the comfort of her wheelchair, citing pain and struggle as reasons not to dance. Instead, she embraced each moment of joy God presented, refusing to wait until everything was perfect. Had Lizzy chosen to wait until her body fully recovered, as it unfortunately never did, she would have missed out on the multitude of beautiful moments God presented to her. If she had deferred living life until she felt completely better, these precious opportunities would have slipped through her fingers.

For me, the lesson is clear—embrace joy, step out, and seize every beautiful moment God offers. God may present opportunities that seem challenging or premature, but don't let them pass. Others are watching, and you never know how your actions to embrace joy can instill hope in someone else.

After Lizzy's spirited dance, she was so happy. Unfortunately, her exertion did bring pain. A quick X-ray ensured no fracture, affirming that Lizzy's act of faith was worth it. Today's message from a precious mom brought a sweet reminder and gave me another lesson from Lizzy. I hope you'll be attuned to the wonderful opportunities God may be presenting to you. May you find the faith to step out in joy, as others may be waiting for the hope you can release to them.

During Christmas, graduations, and other special occasions, we're reminded even more poignantly of Lizzy's absence, a presence we deeply feel is missing. When Lizzy's class celebrated their fifth-grade graduation, we were honored that they included Lizzy in their celebration. As I watched this event, I experienced a tug-of-war between my mind and heart. While my mind acknowledges Lizzy's absence, my heart sees familiar faces and recognizes this is where Lizzy should be. It wonders about the outfit she would have chosen, the friends she would have stood by, and the joy that would have lit up her face. Imagining her smile and excitement, I'm momentarily lost in a world where Lizzy is still with us. As I let my heart explore all these thoughts and emotions, my mind slowly reels my heart back in and reminds it that she is not there to enjoy these moments. My heart obeys, and honestly, the entire experience is incredibly challenging.

Lizzy's birthday was yet another difficult day, brimming with emotions that are difficult to put into words. The support of family and friends who remembered her on that day was invaluable. It was heartening to have several dear friends in Memphis and even school children honoring her memory. Each act of kindness touched us profoundly. One friend, who shared Lizzy's birthday, went a step further by encouraging donations to St. Jude in Lizzy's name—a gesture that deeply touched our hearts.

Acts of kindness like these mean the world to John and me. When others remember Lizzy and include her in their celebrations, it brings a sense of healing. Hearing her name spoken and reminiscing about who she was fills our hearts with warmth and comfort. Our family continues to navigate this journey of grief, and the absence of Lizzy weighs heavily on our hearts. We miss her so much.

Observing the anniversary of a loved one's passing is not something I would wish for anyone. The jagged edges of grief seem to punctuate every aspect of life, mirrored in the cold, rainy weather that seems to reflect our hurt and brokenness. While we want to grieve together and honor the day with something special, the reality is that we each mourn alone in our own way. Our children have grown up and are in the process of finding who they are and how Lizzy's death fits into their story. As a mom, I have to trust that God will help them put the rough edges of their life together and make something beautiful out of all of it.

Standing beside Lizzy's grave with John and the children, we exchanged brief, somber updates of our lives. Some days, the burden of grief weighs heavier than others, and this particular day was cloaked in a veil of cold sadness. When I returned home, I sorted through countless photos of Lizzy and was struck by the overwhelming absence of her sweetness in our lives. Despite her own suffering, captured in precious images, she radiated love and compassion, offering hugs to fellow patients even in the midst of her own pain. It's this extraordinary capacity for love that continued to mesmerize so many people who use the hashtag #bravelikelizzy.

As I navigate this journey of grief, I'm reminded Lizzy wasn't given a roadmap detailing the path to tell her things would all work out. She wasn't promised her pain would instantly go away. The things she lost weren't miraculously restored, yet she remained steadfast in her hope, courageously focusing on others. Her simple acts of kindness, though seemingly insignificant, were magnified by God's grace offering unexpected solace to those in need.

So as I think about the anniversary, I choose to focus not only on the pain but the lessons it taught me. Lizzy's story is far from over; it reminds us that even in our darkest moments, there is hope. Remember to be brave like Lizzy. Know your story is not finished. Although life is always filled with uncertainty, rest assured that all the jagged pieces will begin to fit together. God does make beauty from our ashes. We just need to be patient and trust Him.

CHAPTER 13

Beyond the Shadows

THE IMPACT OF PEDIATRIC CANCER ON SIBLINGS

ALTHOUGH THIS BOOK focuses on Lizzy, we have two other incredible children, Hannah and Daniel. Cancer doesn't just affect the diagnosed child; it ripples through the entire family, disrupting routines, introducing unfamiliar medical terms, and causing emotional upheaval. Lizzy's diagnosis plunged us all into a whirlwind of uncertainty, separating us physically and emotionally. You've already seen how cancer impacted our lives as parents, so we thought it would be important to help you understand how Lizzy's journey affected her siblings as well.

Throughout Lizzy's treatment we tried our best to maintain a sense of normalcy for Hannah and Daniel, but the truth is cancer transformed their lives too. Both of them coped with the stress in different ways, navigating a spectrum of emotions ranging from hope to despair. Despite our efforts to support them, we witnessed the toll that this journey took on their mental and emotional well-being; a toll we never fully anticipated at the outset.

Today, as young adults, both Hannah and Daniel are still navigating their paths, seeking to establish a new sense of normalcy in their lives. We pray earnestly that they will continue to find their footing and seek God's guidance despite the challenges they face. There's no better way to convey their experience than by allowing them to speak for themselves. So without further ado, here are their stories:

Hannah

LIZZY ALWAYS ADMIRED me and wanted to be like me. She trailed behind me like a typical young sister, eager to mimic my every move. It always seemed that whatever I did, she was determined to do as well. Yet, despite my occasional irritation with her constant presence, our bond remained unshakeable. She adored makeup, dress-up, and all things girly. We often spent hours playing with Barbies on the living room floor. Likewise, we enjoyed building LEGOs alongside my brother, forming a trio of playful companions, with Lizzy always at the center. Spending the night in my room was one of her favorite pastimes, as she loved hanging out with my friends, feeling a sense of maturity in their presence. One of my fondest memories with Lizzy was of these late-night sleepovers, where we'd giggle and gossip about her crushes and school adventures, pretending to be asleep whenever mom peeked in.

Lizzy shared my strong-willed nature, yet her outlook on life consistently outshone my own. Like many sisters, we argued a lot, both refusing to concede defeat, resulting in many clashes. But she was always brave and really loving—even before she got sick.

Her optimistic outlook on life was constant. She always seemed to have a smile on her face and to radiate a sense of peace and joy. She treated her friends with kindness, always willing to share a joke or a laugh.

Lizzy was the emotional heart of our family. She would often cry if we argued or didn't get along. She wasn't shy about expressing her feelings, contrasting with Daniel and me, who tended to be more reserved in that regard. She was the one who offered Mom hugs, kisses, and words of love. In a way, her emotional openness served as a counterbalance to our more reserved personalities.

I don't remember the specific moment when my parents broke the news that Lizzy had cancer. Looking back, it all seems to be a blur. But I do distinctly remember the early stages of her cancer treatments when she still had hair, which gradually started to thin. We made visits to see her on weekends, every couple of weeks. I was in high school, so it was difficult for me to always get away. To manage, Mom and Dad took turns being with her, ensuring that one of them was always home.

Whenever we visited Lizzy, it was an opportunity for us to enjoy some fun activities together, like going to the mall or trying out new places to eat. Despite facing challenges, Lizzy maintained a remarkable positive attitude, even more so than I could have imagined. Despite her struggles with anxiety, she rarely complained except when it was time for us to leave. Lizzy was close to both of our parents, but I think there is a special bond between a mother and a daughter. So whenever Mom would have to leave and go back to Missouri, Lizzy would cry. She often expressed her feelings, saying it wasn't fair that we could go home while she had to stay.

It was a shock for me to see Lizzy losing her hair and going bald. With each visit, she seemed to grow weaker and sicker, and

 Making ordinary moments extraordinary: Lizzy, Hannah, and Daniel turn a routine shopping trip into a fun-filled adventure with Mom. 🛍️ 🌎 #FamilyFun #EverydayJoy

that's when the reality of her condition hit me. I struggled to understand why these terrible things were happening to her. It felt like the cancer came out of nowhere, and I couldn't find a satisfactory explanation for why she, of all people, had to endure it. She was just a little kid—why did she have to suffer so much? It was difficult to reconcile the idea that bad things could happen to such a good person. Additionally, I felt a sense of isolation as Mom and Dad's attention was understandably focused on Lizzy, leaving Daniel and me feeling somewhat neglected.

That's when I began to seek distractions, hoping to avoid the overwhelming pain. Anger simmered within me, fueled by the turmoil unfolding in both my life and Lizzy's. To cope, I made choices I now regret, seeking comfort in rebellion against our circumstances. Without fully realizing it, I started to bury the most difficult memories deep within my mind, shielding myself from the raw emotions they evoked. Even today, there are significant gaps in my recollection, a phenomenon psychologists term dissociative amnesia.

I found myself desperately trying to escape the painful reality of Lizzy's illness and our family's turmoil. It felt like my mind had erected barriers to shield me from the overwhelming emotions, leaving me dazed and disconnected. In a misguided attempt to break through this emotional numbness, I turned to risky behaviors and made choices I knew were wrong. Smoking, sneaking out, and general rebelliousness became my outlets, offering fleeting moments of sensation in an otherwise numb existence. As my behavior spiraled out of control, my academic performance suffered, and thoughts of my future evaporated. In a haze of distraction, I lost sight of what truly mattered, craving any semblance of feeling while drowning in the chaos that consumed our family's attention.

The thought of Lizzy's death was unimaginable to me. She was my sister, and in my mind that meant she was invincible. Death seemed like a distant concept; something that happened to others but not to someone as vital to my life as Lizzy.

With no prior experience of losing a loved one, except for my great grandmother who passed away when I was very young, I couldn't comprehend the idea of Lizzy leaving us. It was as if by denying the possibility of her death, I could shield myself from the pain it would bring.

Even as Lizzy's health deteriorated before my eyes, I remained in a state of disbelief, unable or unwilling to confront the reality of her impending passing. In the days leading up to her death, I found myself disconnected from my emotions, trapped in a state of denial and disbelief. I still catch myself instinctively shutting down emotionally, a defense mechanism that I adopted during those difficult times and often struggle to overcome.

I remember when we were all in Memphis getting ready for Lizzy's No More Chemo Party. She thought she was free of cancer and done with chemo. But the doctors did one last scan before sending her home. She was picking out her school supplies and was looking forward to feeling like a normal girl again. As we were at the Target House getting everything ready, Mom got a call. When the phone rang, I had a bad feeling in my heart that something wasn't right. But I wasn't prepared for Mom to deliver the news that Lizzy's cancer had returned. When Lizzy heard the doctor's report, she started screaming and throwing books. She was so brokenhearted that her life was being taken from her. This cruel twist of fate robbed her of a healthy, normal life just when it seemed within reach.

The news that Lizzy wouldn't be coming home was incredibly traumatic for me. Despite the overwhelming emotions inside, I felt numb and detached. I put up a facade of indifference saying, "Whatever," but deep down I was struggling to cope with the pain, unsure of how to protect myself from its intensity.

As Lizzy began her treatments again and her condition worsened, I found myself at a loss for what to feel or think. Everything seemed crushing and unfamiliar, leaving me with a sense of disorientation. In an attempt to navigate this new reality, I resorted to distracting myself, unsure of how to confront the emotions swirling inside me.

My parents couldn't comprehend why I became emotionally distant or why I engaged in rebellious behavior. They were preoccupied and unable to connect the dots. Their attempts to enforce strict rules, limiting my access to my phone or social media, only fueled my defiance. Despite their efforts, I found new ways to rebel, earning the label of the "problem child." Desperate to mask my distress, I sought ways to divert my attention elsewhere.

When Lizzy passed away, my emotional numbness deepened. In an attempt to cope, I found myself in an abusive relationship for a couple of years. The intensity of the relationship provided fleeting moments of sensation in my emotional void. Eventually, the toxicity of the relationship forced me to leave Columbia for my safety. It was then that I sought counseling, where I delved into understanding why my mind shielded me from the full extent of the pain from my sister's death and why I gravitated towards an abusive partner. While I gained valuable insights through therapy, discussing Lizzy's death felt like reliving her loss all over again, reopening wounds that never fully heal.

Attending therapy was emotionally exhausting. I found myself in tears at every session, and the weight of my grief often left me unable to do anything else but sleep for the remainder of the day. While I believe therapy provided some relief and understanding, it was difficult to see its purpose when I knew deep down that Lizzy would never return. The reality of losing her is something I must carry with me for the rest of my life, and it's a burden that weighs heavily on my heart. I struggle to picture a future without her, and it feels inherently wrong to have to navigate life's journey without her by my side.

I've recently resumed therapy, realizing that healing is a gradual and challenging process. Before I moved from Columbia, I found fulfillment in providing home health caregiving. Working with Alzheimer's patients and individuals nearing the end of life felt like a natural fit for me, and I discovered a sense of purpose in helping others. Recognizing my compassion and aptitude for caregiving, many people told me I would be a good nurse. Providing care to others has become a source of healing for me. It's a way for me to feel more connected to life and purposeful in my actions. So I started nursing school and am working toward a degree. Although the idea of becoming an oncology nurse once crossed my mind, I realized it might evoke too many painful memories. Even now, tasks like postmortem care at the hospital remain emotionally taxing for me.

I believe Lizzy would take comfort in knowing that Mom and Dad are channeling their efforts into raising funds to support other children battling cancer. While I'm currently focused on my studies and unable to contribute as much as I'd like, I do what I can to support their cause. My greatest hope is that one day, medical research will discover a cure for the type of cancer that took Lizzy from us, sparing other families from enduring the pain and loss we've experienced. Bringing awareness to pediatric cancer is crucial, as it's often overlooked, and government funding for research falls far short of what's needed. This lack of support feels like a disservice to the countless families who have suffered the devastating effects of childhood cancer. Sharing Lizzy's story allows me to keep her memory alive and feel her presence, even though she's no longer with us physically.

Lizzy was a very strong Christian—especially after she got cancer. She was never really scared of dying. She was heartbroken but was at peace with the fact she was going to heaven. In her final days we would always say to each other, "If I don't see you tomorrow,

I'll see you in heaven." It was a reminder of the eternal bond we shared and the hope of reunion beyond this life.

Since Lizzy's passing, I've struggled with my faith and felt distant from God. I harbored anger towards Him for a long time, questioning why He would take such a young and innocent girl and allow her to suffer for over a year. Witnessing her pain left me grappling with confusion and resentment. This trauma drove a wedge between me and my faith, pushing me further away from Him. However, deep down in my heart, I still hold onto the belief in God's existence. It's a belief born out of necessity, as the thought of never seeing Lizzy again would make my life meaningless. Despite this hope, my relationship with God remains strained. I long for the day when I can reconcile my anger and find comfort in His presence once more, but for now, it's a journey marked by challenges and uncertainty.

To other siblings of pediatric cancer patients, I would offer this advice: cherish every moment you have with your loved one. Allow yourself to feel your emotions, even the painful ones. Capture memories through photos and videos to hold onto. Take time to journal—writing down any thoughts or feelings you want to remember—so you can look back on them in the future and see how much you've grown. It's okay to cry; in fact, it's essential to let those emotions out rather than bottling them up. Grieving is a difficult process, and it's crucial to confront it rather than suppress it, as it may resurface later if left unaddressed. There will be days when getting out of bed feels impossible, when anger towards God consumes you, and that's okay. Lean on your family for support and consider seeking therapy to help navigate through these challenging times. Above all, remember to keep living—for yourself and for the memory of your loved one who has passed away.

Daniel

LIZZY, HANNAH, AND I were an inseparable trio, tied together by a bond stronger than blood. From dawn till dusk, we lived in our own little universe, united by laughter, mischief, and a shared love for adventure. Basketball games in the driveway, cannonballs into the swimming pool, and endless LEGO creations were the fabric of our everyday lives. But it was those early summer mornings when everyone was still asleep that I loved the most. I'd wake up to the gentle rustling of LEGO bricks, the sound amplified by the silence of the house. Rubbing the sleep from my eyes, I'd turn to find Lizzy, wearing her oversized Angry Birds robe, already lost in a world of imagination at the LEGO table in my room. Although she tried to be quiet, excitement betrayed her. Lizzy's efforts at stealth never failed to bring a smile to my face. She was my sister, my best friend, and in those moments, my unwitting alarm clock, signaling the start of another day of endless possibilities.

I know you'll be reading her story from my parent's perspective, so I just wanted to give you a little insight into what it was like to be her brother. Lizzy's positivity was just so infectious that I loved spending time with her—even if she was my little sister. It's no wonder my parents gave her the middle name "Joy;" she radiated joy right from the start. It's crazy how perfectly a name can fit a person. Odd as it may seem, despite being three years older than she was, I looked up to Lizzy as a person. Her ability to find joy in every moment inspired me, and I wanted to find that same zest for living that she carried with her in the beginning, middle, and end of her life.

I remember the time our lives changed dramatically. It started out with a very normal day. It was late at night, and the two of

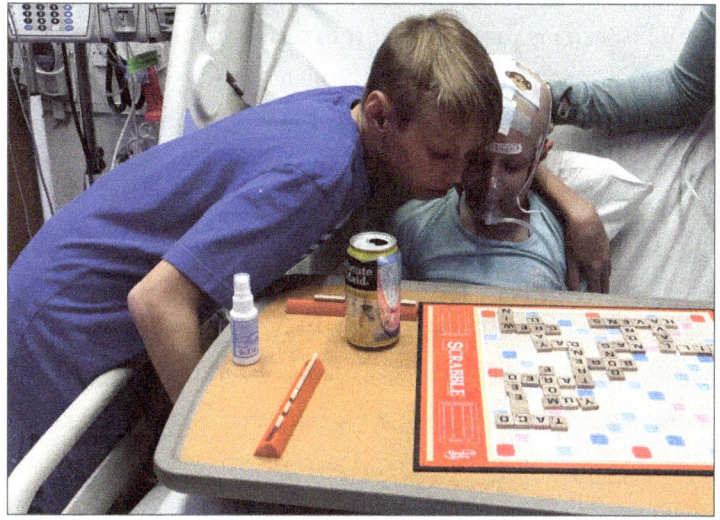

Brotherly love knows no bounds: Daniel embraces Lizzy during a game of Scrabble, bringing comfort and joy during challenging times. ♥ 🎲 Daniel's gentle and loving nature shines through as he proves to be the perfect playmate, always protective and kind. #SiblingBond #StrengthInFamily

us were chasing each other wildly around the bedroom—one of our favorite pastimes. As Lizzy darted around the corner with her characteristic speed, she turned a little too fast and bumped her knee on a table. Tough as she was, she winced in pain, and then started playing again. Over the next few days, I remember Lizzy mentioning how much her knee still hurt. Although she had a bruise from the bump itself, she kept complaining of continual pain. I really didn't think anything of it—just a normal injury. But eventually we realized the hurt in her leg was much bigger than a bruise. When my parents took her to the doctor and got an osteo-sarcoma diagnosis, pretty much overnight our whole lives changed.

Of course, nobody's life changed more than Lizzy's did. She was the one who carried the weight of that terrible, out-of-control diagnosis. Watching the next two years of her life really sucked. I hated seeing my best friend suffer things that *nobody* should have to endure—let alone a kid who ought to be thinking about school and birthday parties. I was in denial for a while, thinking life would eventually just go back to normal, but everything became "real" to me when I saw Lizzy losing her beautiful, blonde hair. Other reminders of our altered reality were constant—whether it was one of our parents always being gone or the absence of Lizzy nearby to share my daily adventures. These were hard realities for my sister Hannah and me to grasp at a young age. Despite the anger and confusion swirling around us, Lizzy held on to the same joy and infectious spirit as always.

The news of Lizzy's cancer hit me like a punch in the gut. Cancer? I had heard stories about people dying from cancer all the time, but that was something that happened to other people. How could it happen to her? I was scared. How could I live without her? My young and carefree world was shattered in an instant and replaced with worry, fear, and dread. Cancer meant death; I knew that much. The thought of losing Lizzy, my confidante and partner in crime, was too much to even think about. And then came the bombshell: St. Jude. I'd seen the commercials of the sick kids who were treated there. Suddenly, the gravity of Lizzy's illness hit me like a ton of bricks. This wasn't just serious; it was a total nightmare.

During Lizzy's absence, I found myself struggling with an overwhelming sense of loneliness. Lizzy and I shared the same school, the same bus rides, and the same treasured moments of play and laughter after school. But when cancer stole her away it felt like a piece of my world had been torn apart. Suddenly, the familiar routine of coming home together, jumping into our favorite activities like basketball and video games, or simply enjoying each other's company, was shattered. Hannah was older and attended a different school, leaving me to navigate the halls and the journey home alone. I took it for granted that Lizzy would be there, and the silence was deafening once she was gone.

Without Lizzy by my side, the house seemed emptier, quieter, and lacking the vibrant energy she brought into every room. With my parents arriving an hour or more after I got home from school, I often found myself alone. Basketball became my lifeline, offering a little bit of normalcy in the middle of the chaos. Honestly, if I hadn't had basketball, I don't know how I could have dealt with it all. Yet, despite the distractions, the ache of her absence lingered, a constant reminder of the empty place in my life. As a young child thrown into the bewildering world of illness and loss, I grappled with confusion and uncertainty. Everything felt unfamiliar, unsettling, and I struggled to make sense of the upheaval unfolding around me. Everything was new to me, and I didn't know what to think or how to deal with it.

One of the greatest comforts during Lizzy's absence was the assurance that she was receiving exceptional care at St. Jude. Knowing that she was in the hands of experts in pediatric cancer treatment at one the best hospitals in the world was huge. Visiting her myself and seeing firsthand that she was safe only boosted my confidence in her well-being. At first she stayed at the Ronald McDonald House. It was such a cool place. The people and the doctors around her were nice too. All of that helped reassure me that I could worry a little less because Lizzy was receiving the best possible care. I really can't imagine her going to any other hospital.

Time went by in a flash. All I could think about was how much I missed her and how scared I was for her. I counted the days until our next trip to Memphis, a city we could only visit every few weeks because of school and my parents' work commitments. But I knew that once we got there we would have an amazing time. There was always so much to do. Sometimes we were lucky enough to receive complimentary tickets to the Memphis Grizzlies basketball game through their close partnership with St. Jude. Other times, we explored landmarks like the Bass Pro Shop Pyramid or nearby areas like Germantown, where we got to see and do fun activities. Lizzy and I would watch television together, and occasionally Mom would push Lizzy's wheelchair to the basketball court so she could watch me play. Simply spending time with her and witnessing her condition firsthand meant the world to me. During the weeks when I couldn't visit, a sense of loneliness would began to creep in. Despite my parents providing frequent updates, it wasn't enough; I longed to be there in person.

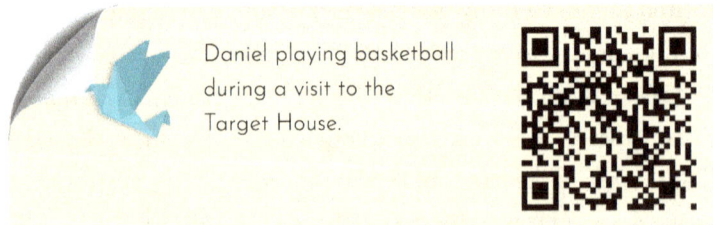

Daniel playing basketball during a visit to the Target House.

When my mom sent me a picture of Lizzy with James Harden, my favorite basketball player at the time, it was super frustrating. She had the opportunity to meet the entire Houston Rockets team, and my mom even sent me a video of the event while I was stuck at home doing schoolwork. I was like, "You're kidding me. Why does she get to have all the fun?" As someone who loves basketball, it was hard not to feel jealous of the exciting opportunities she had. I felt bad admitting my feelings to myself, but sometimes it seemed like Lizzy was living a carefree vacation, constantly getting to do fun things. I longed to be part of those experiences too. Whenever our group chat buzzed with plans to visit a Memphis barbeque joint or to explore a park, I couldn't help but wish I was there instead of being stuck at school. But obviously, at the end of the day, I realized that Lizzy still had cancer. This harsh reality overshadowed any envy or longing for the adventures she had.

By the way, after she passed away, I finally had the opportunity to attend a Rockets game and visit the locker room to meet James Harden. A member of the Rockets staff remembered my parents from their involvement with St. Jude and shared our story with Harden. In a touching gesture, Harden gave me a signed pair of his shoes. It was an incredibly awesome and meaningful moment for me. I still display those shoes on top of the television in my apartment. His kindness during such a difficult time meant so much to me.

Watching Lizzy undergo cancer treatment and enduring chemotherapy was horrible, made even worse by watching her hair fall out and her weight plummet. The sight of her wearing a huge knee brace remains forever etched in my memory. But nothing compares to the sheer dread of the day we found out that Lizzy's cancer had returned. It was in the summer, and the doctors had proclaimed her to be cancer-free. She was about to ring the bell, symbolizing the completion of her treatment. We were packing up her stuff and getting ready for her return to school. She was going to attend Christian Fellowship School again, where she had gone to kindergarten and first grade. We had even purchased her school uniform, complete with polos, so she would be ready for her first day back. We were all so excited that Lizzy was finally getting her normal life back. It had been a long year, but now it was finally over.

We were all together at the Target House when my mom got a call from the doctor saying that the cancer had returned. I'll never forget the sound of Lizzy's cry when she heard the news. It was as if an unearthly shriek of agony pierced the air, followed by her sudden eruption into tears. Witnessing my mom crying only amplified the overwhelming sense of despair. Suddenly my whole world was shaken, and that moment was unlike any grief or pain I had ever experienced. Emotions flooded my brain—profound sadness, aching loneliness, gnawing regret, and intense fear for Lizzy's well-being. I didn't know what to do. So I instinctively sought refuge outside, finding relief in the familiar rhythm of bouncing a basketball. In those minutes of chaos, the basketball court became a sanctuary, offering a tiny bit of control over the turmoil engulfing my life.

Not long after that, my mom and I found ourselves at the mall together. She delicately broached the topic of Lizzy's uncertain prognosis, gently preparing me for the possibility of her passing. It suddenly hit me hard—this situation is extremely serious, and I need to cherish every moment I had left with Lizzy. That day marked one of the darkest moments of my life. Until then, I really didn't think she was going to die. I had held onto a glimmer of hope, believing that she would overcome her long-term health struggles. However, the conversation with my mom shattered that illusion, forcing me to confront the harsh reality of Lizzy's mortality. From that point on, I tried to savor every precious day with her, determined to make every moment count.

Then came the news that Michael J. Porter Jr., the number one recruit coming out of high school, was going to visit Lizzy. He was a big deal at Mizzou, so I was already a huge fan. By then, her condition was getting worse. She struggled to find the strength to move or walk, spending her days confined to the couch. She had little life left, and I could not bear to see this happen to her. She appeared so fragile, almost translucent, with tubes helping her breathe, each breath a struggle. It was one of the worst things I've ever experienced; something I wouldn't wish on anyone.

But when this six-foot-ten guy got there, I was shocked to see him because he was so tall. He was super nice and down-to-earth. He talked to Lizzy for a while and was just so nice to her. Then he gave her a signed pair of his Jordan shoes. The way he treated Lizzy definitely made me like him even more. It made her feel so much better because she had just been cooped on the couch.

So I continued to live and breathe basketball. That's the only thing I had. While friends offered their support, I chose to internalize my grief, keeping it locked away from prying eyes. Instead, I immersed myself in the rhythm of the game and the routine of school, desperately attempting to evade the overwhelming sorrow that threatened to take over. The first week after she died was a blur, marked by moments of silent anguish. I remember being in class with my head down on the desk almost all day, trying to ignore the pain and escape the memory of what happened. It was very difficult, but eventually, with time, it got somewhat better.

I stopped playing basketball after my senior year in high school and shifted my focus to weightlifting. The distraction basketball once provided is no longer necessary as time has softened the raw edges of my grief. While thoughts of Lizzy still linger and occasionally make me sad, I've learned to confront those emotions head-on.

I allow myself to feel the ache, shed tears when needed, and then release the weight of sorrow. Acceptance has become my solace, recognizing that while I cannot change the past, I can choose how to navigate the present.

Lizzy's death taught me not to take life for granted and to enjoy every single moment I have on this earth. We aren't promised endless days. If a happy, joyful ten-year-old can die from cancer, then anything can happen. Every day is a gift, not to be taken for granted, but to be cherished and embraced with gratitude. Life's unpredictability reminds me to savor each moment, for tomorrow is never promised. I want to live every day to the fullest knowing that Lizzy was unable to do so.

Thinking about Lizzy being in heaven brings me comfort. Knowing that she is there with God and is reunited with our grandparents fills me with a sense of peace. She loved God so much. The thought of her in heaven sustains me through life. I can't imagine not believing in life after death. But for now, I can only imagine what our life will be in the future, together with God.

I am still unsure of where life will take me. I have some ideas of what I might want to do in the future, but for now I'm focused on getting a business management degree. Wherever I end up, I want to give my all in everything I do, aiming for 110 percent effort. I want to use the opportunities I have, knowing that Lizzy never had the chance to live out her passion in life.

In the meantime, I'm a regular college student with a job, enjoying time with friends, staying active at the gym, and immersing myself in sports. When times are tough, I often think about what Lizzy would do in my shoes. Surrounding myself with reminders of her, like wearing her "Walk of Faith" bracelet, keeps her memory close and provides a sense of connection and guidance as I navigate life's uncertainties.

Pediatric cancer often flies under the radar in discussions about cancer, overshadowed by more widely recognized types like breast cancer. However, my perspective has shifted dramatically after seeing the devastating impact of pediatric cancer, particularly during my time at St. Jude. Seeing those young kids, brimming with potential, facing a disease that robs them of their futures, was one of the worst things imaginable.

I'm so glad my parents are working so hard to find a cure for cancer and to help other families facing similar journeys. At first I couldn't get excited about their efforts, longing to simply move past the pain of losing Lizzy. But today I have switched my mindset and have realized the profound significance of their mission. Their work not only honors Lizzy's memory but also celebrates the life she lived, serving as a light of hope for others facing similar battles. Realizing that purpose makes their mission so much better. I'm looking forward to continuing to celebrate Lizzy and other people like her in the years ahead. I'll never forget my little sister, and I hope she will be able to live on through me.

Lizzy and I shared a happy-go-lucky and cheerful outlook on life. I try to carry on that spirit, recognizing that we all have the power to either drain joy from others or infuse life with happiness. I strive to uplift those around me and maintain a positive attitude, just as Lizzy did. Despite her challenges, Lizzy found joy in the simple things, and her resilience inspired me. Watching her made me appreciate that no matter how tough life gets, there's always a reason to smile. Her journey taught me that my own struggles pale in comparison, and I'm reminded to be grateful for each day.

CHAPTER 14

Let Your Faith Be Bigger than Your Fear

LIZZY'S WALK OF FAITH FOUNDATION

ROM THE BEGINNING of Lizzy's battle with cancer, we have continually felt the comforting presence of God beside us. Even in our deepest anguish, and perhaps especially in those times, God's guidance remained evident, steering us through uncertainty. Despite navigating a whirlwind of emotions—from grief and sadness to joy and hope—we found solace knowing that God stood steadfastly with us, never once leaving our side.

Throughout our journey, we encountered countless "God moments" where we caught fleeting glimpses of God's purpose, presence, and boundless love. Our community, whether made up of the caring staff at St. Jude, beloved figures like Chip and Joanna Gaines, or friends from home, enveloped us in unwavering love and support. Time and again, we witnessed people uniting and doors opening. Whether it was the timely arrival of financial support in our most desperate moment or the comforting presence of a friend or family member, we could never deny that God was with us. All along the way, to the very end, God's love kept getting bigger and bigger, overwhelming us with its magnitude. Even in the midst of her struggles, Lizzy was able to reach out to those around her and share her light.

Over the course of fifteen challenging months, as we documented Lizzy's battle with pediatric cancer on our Facebook page, we didn't shy away from revealing the harsh realities and ugliness, showcasing both our despair and Lizzy's struggles. From detailing her surgeries and chemotherapy treatments to sharing the moments of hope when we fervently believed she was cured and eagerly planned a No More Chemo Party, to the heartbreaking realization that the cancer had returned, leaving us with no more medical options to explore. For many, our story provided an intimate and eye-opening glimpse into the world of pediatric cancer, serving as their first encounter with its harsh realities.

As Lizzy's life came to a close, we found ourselves surrounded by a multitude of people offering their condolences and support. The community that gathered at her funeral embodied a profound sense of shared grief and solidarity for our family. We were inundated with cards, letters, flowers, and calls from individuals across the country whose lives had been touched by Lizzy's presence. Although we knew that Lizzy's earthly journey had reached its end, the outpouring of love and support continued to resonate strongly. Both of us firmly believed that Lizzy's life and story retained deep significance and purpose, even in her absence.

About two weeks after Lizzy's death, we composed this post with a sense of uncertainty lingering within us. Despite the void left by her absence, we felt a persistent inner prompting that signaled we weren't finished with something, although we couldn't quite discern what that something was.

MARCH 29, 2018

John and I feel a calling to keep Lizzy's light, love, and faith alive on earth. While the exact details are uncertain, we envision creating something on her behalf to continue helping others—whether it be a foundation, a nonprofit, or a ministry. We are committed to avoiding replication of existing efforts, and instead, we aim to support and promote the incredible work already being done by nonprofits such as Pascale Pals, Rally for Rhyan, Faith's Foundation, and many others.

We will let you know as we figure out what we should do in Lizzy's honor. It may take time, and the impact may be modest, but our mission is not to be huge. We simply want for God to be honored, for Lizzy's light to keep shining, and for joy to permeate some of the darkest places. Your love and ongoing prayers for our family mean the world to us. Thank you for your unwavering support. We love you all very much. You've been such a vital part of her journey.

Lizzy's life will endure through our love and the love extended by all of you. Every time you share your love for her, it keeps her spirit alive in some way.

Shortly thereafter, we shared lunch with two dear friends, Sylvie and Jina. Sylvie, inspired by her daughter Pascale's battle with acute lymphoblastic leukemia, founded Pascale Pals, a local volunteer organization aiding families at the MU Healthcare Children's Hospital in Columbia. Jina is a long-time family friend and the owner of Lizzy's favorite restaurant, Jina Yoo's Asian Bistro. Both ladies offered invaluable insight during our conversation. But it was Jina who emphasized the importance of taking action during the community's period of mourning, sparking a discussion about creating a foundation and organizing a 5K race to raise funds for St. Jude. Although neither of us had experience with such large-scale events, we recognized the potential of a race to honor Lizzy's memory while contributing to a noble cause. This sense of purpose, coupled with the support of our wonderful community, motivated us to move forward with this initiative. So, by mid-April, we were ready to share our idea with others on Facebook.

APRIL 18, 2018

We have some exciting news to share soon regarding Lizzy's Foundation. Jen and I are both excited about a potential name, "Lizzy's Walk of Faith Foundation." I've been meeting with credible and trusted advisors to ensure we establish it in a meaningful and impactful way. Lizzy's legacy of compassion, generosity, and faith will continue to touch and uplift countless lives. Stay tuned for more updates.

With just five months until the event, our aim was to host it in September, coinciding with Childhood Cancer Awareness month. To achieve this, we partnered with Ultra Max Sports, an event management company that specializes in organizing and running large race events. Recognizing our tight timeline, they noted that starting in late April—following Lizzy's passing in March—put us at a disadvantage. While they found the concept commendable and Lizzy endearing, they cautioned us to keep our expectations low citing the saturation of 5K events within the nonprofit sector. They expected no more than two hundred people to register for the race. However, they failed to grasp the depth of our conviction, the power of community, and the remarkable outcomes that can unfold when guided by faith. Here is what we posted on Facebook:

APRIL 28, 2018

We have some very exciting news and would love for you to be a part of it! Yesterday, John and I met with Ultra Max Sports to nail down a tentative date for Lizzy's 5K Walk/Run of Remembrance. It looks like it'll be on Saturday, September 29th—just five months from now. We'd be thrilled if you could mark your calendars! It's especially meaningful to us that we can host it in September, as it's Childhood Cancer Awareness month.

This walk/run is more than just an event—it's a heartfelt remembrance of Lizzy and a tribute to all children in our community who have lost their battle with childhood cancer. We're also using this platform to raise awareness about pediatric cancer and the urgent need for funding. We would like this to become an annual event. This year, all proceeds will go to St. Jude, a cause incredibly dear to us. In the future, we may also support other pediatric cancer research organizations, guided by where the need is greatest. St. Jude's commitment to sharing their research globally resonates deeply with us.

We are so excited to be a part of this event. We want all families who have had to encounter childhood cancer to feel this walk/race is for them. There is so much that we envision for this walk, and we'll definitely need your help to make it happen.

Ensuring wheelchair accessibility is a priority for us. Lizzy's time in a wheelchair made us acutely aware of the importance of this. She had compassion for other children who were in wheelchairs. It's something we'll prioritize for her foundation.

Speaking of which, we'll soon have Lizzy's Walk of Faith Foundation up and running. We are partnering with the Columbia Foundation, a trusted organization in our community, to ensure secure donations with tax benefits.

We've been overwhelmed by the love and support we've received over this past year-and-a-half. Many have expressed a desire to contribute tangibly, and we're inviting those with a heart for Lizzy's cause for a cure to join us in this vision. Here are a few ways you can get involved:

1. Help us design the website for Lizzy's Walk of Faith Foundation.
2. Use your creative talents to design logos for the race T-shirts and promotional materials.
3. Share your ideas on how we can best promote Lizzy's 5K walk/run in September.

We'll be creating a Facebook event for the 5K soon and will keep you posted on its progress. All of this brings me so much joy and healing. It's a way for me to keep Lizzy's memory alive and share her story with the world. As long as we continue to see the impact and feel God's presence in this endeavor, John and I are committed to carrying on Lizzy's Foundation. We are grateful to already have the support of wonderful businesses and individuals who are eager to sponsor the race and be part of Lizzy's legacy. I am looking forward to this remembrance walk/run and hope it brings comfort to many families while raising money to help find a cure. Thank you for your love and support! As we continue to navigate this journey, I hope you all find moments of joy and peace in your day.

There were so many things to do and so many decisions to be made. At that point, there were two directions we could have taken. We could have made this a St. Jude race, or we could make it Lizzy's race. Our heartfelt desire was to immortalize Lizzy's name and establish a foundation in her honor. However, we were grateful to receive St. Jude's blessing allowing us to put their logo on our T-shirts and signage. Donations were initially channeled through the Columbia Community Foundation. However we soon realized this arrangement limited giving as we could only write checks to other nonprofits. While we wanted to give to entities like St. Jude, we also wanted the freedom to support families directly affected by pediatric cancer.

So with guidance from trusted advisors, we took the decisive step of establishing Lizzy's Walk of Faith Foundation as a 501(c)(3) entity, allowing us the autonomy to fulfill our philanthropic vision.

Preparing for that first 5K event was a lot of work, but it helped with our healing. Despite the dire predictions of the event planner, we went ahead with the race. By September, Ultra Max was just blown away by how many people ended up registering. They were printing T-shirts as fast as they could. That first year, more than five hundred people registered. A lot of the participants were virtual runners, but between two and three hundred people showed up at the event. We raised about $30,000 and gave it all to St. Jude.

Since then, both the race and Lizzy's legacy have continued to flourish. We often found ourselves wondering whether we could match the impact of the inaugural year, especially considering the profound emotions surrounding Lizzy's passing. Yet, to our amazement and joy, not only did we meet the previous year's success, but we exceeded it. In the second year, despite maintaining a similar number of runners, our fundraising efforts yielded approximately $45,000, igniting a sense of momentum and determination within our community.

However, the unforeseen challenge of the COVID-19 pandemic emerged during the third year, casting uncertainty over our plans. Despite initial hopes that the pandemic would be over by September, the reality forced us to pivot to a virtual format just a month before the race. Undeterred, we mobilized to ensure that the spirit of the event remained intact. Though devoid of physical participants, we orchestrated a vibrant virtual experience, complete with T-shirts, promotional materials, and a virtual race day with live streams on social media.

Despite the unprecedented circumstances, the outpouring of support was overwhelming. Even without traditional race participants,

Grateful for every step taken in Lizzy's honor at the Walk of Faith 5K Walk/Run. ❤️ 👟 Putting together this event is a labor of love, but seeing each participant cross the finish line makes it all worth it. Thank you for joining us in making a difference! #WalkOfFaith #CommunitySupport

over a hundred individuals defeated the odds to join us in person, while hundreds more participated virtually. This remarkable turn-out underscored the unwavering dedication of our community to Lizzy's cause, resulting in a staggering $50,000 raised.

In subsequent years, our events have only continued to grow. In 2021, a record-breaking 459 participants joined the cause, contributing to an astounding $75,000 raised. Buoyed by this success, we set an ambitious goal of $80,000 for 2022, only to surpass it in spectacular fashion. With over eight hundred participants, we raised an incredible $104,000. The next year we were blown away when the race brought in $140,000, further solidifying our belief in the power of collective action and the enduring legacy of Lizzy's Walk of Faith Foundation.

We often describe Lizzy's vibrant personality as "a party waiting to happen." With her love for fun and outward-focused nature, it was essential that our 5K walk/run captured Lizzy's essence of positivity, encouragement, and zest for life. Set against the backdrop of a local park in Columbia, we created an event that reflected Lizzy's favorite things: vivid colors, upbeat dance music, and the aroma of fresh popcorn permeating the air. Our aim was to have a lively and festive atmosphere filled with energy and excitement.

Lizzy's first Walk of Faith 5K Walk/Run.

To achieve this, we enlisted the help of various entertainers and performers, including magicians, fire jugglers, face painters, and costumed characters, all dedicated to enhancing the joyous ambiance of the event. Additionally, we reached out to sororities and fraternities at the University of Missouri (Mizzou) who were eager to contribute to a cause that resonated with them. As runners started the race, they were greeted with cheers from the spirited "Mizzou Golden Girls," setting the tone for an exhilarating race experience.

In subsequent years, we have amplified the festivities by introducing an array of attractions, including food trucks, exotic cars, pop-up tents, and even fire trucks, ensuring there was something for everyone to enjoy. The event is a vibrant tapestry of entertainment, featuring baton twirlers and even a Guinness World Record holder showcasing his remarkable talent for kicking a hacky sack footbag.

Amid the excitement, we also take time to honor and recognize individuals and businesses that have steadfastly supported Lizzy's mission. The coveted "Lizzy Awards" celebrate their unwavering dedication, alongside accolades for the largest team and other notable achievements. Yet above all our primary focus is fostering a sense of camaraderie and community spirit, ensuring the event is not just a race, but a jubilant celebration shared among good-hearted individuals united by a common cause. Oh, how we wish Lizzy could witness this joy-filled celebration!

We were deeply committed to ensuring that the mission of the foundation resonated with Lizzy's own aspirations and values. With this in mind, we promptly clarified our purpose, recognizing it as twofold: first, to raise money dedicated to advancing pediatric cancer research, and secondly, to provide tangible support to families navigating the difficult journey of pediatric cancer treatment. It was vital to us that Lizzy's legacy be one of hope, compassion, and tangible assistance to those enduring similar challenges. So our mission statement crystallized around the dual objectives of funding critical research initiatives and offering direct support to families confronting the profound impacts of pediatric cancer. By embracing this vision, we aimed to honor Lizzy's memory in a way that reflected her enduring spirit and unwavering compassion for others.

In the final days before her passing, Lizzy, despite the overwhelming physical and emotional strain, displayed remarkable courage and selflessness. With the oxygen machine humming in the background and tears glistening in her eyes, she made a heartfelt declaration: she wanted to donate her tumors to St. Jude for research. It was a profound act of compassion, driven by her desire to spare other children the pain she had endured. Lizzy couldn't bear the thought of any more families hearing those devastating words—that there is nothing more that could be done. She envisioned a future where

Grateful for these amazing young hearts who joined Lizzy's Walk of Faith Junior Board. 🧡 Together, they've wrapped presents for St. Jude, lent a hand at the 5K, and turned grief into action. 💥 #JuniorBoard #LizzysWalkOfFaith

no parent would have to endure the heart-wrenching separation from their child. That was her heart—to make a difference in the fight against pediatric cancer.

Today, Lizzy's tumors serve as invaluable specimens, studied by researchers around the world to help unravel the mysteries of osteosarcoma and develop effective treatments. Her legacy extends beyond mere tissue samples; there are now several research studies bearing her name, a testament to her spirit and enduring impact on the medical community. Lizzy's fierce will to live was only matched by her compassion for others. She couldn't bear the thought of any other children suffering the agonizing grip of osteosarcoma.

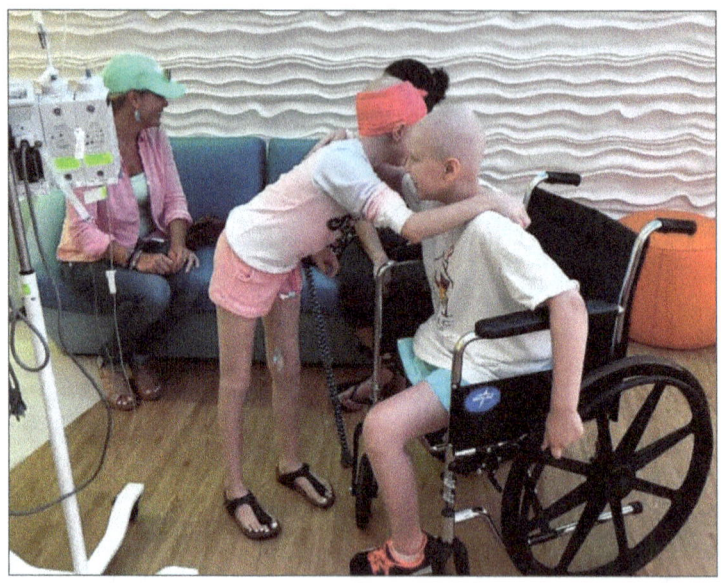

A heartfelt embrace between Lizzy and her
dear friend Kadence Castillo, who shared
a similar journey battling osteosarcoma.
Kadence's passing deeply affected Lizzy,
igniting a passion in her to support and
uplift other children facing similar struggles.
Their bond transcends time and space. 🧡
#ForeverInOurHearts #ChildhoodCancerHeroes

Osteosarcoma presents a formidable challenge in the realm of
pediatric oncology. Its complex nature, characterized by a multitude
of mutating cells, renders it resistant to conventional treatments.
As chemotherapy drugs wage their war against the cancerous cells,
osteosarcoma adapts and evolves, thwarting attempts to get rid of
it. The quest for viable treatments for this horrible, horrible cancer
is definitely an uphill battle.

It is exciting that there have been so many advancements made in treating adult cancers. It brings hope that similar advancements can also be made in treating childhood cancers. Unfortunately, the treatments used for adult cancers do not always work for children. Children often need a different protocol—just like Lizzy did. Today, only 4 percent of the National Cancer Institute's budget goes to pediatric cancer research. That's why families like ours and other nonprofits raise money for research—because hospitals need that money to find better treatments for children. How we wish there had been a trial open for a treatment with fewer side effects and that held the possibility of curing her disease. Pediatric cancer is the leading cause of death by disease in children. One in five children with cancer in the United States will not survive it. When children do survive, they are often left with many side effects from the chemotherapy because it was made for adults.

Regrettably, we are aware of too many parents desperately seeking alternatives, driven by the realization that decades old toxic medication has proved ineffective for their precious child. Parents are resorting to drastic measures, including selling their homes, in pursuit of potential solutions. But unfortunately, even extreme measures do not always provide a definitive answer. No family should have to face such extremes in search of treatment options.

The chemotherapy and treatment protocols used to help Lizzy closely mirror those used thirty years ago for osteosarcoma. While these traditional approaches have worked for some, the accompanying side effects are horrible. This is acceptable when the treatment is successful in healing osteosarcoma. However, for cases like our daughter Lizzy where the standard protocol proves ineffective, the urgent need for alternative options becomes glaringly apparent. We need other solutions right away for those who do not respond favorably to the conventional approaches, ensuring a more comprehensive and adaptive approach to combating osteosarcoma. It is our fervent hope to discover additional treatments that can offer hope and healing for those like Lizzy who do not respond positively to conventional approaches.

Our partnership with the Osteosarcoma Institute (osinst.org) in Dallas is fueled by this aspiration. In honor of Lizzy's unwavering passion for science, we established "Lizzy's Osteosarcoma Science Fund" as an initiative under the Partnering for Progress program, dedicated to advancing osteosarcoma research. Donations to this fund are put into action immediately, driving forward our mission to address the specific challenges posed by osteosarcoma.

Recognizing the urgent need for targeted research, we selected a study led by Dr. Brian Crompton, a distinguished pediatric oncologist at Boston Children's Hospital and the research co-director of the Solid Tumor Center at Dana-Farber Cancer Institute. Dr. Crompton's groundbreaking research focuses on the efficacy of liquid biopsy in monitoring osteosarcoma treatment. Currently, patients undergo chemotherapy without knowing its effectiveness, making this study particularly crucial. The liquid biopsy technique offers a promising avenue for tracking chemotherapy's impact within the critical initial three-month treatment window, providing invaluable insights into treatment response and potentially uncovering biomarkers for early detection.

Every six months, we receive detailed progress reports on Dr. Crompton's research, offering a glimpse at the strides being made in the fight against osteosarcoma. Knowing that progress is happening would undoubtedly bring joy to Lizzy, who had an insatiable curiosity and a deep desire to see positive change. Imagining her giggling, smiling, and laughing at the prospect of advancements in osteosarcoma treatment fills us with a profound sense of determination to continue our mission in her memory.

The second objective of our foundation is to provide practical assistance to families navigating the difficult journey of pediatric cancer treatment. During her time at St. Jude, Lizzy encountered numerous healthcare professionals, including a compassionate psychologist. One memory stands out: after approximately two months in the hospital, with her life irrevocably altered, Lizzy was asked a simple but profound question by the psychologist: "What is the hardest thing for you about being at St. Jude?" We all thought Lizzy's answer might involve being away from her siblings or friends, having cancer, or a number of other things. But, without hesitation, Lizzy's response cut straight to the heart: "Seeing all of the other sick kids in the hospital." Her immediate thought went to the other kids—children who were in wheelchairs, on crutches, missing limbs, or bald.

This moment crystallizes the driving force behind our foundation's mission—our firsthand witness to the profound suffering caused by cancer. We are doing this because of what we've seen. We've witnessed the heartache that people go through because of cancer and are driven to make a difference in the lives of those affected by pediatric cancer. Our purpose is clear: to honor Lizzy's memory and the profound impact she had on others by extending support to families navigating similar journeys.

Lizzy's diagnosis had a profound effect on our family's finances. We didn't have medical bills because our child was at St. Jude, but we still grappled with the financial responsibilities of maintaining a household, including mortgage payments and daily expenses. The resulting financial strain was formidable. Without the unwavering support of family and friends, we wouldn't have made it.

This underscores a larger issue: St. Jude cannot accommodate every child in America battling cancer. Many hospitals and insurance policies fall short, leaving families with unexpected bills or agonizing decisions regarding treatment. Our mission is to provide money directly to families, empowering them to allocate resources where they are most urgently needed. We try to give cash because, while gift cards are a thoughtful gesture, their utilization can sometimes become burdensome. Cash allows families to use the help where it is needed most. In recent years we have been able to give families money to help with the additional expenses of the holiday season. It heartens us to be able to give back. We also provide personalized care packages for recently diagnosed children who are referred to us by the Osteosarcoma Institute.

Lizzy had an incredible passion for helping other children who were battling cancer. During her Make-A-Wish trip to Disney World, despite being in a wheelchair herself, she insisted on being wheeled over to greet other children in wheelchairs. It sometimes led to awkward encounters with their parents, who couldn't quite grasp Lizzy's deep empathy. However, Lizzy would patiently explain her actions, that she "knew how they felt" and wanted them to know she was there with them. One memory from that time stands out: while at a store, Lizzy urged me to approach a little girl in a wheelchair. When we got to her, Lizzy reached into her purse and offered her last $10 bill. Witnessing her selfless generosity left us momentarily speechless, but we realized we had to honor Lizzy's heartfelt gesture. Her willingness to give everything she had to someone else deeply resonated with us. It's moments like these that drive our mission. We want not only to carry on Lizzy's legacy of compassion and generosity but also to bring joy knowing that her spirit lives on through our actions.

Driven by our firsthand experience, our vision for Lizzy's Walk of Faith Foundation is rooted in the desire to extend a helping hand to families grappling with similar challenges. We aim to stand alongside them, alleviating the burdens they face so they can devote their energy and attention to their child's care and well-being. At the heart of our foundation's initiatives is the "Table of Remembrance," a tribute to families who have recently lost a loved one to cancer. Each 5K race hosted by our foundation features this table adorned with photographs and mementos, serving as a touching homage to those who have endured the devastating loss of a family member.

Additionally, we use these races as opportunities to honor other children who have battled pediatric cancer. By showcasing their stories and experiences, we aim to provide them with a platform and a voice, recognizing the courage and resilience they have demonstrated in the face of adversity. It is always our favorite part of the day. One memorable instance from our inaugural race was when we honored Bailey, an osteosarcoma patient who was with Lizzy at St. Jude. There was a deep connection between our families because Bailey was Lizzy's "battle buddy." They both had the same type of cancer and had many of the same treatments. His family traveled from Memphis to join us, and we gave him a specially designed "Lizzy Medal" in recognition of his bravery. We remember putting the medal around his neck and almost feeling Lizzy's presence with us. Witnessing the community come together to uplift Bailey and other children like him is an incredibly moving experience—one that encapsulates the spirit of solidarity and support that defines our foundation's mission.

Despite the bittersweet moments of honoring these courageous individuals, our ultimate wish is for a world where childhood cancer is eradicated entirely. Yet until that day arrives, we remain steadfast in our commitment to support and advocate for families affected by this devastating disease, ensuring that no child or family faces the journey alone.

Faith was always a guiding force for Lizzy, and it remains an integral part of our foundation's mission. We aim to assist individuals from all walks of life, irrespective of their religious beliefs, as Lizzy's journey was a testament to the power of faith for all involved. It was a walk of faith for her. It was a walk of faith for all of us. If you would like to help, we invite you to join us at Lizzy's Walk of Faith 5K Walk/Run in September or to contribute to the cause by donating. More information can be found on lizzyswalkoffaith. org or our Facebook page.

Lizzy graced this earth for ten remarkable years, leaving an indelible mark with her boundless generosity, unwavering spirit, and relentless determination to help others. Her passing marked the end of a prolonged battle against cancer, during which she endured fifteen months of treatment, navigating a long protocol of chemotherapy sessions and surgeries. Through it all, she was steadfast in her faith in God and in her love for others. Though she lost her physical battle, she lives on through the countless lives she touched with her kindness, generosity, and compassion.

Establishing a foundation to honor Lizzy's legacy of compassion, generosity, and faith has been our great privilege. It has provided us with a source of healing and a means to give back to others. The overwhelming outpouring of love from our community fills us with gratitude and joy. As we continue our journey, we are reminded that until there's a cure, we have to keep giving.

As we walk the winding paths of life on this side of heaven, our resolve remains steadfast. We are reminded of Lizzy's selfless act at the St. Jude Marathon, where despite her own pain, she extended

A touching moment captured at our 5K event as Emma Brengarth, a survivor of Ewing sarcoma, presents an award to Clarke O'Neill, a brave Wilm's tumor survivor. Clarke's mom, Alli, founded Clarke's Creature Comforts, spreading joy to fellow warriors. 🎗️ 🧡 #CelebratingSurvivors #PediatricIllnessAwareness both arms to encourage others with a simple high-five. Her legacy continues to illuminate our path forward.

In honoring Lizzy's memory, we pledge to continue our mission with renewed fervor and intentionality. Until a cure for pediatric cancer is found, we will persevere in our efforts to uplift and support those in need. Together, let us forge ahead, united in our commitment to making a meaningful difference in the lives of others.  #LiveLikeLizzy #BraveLikeLizzy

To honor Lizzy's legacy and continue the fight against childhood cancer, help spread the word about Lizzys Walk of Faith Foundation. Scan one of the QR codes below to make a donation. Together we can make a difference.

PAYPAL

VENMO

 Lizzy featured in video segments by Life Church, The Crossing Church, and the Osteosarcoma Institute.

THE PAPER CRANES

YOU MIGHT WONDER why the pages of this book are filled with so many pictures of origami paper cranes. Throughout the years, paper cranes have become a symbol of hope, healing, and peace for children with childhood cancer. This idea originated from a Japanese legend that promises that a wish will be granted to anyone who folds a thousand origami paper cranes.

Lizzy's best friends, Frank and Jacei, were inspired to fold paper cranes after their teacher read them the book, *Sadako and the Thousand Paper Cranes*. The book is about a twelve-year-old girl who developed leukemia as a result of radiation from the atomic bombing of Hiroshima, which occurred when she was just two-years-old. Sadako's brave attempt to fold a thousand cranes before her passing deeply touched Frank and Jacei.

Motivated by Sadako's story, Lizzy's friends decided to embark on their own mission to create a thousand cranes to support Lizzy in her cancer battle. They believed in the power of the cranes and hoped for a miracle that would cure their friend.

Shortly before her death, Frank randomly asked Lizzy if there was an animal that he could use to remind himself of her whenever he saw it. He mentioned a fox, a bunny, or a crane. Lizzy said that she wanted him to remember her whenever he saw a crane.

At Lizzy's funeral, Frank spoke about their quest to find the miracle of the cranes for Lizzy. He explained how he struggled with God to understand why this miracle didn't happen for Lizzy. However, he recounted that he finally found peace and a realization that Lizzy's life was the miracle he had prayed for. Lizzy's laughter, kindness, and friendship had been a beacon of light for everyone around her.

As a tribute to Lizzy, Frank and Jacei handed out the paper cranes they had folded to everyone attending the funeral. Each crane represented their love for Lizzy and their belief in hope and resilience. Ever since then, we think of Lizzy whenever we see a paper crane. Her story and the cranes remind us to cherish every moment and to find strength and hope, even in the face of adversity.

QUESTIONS FOR DISCUSSION AND CONTEMPLATION

CHAPTER 1

1. Describe Lizzy's personality. What traits stand out to you, and how do they shape her character? Does she remind you of a child you know?
2. How does Lizzy's faith influence her actions and her interactions with others?
3. In what ways does Lizzy's presence impact her family's life?
4. Read Matthew 5:14-16. How do you think Lizzy's faith journey as depicted in this chapter reflects the biblical principle of spreading light and joy to others? Have you ever seen this principle reflected in other people?

CHAPTER 2

1. What initial signs prompted John and Jennifer to take notice of Lizzy's condition? How did Lizzy initially react to her symptoms, and why did she not fully understand the severity of her situation?

2. How did Lizzy and her family prepare for their journey to St. Jude, and what challenges did they face during this time? Have you ever known someone who was treated for cancer? Describe the challenges they faced.

3. Thinking about the events described in Chapter 2, how did the family's perception of normalcy change, and what emotions did they experience during this period?

4. Read James 1:2-4. How do John and Jennifer's reactions to Lizzy's diagnosis illustrate the biblical theme of trusting God's plan even in the midst of unexpected challenges?

CHAPTER 3

1. Describe the initial emotions John experienced upon arriving at St. Jude Children's Hospital with Lizzy. How did the statue of Danny Thomas contribute to these emotions?

2. Describe the impact of Lizzy's treatment on John's and Jen's work situations. How did they prioritize Lizzy's needs over work obligations? What financial impacts have cancer treatment had on patients you have known?

3. Reflect on the statement, "Despite the hardships of sickness, there was a strange sense of joy associated with it," in the context of the chapter. How did the family adapt to the new normal of life at St. Jude?

4. Considering the theme of hope amid despair in the chapter, discuss how the Bible talks about perseverance through trials, such as the story of Job or the apostle Paul's experiences, and how it provides encouragement and perspective during difficult times (Job 23:10, Romans 8:18).

CHAPTER 4

1. Lizzy's family chose to share her journey publicly through social media. What do you think the impact of sharing such personal experiences can have on others, both within and outside of their community?

2. Reflecting on the journey documented on Lizzy's Facebook page, what insights can be gained about the challenges faced by pediatric cancer patients and their families?

3. Reflect on the moments of joy and celebration shared on the Facebook page, such as receiving positive medical reports or enjoying outings together. How did these moments provide hope and encouragement during challenging times?

4. How did Lizzy's community of friends, family, and supporters impact her journey through pediatric cancer? What specific acts of kindness stood out to you the most?

5. Lizzy's journey through cancer is marked by moments of divine intervention, unexpected blessings, and the presence of God in her pain and suffering. How does Lizzy's story echo the biblical narrative of God's faithfulness, compassion, and redemption in the midst of suffering (Psalm 34:18, Romans 8:28)?

CHAPTER 5

1. Explore the theme of hope throughout the chapter. How do Lizzy and her family maintain hope during the darkest moments of her treatment?

2. Reflect on the impact of medical procedures and treatments on Lizzy's daily life. How do these experiences shape her perspective on her illness and treatment?

3. Lizzy's father, John, mentioned feeling a mixture of emotions when witnessing his daughter's head being shaved. Can you

relate to these conflicting emotions? How do you think parents cope with seeing their child undergo physical changes due to illness?

4. Reflect on the significance of milestones and victories, no matter how small, in Lizzy's journey. How do these moments impact her and her family's outlook on her treatment and recovery?

5. Romans 12:12 instructs believers to "Be joyful in hope, patient in affliction, faithful in prayer." How do Lizzy and her family demonstrate these qualities throughout their journey, and what lessons can we learn from their example?

CHAPTER 6

1. How did Lizzy's family cope with the emotional toll of her illness, particularly during holidays like Easter?

2. How did Lizzy and her family demonstrate faith and trust in God throughout their journey with cancer?

3. How did Lizzy's family handle setbacks such as fever and infection during her treatment process, and what role did prayer play in their response?

4. Explain Lizzy's family's reaction to the news of additional tests and the possibility of further treatment. How did they maintain hope and resilience in the face of uncertainty?

5. What role do celebrations like the No More Chemo Party play in acknowledging and marking the milestones achieved during a patient's treatment journey? How might the postponement of such a celebration affect the emotional well-being of the family?

6. How does Lizzy's family's journey through her illness challenge and strengthen their faith, reflecting themes of testing and perseverance found in the Bible (James 1:2-4)?

CHAPTER 7

1. How do you think Lizzy's siblings are handling Lizzy's illness, and what support do you think they might need?
2. What can be learned from Lizzy's story about facing challenges and finding hope in difficult times?
3. What emotions do you think Lizzy's parents are experiencing as they navigate this new phase of her treatment?
4. Despite the challenges Lizzy faces, her family continues to hold on to hope for her healing. How does Hebrews 11:1 ("Now faith is confidence in what we hope for and assurance about what we do not see.") resonate with their perspective, and how can it inspire us to maintain hope in the midst of adversity?

CHAPTER 8

1. Reflect on Lizzy's resilience and courage throughout her journey. How did she find purpose and meaning even while suffering?
2. What was the emotional significance of Lizzy's participation in *The Today Show's* "Thanks and Giving" holiday campaign, considering the timing of her appearance during her relapse and treatment?
3. Discuss Lizzy's meeting with Chip and Joanna Gaines and their involvement in renovating the Target House at St. Jude. What was the significance of their partnership, and how did it affect Lizzy and her family? How did Lizzy impact Chip and Joanna?
4. The chapter emphasizes the impact of Lizzy's advocacy and storytelling on raising awareness for pediatric cancer research and the mission of St. Jude. How does Lizzy's example illustrate the biblical principle of using one's voice and platform to make a difference in the lives of others (Esther 4:14, Matthew 5:16)?

How did Lizzy's advocacy inspire others to join the fight against childhood cancer and support families facing similar struggles?

CHAPTER 9

1. How does Lizzy's unwavering faith impact her journey and the way she faces her illness?

2. Lizzy's wish to give back to others, even in the midst of her own struggles, is a recurring theme. How does her generosity and compassion inspire you?

3. Lizzy's Make-A-Wish trip to Disney World provides a temporary escape from her illness. How do you think that experiences like this impact individuals facing serious illness, and why are they important?

4. Psalm 23 is a well-known passage that speaks of God's presence and provision, even in the darkest valleys. How does Lizzy's journey reflect the themes of this Psalm, and how does her faith sustain her through difficult times?

CHAPTER 10

1. How do moments like Lizzy's conversation with her grandfather and the family's interactions with visitors during her final days shape their understanding of life, death, and the importance of love and connection?

2. Lizzy's journey toward heaven prompts deep theological reflections on topics like faith, suffering, and the nature of God's kingdom. How do Lizzy's experiences resonate with biblical narratives of faith, perseverance, and the hope of eternal life (Hebrews 11:1, Romans 8:18)?

3. How does Lizzy's legacy inspire you to live your life differently or to appreciate the blessings you have?

4. Describe the significance of Colin and the other young pallbearers' role in Lizzy's funeral. How does their support exemplify biblical principles of friendship, love, and bearing one another's burdens?

5. Lizzy's family found solace in their faith in eternal life and reunion with loved ones in heaven. How does this belief align with Jesus' words in John 14:1-3, where he promises to prepare a place for believers in his Father's house and assures them of his eventual return to take them to be with him?

CHAPTER 11

1. John mentioned societal expectations regarding grief and coping mechanisms. What biblical examples or teachings offer guidance on how to support one another through grief?

2. John discussed the idea of embracing each day to the fullest, echoing the sentiment of living with purpose and gratitude. What biblical teachings support this approach to life, especially in the face of loss and grief?

3. Reflecting on the family's grief journey, what biblical passages or stories provide comfort or guidance for navigating the loss of a loved one?

4. Like Abraham, Lizzy's father experienced a profound shift from fighting for his daughter's life to surrendering to God's will. How does this transformation mirror Abraham's willingness to submit to God's command, even at great personal cost (Genesis 22:1-19)?

CHAPTER 12

1. Lizzy's mother describes the emotional weight tied to Lizzy's belongings. How do these tangible items serve as triggers for her grief? Can you relate to this experience in any way?

2. Jennifer reflects on the decisions and preparations made before Lizzy's passing. How do these preparations impact the family's ability to navigate the immediate aftermath of her death?

3. Jennifer discusses the unpredictability of grief, comparing it to waves that arise when triggered. How do these triggers manifest in her life, and how does she cope with them?

4. Lizzy's mother found comfort and hope in Matthew 5:4 ("Blessed are those who mourn, for they will be comforted.") and Psalm 34:18 ("The LORD is close to the brokenhearted and saves those who are crushed in spirit."). What other passages have brought you comfort in the midst of grief?

CHAPTER 13

1. What were some of the coping mechanisms used by Hannah and Daniel to navigate the emotional upheaval caused by Lizzy's illness?

2. In what ways did Hannah's and Daniel's experiences with Lizzy's cancer treatment differ from their parents' perspectives?

3. How did Hannah and Daniel grapple with questions of faith and spirituality in the face of Lizzy's illness and eventual passing?

4. In Matthew 11:28-30, Jesus says, "Come to me, all you who are weary and burdened, and I will give you rest." How do you see this verse reflected in Hannah's and Daniel's experiences as they navigate the challenges of Lizzy's illness?

CHAPTER 14

1. In what ways did Lizzy's legacy extend beyond her passing? How did her selflessness and compassion continue to inspire others?

2. How did John and Jennifer address the financial and emotional challenges faced by families dealing with pediatric cancer? What initiatives did they undertake to support these families?

3. What impact did Lizzy's tumor donation have on pediatric cancer research? How does her contribution continue to influence advancements in treating osteosarcoma?

4. How does Lizzy's story inspire you to take action or contribute to causes that are meaningful to you? What lessons can be learned from her life and legacy?

5. Lizzy's favorite scripture was Psalm 91. How does the experience of feeling God's presence and protection throughout the journey through Lizzy's illness resonate with the assurances given in Psalm 91, particularly regarding God's promise of shelter and deliverance in times of trouble? In what specific moments or aspects of this book do you see parallels with the comforting imagery and promises described in Psalm 91?

www.ingramcontent.com/pod-product-compliance
Lightning Source LLC
Chambersburg PA
CBHW061559120626
46550CB00004B/1545